AF394333

RUSSIAN CRIMINAL TATTOO
ENCYCLOPAEDIA

VOLUME I

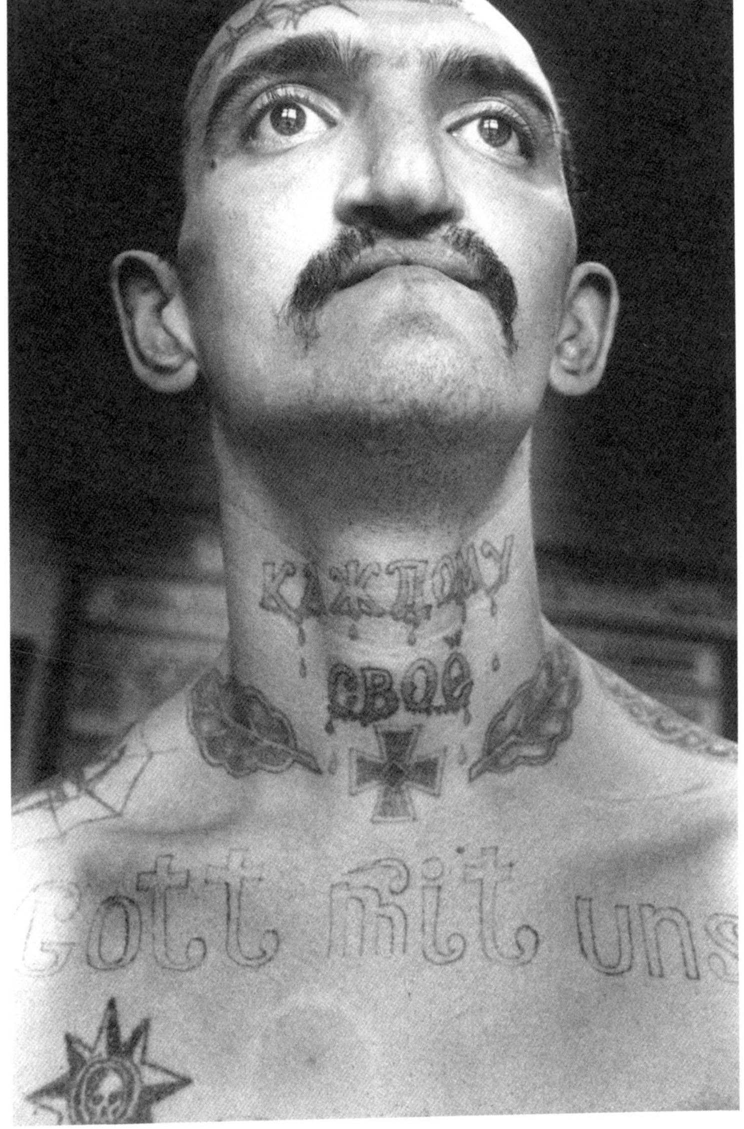

КАЖДОМУ
СВОЁ
Gott mit uns

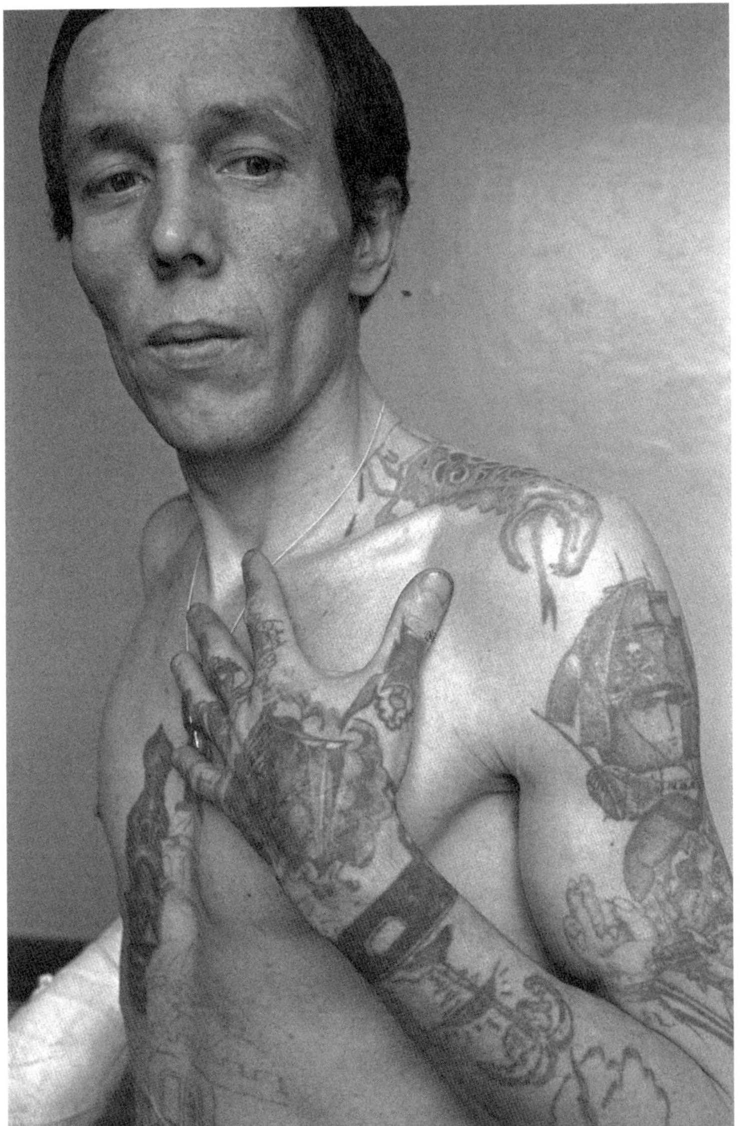

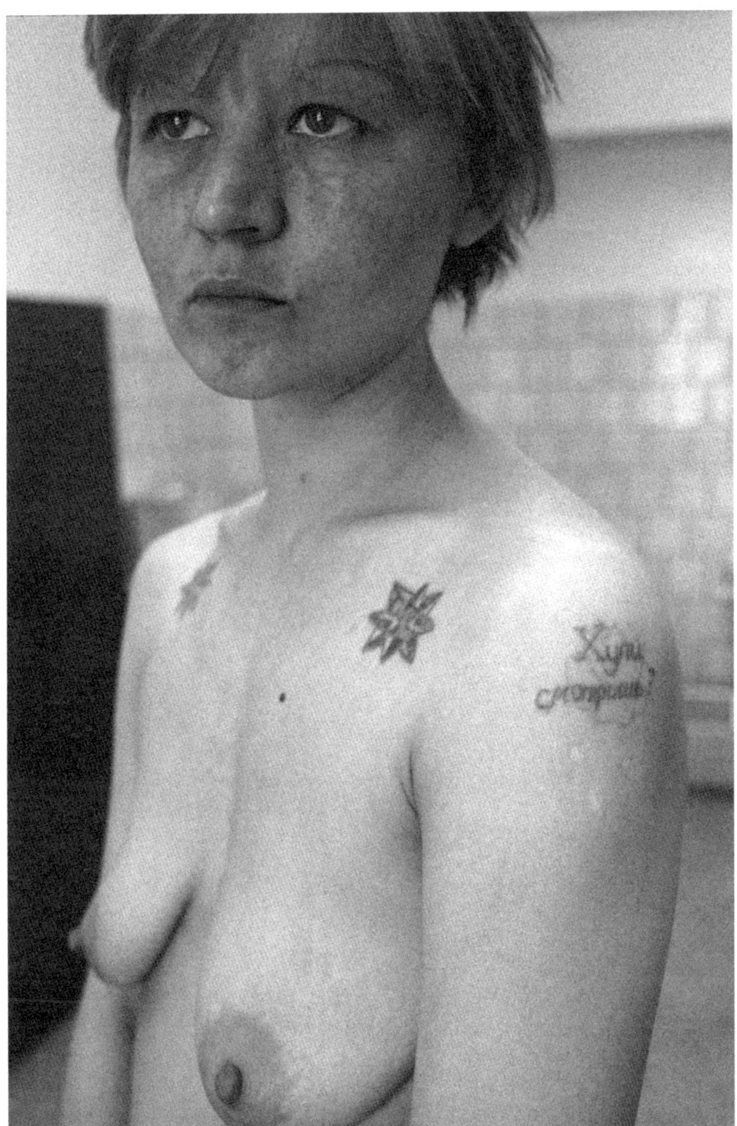
Хули
смотришь?

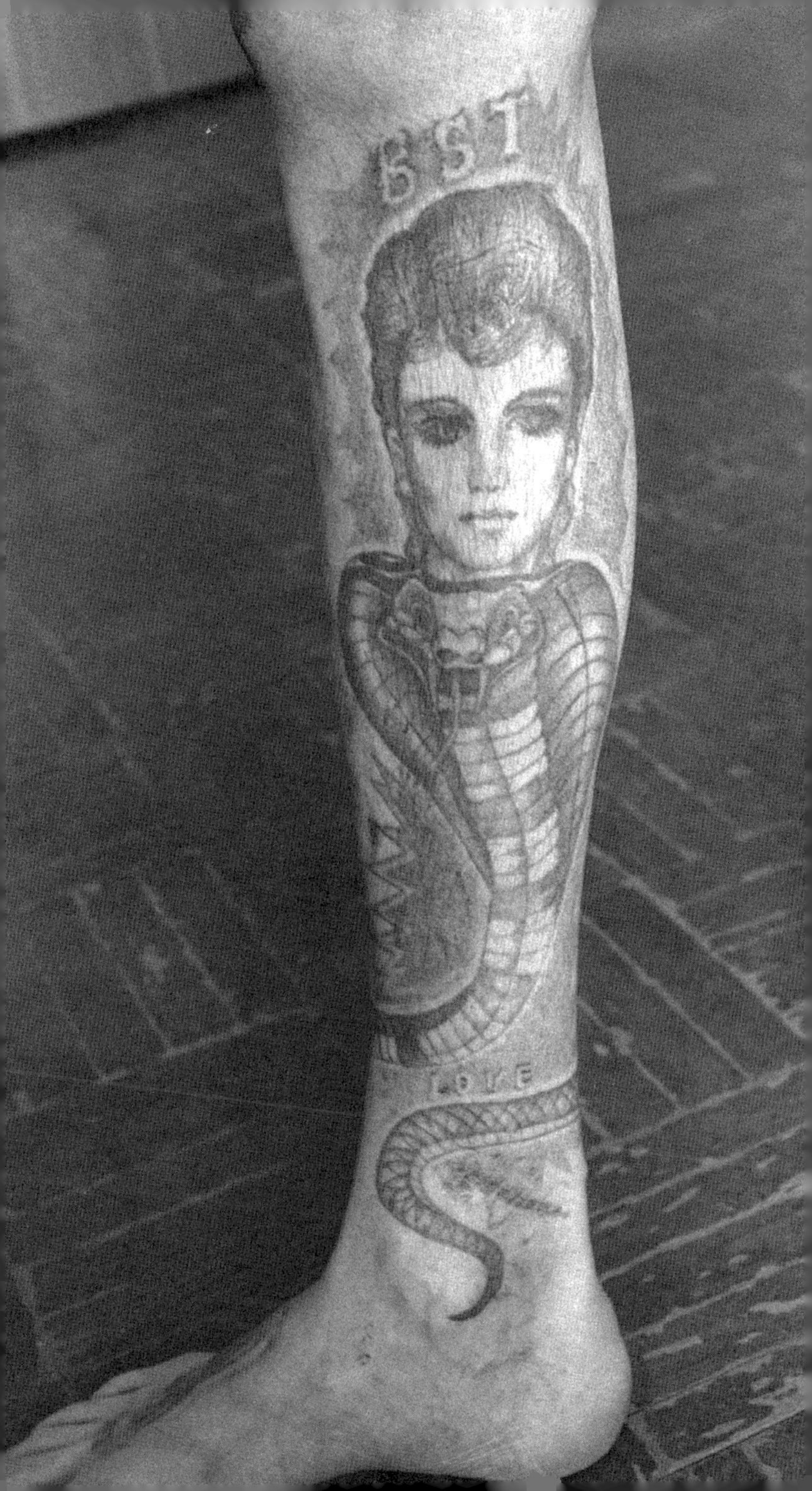

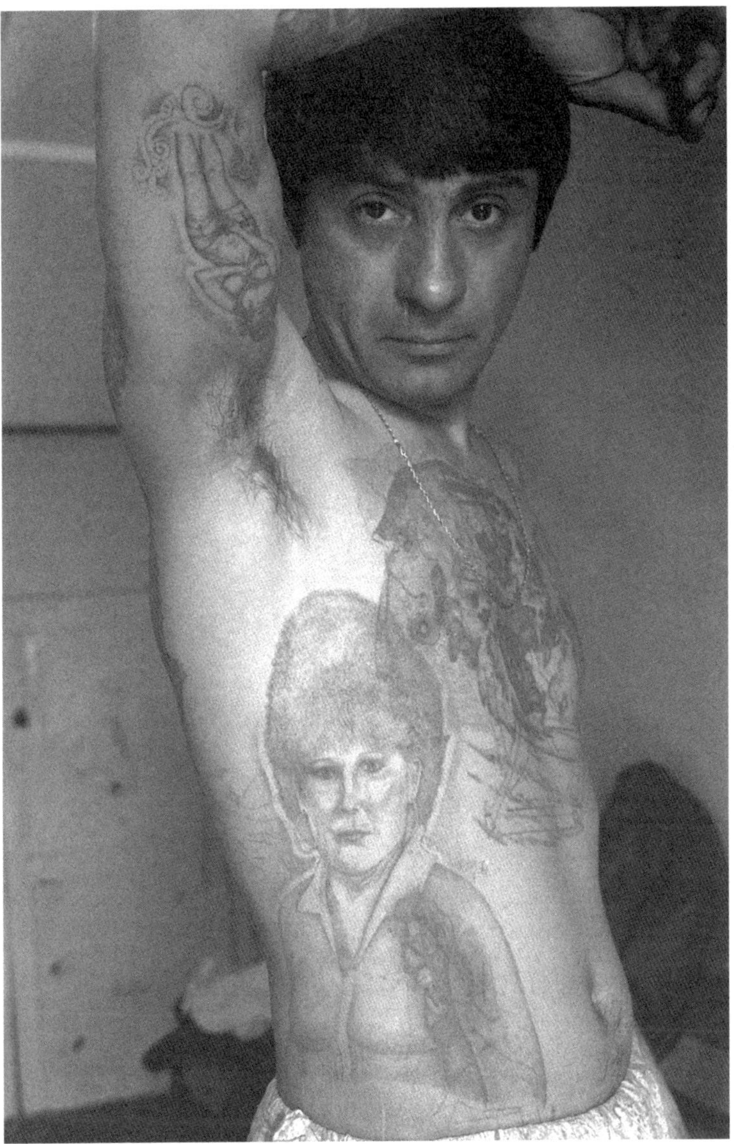

DRAWINGS AND TEXT Danzig Baldaev
PHOTOGRAPHY Sergei Vasiliev
INTRODUCTION Alexei Plutser-Sarno

DESIGN AND EDIT Murray & Sorrell FUEL
EDITOR Honey Luard
TRANSLATOR Andrew Bromfield
CO-ORDINATORS Anna Benn, Julia Goumen

Russian Criminal Tattoo Encyclopaedia

Volume I

FUEL

Contents

Foreword 16

Introduction 26

Photographs. Section One 55

Drawings. Male Tattoos 115

Drawings. Female Tattoos 293

Photographs. Section Two 331

Foreword

Danzig Baldaev

According to calculations made by my father, the eminent Buryat folklore specialist and ethnographer, Sergei Petrovich Baldaev, at least fifty-eight members of his and my mother's families died in the torture chambers of the OGPU (United State Political Administration) and the NKVD (People's Commissariat of Internal Affairs), either in exile or in prison camps. These were educated people – doctors, technicians, teachers, engineers, land and mine surveyors.

On both my mother and father's side I am descended from baptized Buryat-Mongols, people who were rich, brave and strong. My paternal grandfather Pyotr died in Bokhan jail at the age of ninety-six after being interrogated using 'the Leninist method of physical persuasion'. This was a man who, for amusement, would carry his horse Khurdankhara, on his shoulders. The horse had once saved his life by outrunning escaped convicts from the central prison at Alexandrovsky.

My mother, Stepanina Yegorovna Bazhicheeva-Baldaeva, was very strong and hard-working, and she had plenty of natural courage. One winter's day when she was only sixteen, she was riding back home from Irkutsk with a string of sixty to seventy sledges. The Russian and Buryat Mongol peasants she was travelling with had sold their produce and so they were carrying money. They were attacked by convicts and robbed of money, clothing and horses. My mother grabbed a twelve-round Winchester semi-automatic, and as two convicts with axes rushed towards her she shot them at point-blank range. She shouted, 'Men, tie them up!' and then shot a third who was trying to escape. More than twenty criminals were bound and delivered to the Alexandrovsky central prison. My mother was given a reward, but she donated every last Kopeck to the school in Bokhan that she attended as a child.

By agreement with the Tsarist military administration, my grandfathers sold wheat, oats and cattle to the provision depots in Irkutsk. During the Russian-Japanese War, together with other affluent people, they opened free soldiers' canteens at the Cheremkhovo and Usolie-Sibirskoe

railroad stations. Then, during the Civil War, the family was torn apart. My uncle Alexander fought for the Reds and was rewarded with a golden sword for his part in the rout of Baron Ungern's forces and the capture of the Baron. For this the Order of the Red Banner was affixed to the hilt of his sword. He was also awarded the Order of the Pole Star by the government of the young Mongolian People's Republic. My younger uncle, Mikhail, was awarded the soldier's Order of St. George by Ataman Semenov for personal bravery, and for his part in the taking of Chita he received the officer's George Cross. When the Fifth Red Army advanced and Ataman Semenov retreated into Manchuria, my uncle Mikhail collected weapons, ammunition and provisions from the stores depots in Chita, and withdrew into the Muisky Valley to protect the gold prospecting co-operatives. Both uncles and their elder brother Pyotr, who did not participate in the war, were killed by the communist authorities. When my father went to the Ulan-Ude KGB in the 1960s to ask them to return the golden sword, a family heirloom, together with the Order of the Pole Star, the head of the office asked him, 'Why? Do you want to use that sabre to cut off the heads of NKVD employees?'

Another uncle of mine, Georgy, who graduated from the Cheremkhovo Commercial College before the revolution, worked as the senior bookkeeper in the Special Timber Section of the State Camp Administration (GULAG) of the People's Commissariat for Internal Affairs (NKVD). The family of my mother's uncle Miron almost all died from hard physical labour, hunger and disease, in the village of Irbeisky in the Krasnoyarsk Territory. The Poor Peasants' Committee of the settlement of Khokhorsk (thirty drunkards and idlers), totally ruined this rich village of 120 homesteads.

I also became the son of an 'enemy of the people'. My father was arrested following the denunciation of a down-and-out who had tried to court my mother before she married. My younger sister and I were placed in children's homes. I was lucky, I found myself in the October Revolution Children's Home in the village of Ikei in the Tulunsky district of the Irkutsk Region. There were 156 children of 'enemies of the people' there – children of command staff from the Independent Far Eastern Red Army and the Urals Military District, as well as children of the Irkutsk intelligentsia. Many of them came from noble backgrounds and spoke several European languages. The Young Pioneer leaders called us 'little enemies', and demanded that we speak only Russian, claiming that foreign languages encouraged anti-Soviet thoughts.

They checked all of our post. When the school suddenly surprised everyone by heading the list for academic achievement, the NKVD was not pleased. A 'comrade' came to visit us and a model re-examination was held, which we 'enemies of the people' passed with flying colours. At a meeting afterwards the comrade said, 'Now you know how well the enemies of the people have prepared their children and how much

damage they can do to our workers' and peasants' state. But we won't let them into the institutions of higher education!'

All this happened in 1938, after my father was convicted of promoting Russian Tsarism. A newspaper article he had written in the 1920s supported the idea of opening Russian schools alongside Buryat-Mongol schools and teaching Russian culture. All his life my father, a researcher whose work was valued by major scholars, had collected gems of Buryat-Mongol folklore, customs and genealogies. He was the first director of a Buryat-Mongol school, a graduate of the Moscow Institute of Peoples of the East, and a postgraduate student of Academician N.Ya. Marr, who had intended to keep him on to teach at the institute. But the Poor Peasants' Committee of Khokhorsk settlement was sent to Moscow to demand that my father be excluded from the institute for being the son of a rich man. I remember how my father and I visited Lenin's wife Nadezhda Krupskaya, who had ordered the exclusion, at the People's Commissariat of Education. A demand for my father's transfer from the institute had come through the Central Executive Committee of the All-Russian Communist Party (Bolsheviks), from a close friend of his, the first secretary of the Regional Committee of the All-Russian Communist Party of the Buryat-Mongol Autonomous Soviet Socialist Republic, M.N. Erbanov, who wanted him to establish institutes, technical colleges and schools in the republic. Erbanov, one of the ill-fated delegates to the 17th Party Congress, was shot in 1937. In beating a confession out of him, the NKVD broke his arms, legs and jaw.

My father used to tell me that in Sanskrit the word *Rossiya* (Russia), means 'experimental country or field of Satan'. A soothsayer told my father, 'At present the fiends and devils have nothing to be afraid of. They used to fear priests, shamans, churches, monasteries, mosques and temples, but now in human form they have become communists, NKVD men, informers (the petty devils), and members of Poor Peasant Committees'. In 1940 my father was released 'for lack of evidence'. They gave him a flat on the outskirts of Ulan-Ude, returned a few pieces of furniture, (the most valuable things, such as furs, gold and silverware, were not given back), and allowed him to work. But in 1948 he was summoned by the First Secretary of the All-Russian Communist Party of the Buryat-Mongol Autonomous Soviet Socialist Republic, a certain Kudryavtsev, (the son-in-law of G.M. Malenkov), who wanted to exploit my father's status as a scholar in order to settle scores. He demanded that my father write a devastating article denouncing more than twenty-five people for being both pan-Mongolists and flunkies of the West. There were five or six Buryat-Mongols on the list, all the rest were Russians, Ukrainians, Jews and Tatars. This sham 'internationalism' was clearly a deliberate attempt to sow the seeds of national discord, which the communists hoped would allow them to carry on a policy of 'divide and rule'. As an adult, I visited prisons and camps in republics

right across the country and I saw the results of this policy, which has been responsible for so much bloodshed in our time.

When my father refused to write the article, he was immediately reminded that he was an 'enemy of the people'. That night he left for Leningrad to stay with his eldest daughter, who was married to a sea captain. During the two years that he lived with her without being officially registered, this famous scholar earned a living sawing up firewood for the Municipal Heating Department, labouring in a canteen, nailing together crates at a packaging depot, digging vegetable gardens for the rich owners of dachas, and unloading railway wagons. But my father spent all his free time in the Saltykov-Shchedrin Public Library, pursuing his scholarly work, (his old friend professor M.K. Azadovsky got him a ticket to the reading room). One day I showed my father a copy of some tattoos from the 'Crosses' (solitary confinement cells), where I worked as a supervisor, and he said to me, 'My son, collect the tattoos, the convicts' customs, their anti-social drawings, or it will all go to the grave with them'. He taught me the methodology for documenting prison folklore and how to encode material, which was essential to this dangerous undertaking.

For thirty-three years I, a ward of a home for children of 'enemies of the people', an artist with an incomplete education who fought in the Second World War, worked in the Ministry of the Interior. For all those years I collected material on the language and folklore of the criminal world. Thanks to a free ticket, I travelled four times from Leningrad to Vladivostok and visited dozens of corrective labour camps and colonies. I went to Central Asia, the Caucasus, Ukraine, the Russian North and the Baltic, although I never went to Kolyma. I made several attempts to publish what I had collected and met with some success – a dictionary of prison and camp slang with tattoos was published by 'Outskirts of Moscow'; a work on slang and tattoos for professional use was published by the Criminal Investigation Department of the State Office of Internal Affairs of the Leningrad Region. I was reported to the KGB, but unexpectedly they supported me. They realised the value of being able to establish the facts about a convict or criminal: his date and place of birth, the crimes he had committed, the camps where he had served time, and even his psychological profile. While I served in the St. Petersburg Criminal Investigation Department of the Ministry of the Interior, I caught more than 300 thieves, robbers, murderers and rapists.

However, I didn't intend my work to be purely for professional use. It is appropriate that P. Belov's book, *The White Sea Canal*, is based on my tattoos. As in a mirror, everything the country has gone through has been reflected in prison and camp life. Is it a distorted mirror? I don't think so, despite all the naivety, superstition and perversity that is typical of the convict's way of thinking. Ideological lies, skilfully devised international conflicts, the humiliation of people, the denial of the right to a dignified

life – or to life itself. These are the sins of the state. They are manifest in the world of the prisons and camps, in the terrible plague patches of tattoos, in the obscenities of thieves' jargon, the criminal obsessions and depraved notions of the structure of society and social ideology.

For a long time all of us lived under the leadership of villains, tricksters and bandits. Thank God those times are slowly receding, although all sorts of 'bosses' and 'little bosses' continue to oppress us. It seems that until they have divided up amongst themselves everything created by our fathers and grandfathers, they are not going to do anything about fighting organised crime and corruption.

It is a pity that I am over seventy years old, but at the same time it is good that I have managed to 'scoop-up' some of the filth from our slavish past that is now disappearing and record it, 'in all its glory', for future generations.

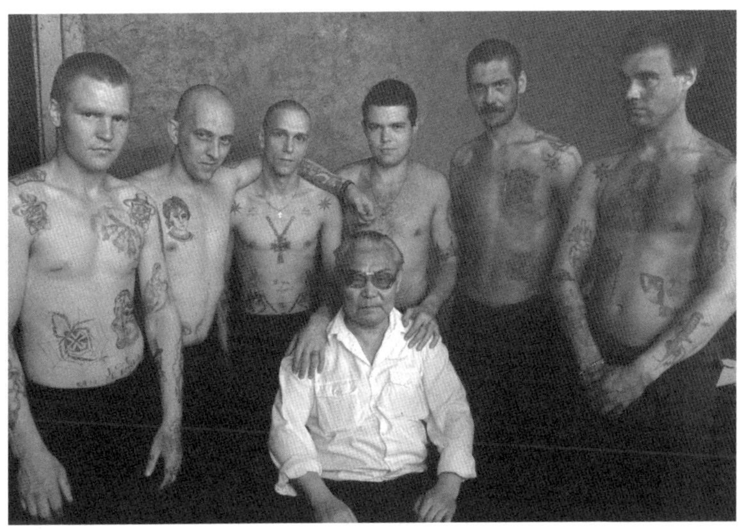

Danzig Baldaev (seated) and criminal 'authorities'.
ITK Settlement No.9, Gorelovo Leningrad Oblast, 1989.

Introduction

**The Language of the Body and Politics:
The Symbolism of Thieves' Tattoos**

Alexei Plutser-Sarno

'A tail coat with decorations'

Strange as it may seem, the tattoo-covered body of a *vor v zakone* (legitimate thief), is primarily a linguistic object. Tattoos are a unique language of symbols and the rules for 'reading' them are transmitted via oral tradition. Esoteric in nature, this language resembles thieves' argot and it performs a similar function by encoding secret information to protect itself against uninitiated outsiders. In exactly the same way as argot is a masked language, neutral words with coded meanings, tattoos convey 'secret' symbolic information through the use of allegorical images which at first glance may seem familiar to everyone, (a naked woman, a devil, a burning candle, a dungeon, a snake, a bat, etc.). This is a language that is both highly socialised and politicised. A thief's tattooed body is like a 'depiction' of a full-dress uniform, covered with regalia, decorations and badges of rank and distinction. In thieves' jargon the traditional set of tattoos is known as *frak s ordenami* (a tail coat with decorations), an expression that is included in Danzig Baldaev's dictionary of thieves' slang.[1] We can, in fact, speak about a uniform in literal terms. For example, there are numerous shoulder tattoos which depict genuine epaulettes or shoulder-straps with stars or skulls. Sometimes even German shoulder-straps from the Führer's army can be found. Bodies are decorated with rings, crosses on chains, shackles, bracelets, star-shaped badges and crowns. Transverse lines encircling the fingers are actually called *perstni* (rings) in thieves' jargon.

In effect, these tattoos embody a thief's complete 'service record', his entire biography. They detail all of his achievements and failures, his promotions and demotions, his 'secondments' to jail and his 'transfers' to different types of 'work'. A thief's tattoos are his 'passport', 'case file', 'awards record', 'diplomas' and 'epitaphs'. In other words, his full set of official bureaucratic documents. Therefore, in the world of thieves a man with no tattoos has no social status whatsoever. In the thieves' argot such a man is known as a *petushok* (cockerel), and in a prison camp he immediately acquires the status of a *chukhan* (stooge). New arrivals

in 'the zone' (prisons and camps) are first of all divided into *rakovye sheiki* (crayfish necks), or 'old hands' who have tattoos, and 'cockerels' who don't. 'I became a "crayfish neck" the moment I took my shirt off. The overseer spotted an ace of clubs on my shoulder, squinted at it and waved his hand to tell me: come out here! "Cockerels" to the "cockerels", and "crayfish necks" on one side'. That's how the procedure is described in the language of thieves.'[2]

Anyone not initiated into the secret meaning of thieves' tattoos takes them for a chaotic jumble of symbols. But in reality a thief's body is anything but a random assortment of unrelated 'pictures'. It is a statement organised in a highly complex manner, some parts of which are the voice of a man expressing his own thoughts, feelings or memories. For example, 'Mother, forgive me' or 'I won't forget my own dear mother!' Tattoos can also convey specific messages, as when thieves send letters into the zone tattooed on the body of a 'courier', who deliberately 'takes on' the appropriate crime and is thereby delivered to the correct part of the zone. He becomes a living letter, his body is the speech of the criminal boss or 'authority'.

Tattoos most often represent the language of the entire world of thieves, they are a means of socio-political communication, a kind of thieves' mass media and a 'courier' often carries on his body a message from the community of thieves to the entire zone. Tattoos act as symbols of public identity, social self-awareness and collective memory. They shape stereotypes of group behaviour and set out the rules and rituals necessary for maintaining order in the world of thieves. For instance, tattoos with a proverbial text like: 'The most important man in the zone is the legitimate thief', and tattoos including various acronyms: the letters of the Russian word *Bog* (God) stand for 'I shall rob again'; the word *zhuk* (beetle) for 'I wish you successful robbing'; the word *list* (leaf) for 'Flatten narks and stool-pigeons'; the word *mir* (peace) for 'Shooting will reform me'; the abbreviation *NKVD* (People's Commissariat of Internal Affairs), for 'Nothing is stronger than thieves' friendship' and the word *sliva* (plum) as 'Death to narks and all activists'. These tattoos express an entire legal code for the world of thieves, they set the rules for their wearer's behaviour in the future and the interpretation of their past.

Some tattoos may be regarded as the voice of the outside world, such as 'You can't escape your fate'. Some refer to what a man is going to suffer in the future. The acronym *OGPU* (Unified State Political Administration) stands for 'O God, help me to escape!' Texts like this can dictate the future, since the man wearing them accepts them as a programme of behaviour to be acted out. In this way a tattooed body is capable of ordering life and shaping fate. A man becomes totally dependent on the symbols of his tattoos. And since tattoos possess a distinct 'ritual magic' subtext that manifests itself in various 'talismans' such as 'God is with you', tattoos effectively transform a man into the hero of his own criminal 'myth'. A living person is transformed into a character in the world of tattoos.

In the world of thieves, anybody who misappropriates the tattoos of a 'legitimate thief' is killed. Tattoos can only disappear together with the man or a part of his body – 'If they discover that a tattoo is phoney and was only made out of bravado, savage retribution awaits the transgressor of convention, from the amputation of a finger with a false ring to conversion into a despised "cockerel".'[3] Other types of false but less 'high-ranking' tattoos are removed together with the skin, but their owner may be left alive, 'The question that criminal "authorities" in the zone ask new arrivals in a corrective labour camp or colony is: "Do you stand by your tattoos?", and if his tattoos do not reflect his rank, they force the prisoner to remove them with a knife, sandpaper, a shard of glass or a lump of brick. And for insubordination and failure to carry out the instructions of "legitimate thieves" the bearer of the tattoos is subjected to ferocious beating as an impostor.'[4] All this indicates that the tattoo is regarded as an inalienable and highly valued 'body part', and a man is regarded as part of a universal 'tattoo text'. Any deception here is considered as blasphemy, a violation of the true sacred language. The intimate corners of the human body are transformed into a forum for the public 'politics' of thieves.

The difficulty in 'reading' tattoos lies in the fact that the regions of the body are already charged with meaning, so that the meaning of a tattoo changes, often to its opposite, depending on the part of the body to which it is applied. A female head on the stomach is the mark of a prostitute, however a female head on the chest is a juvenile convict's badge of initiation. At the same time, unlike ordinary speech, in which words are arranged in linear sequence, in convict tattoos signs at various levels are interpreted as being set inside each other. The tattoo text is not linear, but volumetric and multidimensional. Tattoos can incorporate the most varied kinds of signs, including verbal, representational, allegorical and symbolic. Due to the complexity of this language, people who are experienced in 'reading' and making tattoos acquire additional status in the world of thieves, just like those who are masters of *blatnaya fenya* (criminal spiel). In thieves' jargon they are known as *kol'shchiki* (prickers), or more accurately 'zone prickers', since tattoos are most often applied during terms of imprisonment.

The needle for applying tattoos is called an *peshnya* (ice pick), *pchyolka* (bee), *shpora* (spur) or *zhalo* (sting). The device for applying tattoos is made from a mechanical or electric razor and its argot names include *mashinka* (typewriter), *bormashina* (dentist's drill), and *shveinaya mashina* (sewing machine). The ink is called *mazut* (fuel oil) or *gryaz'* (dirt). *Mazut* also means the most valuable food products in the prison camp zone: tea, fat and jam. The pigment is thus equated with the zone's highest material values. The tattoo itself is called a *reklama* (advert), *regalka* (regalia), *raspiska* (painting) or *kleimo* (brand).

The tattooed body as a whole is involved in a continual 'dialogue' with the world that surrounds it. Tattoos require their owner to conform

to certain mimetic, gestural, verbal and behavioural stereotypes. In addition, tattoos also set the rules of behaviour towards others. An individual interacting with a thief is obliged to strictly conform to his own complex stereotype. Thieves' tattoos are therefore capable of structuring the entire socio-political space of the 'community' of thieves. But in Russia every businessman pays his 'tribute', every politician has his *krysha* (roof), or protection, and the language of thieves has long since permeated the whole of society. As a central element of the language of thieves, tattoos subjugate all the space around them. The *pakhany* (body language) of the main criminal bosses, is capable of structuring the life of the whole country.

We live in a virtual age, where written language has become electronic and books, libraries, presidents, prisons and humans have all become just one item in a list of possible realities. The value of high literary culture has been relativised. We have been made aware once again of the conditional nature of any world that exists, we have sensed that all the sacred written texts exist in only one of a multitude of imaginable realities. And of course, tattoos also exist in three realities: on the human body, on the Internet and on paper, more specifically in this publication.

It is paradoxical that the desacralisation of high literary culture has resulted in a higher status accorded the 'natural' world. The entire 'natural' world as a text has regained some of its former grandeur. The desacralisation of the cultural 'centre' has resulted in an expansion of 'the boundaries of culture' and an increased interest in its 'peripheries'. The language of palmistry, of astronomy, the physiognomy of the human face and the tattooed body are once again considered worthy of serious attention. We have remembered that alongside the triple reality, natural world/world of art/virtual world, there is another, fourth world just as mysterious and yet little studied. A world beyond the bounds of literary invention, beyond the limits of electronic space, beyond the boundaries of handmade 'nature'. The 'natural', 'everyday' world has also turned out to be a duality, since it is entirely covered with the mysterious text of graffiti: inscriptions, words, symbols, drawings, poems, names, dialogues and signs. But a 'natural' object entirely covered by texts can lose its 'naturalness'. In the coordinate space of this 'text' the conditional character of civilisation becomes entirely 'virtual'.

'Preserve thy poor servant Alexei'

One genre of tattoos is the so-called 'autograph'. As a rule this is the name of the 'bearer of the tattoo' or a symbol standing in its place. Such tattoos are also widespread outside the world of thieves, and they are often regarded as a sign of an uncultured person. In modern civilisation the body is an extremely precious object that must not be damaged. From this standpoint a tattoo on a body defiles it. It is like the inscription

'Vasya was here' on a Raphael Madonna, or the dollar sign drawn by Alexander Brenner on a painting by Malevich. But from a different perspective, if the human body was created by God, then what is written on it is just as sacred as the inscription on an icon or the letters on a Christian cross. A tattooed autograph becomes a living word addressed to God. It is a signature that contains the author's 'self' in involute form, it is congruent with the soul.

In fact, the tradition of these autograph-captions was widespread in Old Russia. They were even applied to church walls. The church was already waging a struggle against them in the 11th century, when graffiti of pagan origin on church walls 'were removed by devotees of the church...',[5] since they were regarded as being inscriptions on the body of Christ: the church was both the 'body' of the Lord and the 'body' of the church community. This 'holy' war against 'tattoos' on churches was sometimes even conducted on the church walls themselves. For instance, it was the Christian zealots who were responsible for the 11th century inscription 'May Your Hands Wither',[6] made on the church's 'body' by one of the champions of its purity.

Many of the graffiti strewn across the walls of churches in Old Russia were the 'autographs' of the people who wrote them, and from the churches' point of view were considered to be innocent. Every Russian town is covered with them. A.A. Medyntseva remarks in her book that, '...autographs were equated with prayer, which is confirmed by the images of crosses or churches that often accompanied an autograph'.[7] A tattoo on a human body can be regarded as a prayer addressed to God in exactly the same way. The idea that a simple cross can be a sign of prayer was also first expressed by Medyntseva: 'The numerous representations of crosses unaccompanied by inscriptions that are often to be found on the walls... are also people's prayers...'[8]

The crosses of various shapes and sizes found on the body of a thief may convey different meanings. Some crosses are badges of a thief's *mast'* (suit) or caste, some record his 'trips to the zone', some are oaths of vengeance, some are symbols of devotion to the idea of 'thiefhood', some are emblems of his speciality as a thief, and some symbolise the need to preserve one's honour as a thief, even unto death. But the language of tattoos also includes crosses that are prayers and talismans.

In the world of thieves' tattoos, when a simple and unremarkable event from the life of a thief is engraved on his body it becomes a fact of universal sacral history and ceases entirely to be a 'personal matter'. The tattooing of a name or nickname derives from the same desire to 'chronicle' one's own life. The corpus of modern thieves' tattoos devoted to historical events is immense. Practically the whole of modern Russian history has been drawn on the bodies of Russian convicts.

A tattoo is not simply a 'human voice' engraved on a body, it is not the replica of a voice, it is the voice of the body as a 'thing', as an object, it is

the *vox rei*. The body dies as it is reified, becoming an object, and it comes to life again as a talking thing. The main feature of such tattoos is that they 'speak' in the first person and address the viewer. They include, for instance, tattoos on the feet that read, 'Wash and dry!', or tattoos on the eyelids that read, 'Do not wake me!'. In this context prayers and talismans, such as the tattoo which uses the acronym *OGPU* with the meaning 'O Lord, help me to escape', can also be regarded as the 'speech' of the body or even of its parts. In such ritual tattoos the various elements of the body, the legs, arms, eyes, buttocks, may be personified, as in tattoos on the eyelids that say, 'We're sleeping', or on the feet that say, 'We're tired of walking', or 'They're tired from the long journey', or 'They're tired of walking under armed escort'. One tattoo applied to the insteps of the feet reads, 'They drag me along under armed guard'. Here the body speaks about the feet as a separate entity.

And so, when the self-contained space of the body is entirely covered with magic inscriptions, its status changes fundamentally. It is transformed into a site for the performance of ritual enactments. Such tattoos are regarded as a source of power that force the world beyond to react to the object with which it comes into contact. Tattoos of this type include 'talismans' with texts such as 'Preserve thy servant Alexei'. Images of scarab beetles are one of the oldest of thieves' talismans. Other well-known ones include: 'May the Queen of Heaven grant me a thief's luck' and 'Preserve me from narks and the court'. Talismans also include many images of the Holy Virgin: 'Mother of God, forgive my sins', 'Mother of God, save and preserve Thy son, a sinful servant' and of the Lord God 'Holy Father, save and preserve this servant of God'. Talismans also include numerous images of guardian angels, including some guarding the flame of a candle. Images of churches make up a distinctive category of talismans. Of course symbols of this kind may carry a whole multitude of meanings, for instance, the domes of a church may indicate the number of years spent in imprisonment or the number of 'trips to the zone'. Danzig Baldaev himself classifies images of churches and monasteries as 'talismans': 'The talisman tattoo of an authoritative thief is an image of Jesus Christ, the Virgin Mary, angels, archangels, saints, a church, a monastery or a cross'. He also includes images of skulls in the same category: 'A talisman is the tattoo of an "authority" in the criminal world with an image of Jesus Christ, the Virgin Mary, angels, archangels, saints, a church, a monastery, a cross, a human skull...' Apparently, tattoos that are connected with religious themes and death always have a hidden subtext although, as we have said, all of these symbols have multiple meanings, and a skull, for instance, may also signify a man's specific rank as a thief. In thieves' jargon this meaning is one of the fundamental ones, as Danzig Baldaev confirms: 'A skull tattoo indicates that the owner is an "authority".' In addition a skull is a symbol of death, as are images of crosses, axes, scythes and snakes. But a snake is not only a symbol of

deadly fate, it is also a symbol of the wisdom of the thieves' laws.

The theme of death is represented in tattoos by three main assertions that signify the absence of any fear of death: 'A thief is not afraid of death', the constant closeness of death, its presence in life, 'I am deathless death, always near!' or 'Death is always waiting for me', and our primordial relationship to death 'I am already a corpse'. This gravitation towards death, 'I was born to die', represented by an image of a skull on a cross, is a basic principle of the thief's view of the world and the skull depicted in convicts' tattoos expresses a fundamental concept of thiefhood. It is obvious that a thief who is afraid of death is no longer a thief, if only because in the world of thieves there is no death in the usual sense of the word.

The theme of death is also expressed in the widespread 'genre' of initiatory tattoos, which are applied to juveniles when they reach adulthood. These feature female heads, sometimes accompanied by a tulip or a rose, a dagger or barbed wire, a glass of wine and various symbols of a thief's 'suit'. Young thieves can only embark on their careers after undertaking the appropriate prison rites of consecration and having had these tattoos applied. The significance of this ritual is increased by the fact that the initiation is a symbolic death – as a juvenile who has gone through the rites is considered to be already dead. In order to become a thief, one has to die twice, first by abandoning the 'world of juveniles' and second by leaving behind the 'world of will'. The language of tattoos tells us that thieves regard themselves as characters from the world beyond. Prison itself is symbolically regarded as a grave, and visiting it is a major part of the life of a thief.

'Chummy devils'

The clear politicisation and social significance of thieves' tattoos leads researchers to categorise a large number of them as anti-Soviet and anti-communist. In fact the world of tattoos includes all the major Soviet political leaders, who also often speak in the first person. There are images of Yeltsin ('I'm not a punk like Mishka Gorbachev, who drinks nothing but *ryazhenka*'), Lenin ('The chief boss of the CPSU'), Stalin ('Head of the camp of socialism. GULAG. NKVD'), Andropov ('the boss of the Soviet system'), Brezhnev ('The chief arse of the Kremlin'), and Gorbachev ('The slave of Marxist-Leninist lies and deceit. Misha stop talking through your arse... Give convicts more rations and cut their sentences'). In this last example the tattoo addresses the president, rather than the reverse. Note that in the opinion of L.A. Milyanenkov, the common image of Lenin is also a concealed acronym for *VOR* (thief), since the Russian word is made up of the first letters of the words 'Leader of the October Revolution'.[9]

Tattoos of this kind are full of strange political slogans and Soviet symbols. But the hammer and sickle are merely emblems of an 'alien'

power as the world of thieves acknowledges no power except that of the thieves' own 'authorities'. In the language of thieves' tattoos the devil, Stalin and the red banner are all equivalent symbols taken from a world hostile to thieves. The five-pointed star, hammer and sickle, swastika, even the mark '666' are also almost synonymous here. The endless images of devils or of Lenin with horns and a tail cause no surprise. Members of the MVD (the Ministry of the Interior, which operates the militia, or police force), and the organisation itself are always represented in the form of a devil. Stalin also appears in the guise of Satan. The 'head boss' may also be represented as a vampire or a bat. One tattoo actually has the inscription: '...his image "The Bat" is the symbol of Satan'. And of course the image of Karl Marx may also be adorned with devil's horns.

For thieves there are no contradictions in this apparent chaos of images. Many of these anti-communist tattoos actually have no connection with political dissidence. The communist symbolism merely signifies a refusal to collaborate with the powers that be. These signs repudiate 'the system'. Not, of course, in favour of democracy but in favour of the power of the 'law of thieves'. For instance, a skull with a sickle on its forehead and eagle's wings is a sign of a thief's authority. Politics has nothing to do with it. Such tattoos are only the formulaic oaths of denial of external authority: 'I won't graft for the CPSU in the zone, I'm no Soviet serf!'. They are the symbols of the thief's traditional refusal to collaborate with *menty* (the fuzz), as in the tattoo with the inscription: 'Greetings to the Kremlin from Kolyma', showing a skeleton clutching an erect penis in its hands. They are symbols of a refusal to be subjugated, a declaration of war on *menty*, but they are not anti-communist slogans as such. In the language of thieves this is known as 'a grin at the authorities'. It is no accident that the hammers and sickles in these tattoos are often surrounded by wreaths of barbed wire.

Thieves' tattoos are not patriotic either. For example, an image of St. George battling the dragon is yet another symbol of resistance to the diabolical power of 'the fuzz'. A typical tattoo of a criminal 'authority' shows a thief in the form of a lion biting a pig-like devil who represents the world of 'the fuzz'. In thieves' argot the word *chyort* (devil), actually means someone who does not belong to the thieves' world, specifically 'an employee of the agencies of the Ministry of the Interior (MVD)', and the phrase *chyortovaya rota* (devil's company), refers to MVD staff. *Cherti kumovskie* (Chummy devils) are convicts who collaborate with the camp management.

'The suit of clubs'

The concept of a 'suit', meaning 'clan' or 'caste', is central to thieves' jargon. This word embraces multiple collective values: the entire class of thieves, a group of thieves, a community of thieves with a particular speciality

or that speciality itself, and a thief's fate, happiness and luck. In this argot 'to hold the suit' means 'to have power over the community of thieves, to control them, maintaining order and the observance of the law of thieves'. Danzig Baldaev speaks of *mast muzhikov* (the suit of men), *mast blatnykh* (the suit of criminals) and *mast kozlov* (the suit of jackasses), which shows that a 'suit' may signify a section of the camp community who are not thieves in the narrow sense but are united by a particular trait (the suit of jackasses), or a category of individuals who have ended up in prison but do not belong to the community of thieves (the suit of men). However, of course, they all form part of the same social system.

The main symbol of a 'legitimate thief' is the suit of clubs or the suit of spades and the most 'noble' cards in the deck are the King of clubs and of spades. In thieves' jargon the King of clubs was sometimes called 'St. Nicholas'.

The basic 'thieves' signs' also include images of skulls, wings (most often those of an eagle, sometimes those of a bat), the sign of the cross (with one, two or three cross pieces) and the image of the crown of the king of thieves. The symbols of authoritative 'legitimate thieves' also include several animals – a cat, a panther, a lion, a leopard, a tiger (the symbol of a 'tiger of the zone', an authoritative 'executioner'), a snake and an eagle. As Danzig Baldaev has suggested, an eagle may also indicate an escapee from a camp. A tiger is also an *otritsala* convict (anti-social), and in thieves' argot the word derived from 'tiger' (*tigryatnik*) is therefore a synonym for the concept of rejection of *otritsalovka* (authority). Such words are used to refer to a group of thieves that have adopted certain rules of behaviour, as well as the places in a corrective labour camp where they may be isolated. These meanings are given in Danzig Baldaev's dictionary: '*Tigryatnik* – 1. The same as Television... 2. The same as *Otritsalovka* 3. A cell in a punishment block where anti-social convicts are held...'.

One of the most widespread symbols used by thieves is a cat, which symbolises agility and a thief's luck. A less common symbol for a thief is the wolf: 'A wolf is a friend and brother to a wolf'. A 'pen' (knife), sword, dagger and grinning 'beast' are symbols of a thief's power, strength and ruthless attitude to enemies of the world of thieves. Any member of that world who sees a tattoo with a lion, the suit of clubs and wings will recognise its owner as a thief. Likewise, a tattoo with a tiger, a crown, a cross, wings and the suit of spades will tell him that its owner is an 'authority'. Wings are one of the basic thieves' signs. Combined with a cross the majestic eagle (now the crest of Russia), becomes a symbol of a thief's prestige.

Yet another extremely important thieves' symbol is the word *mat* (mother), tattooed or spoken. Where a thief has rejected his family and blood ties as a matter of principle, his real mother is only an abstract idea, a positive focus in the hostile *grazhdanka* (civilian world). She is a romantic memory from a former life: 'Do not wait for me, your good son, mother...'

The thief's true mother is the so-called *vorovskaya mama* (thief's mum), also referred to as *makhan, makhanka, pakhanka* or *pakhansha*. Like a thief's *brat* (brother), she is very rarely a blood relative. When relationships between thieves do correspond to blood ties it is no more than a coincidence. Just as in argot *vorovskaya semya* (a family of thieves) is a group of thieves without any ties of blood. A 'thief's mother' is either an older female *vor v zakone* (legitimate thief) who maintains the old traditions and controls a group of thieves, (this is a rare occurrence), the madam of a brothel and thieves' *malina* (den), a keeper of thieves' loot, or a dealer in stolen goods. And so a 'thieves' mother' means, firstly, a specific position in the world of thieves and, secondly, a symbolic 'mother' to thieves, the progenitress of the tribe of thieves, the transmitter of the thieves' laws. A mother is a 'ritual' character, it is in this sense that the word is used in the thieves' oath: *klyanus' mamoi* (I swear on my mother). This symbolic personification of the 'mother' is central to the thief's concept of truth and honour.

'The suit of hearts'

The next category of tattoos is the erotic tattoo. In generic terms, such tattoos are undoubtedly related to ritual texts and are not simply 'indications of the object of love'. Even the universally familiar image of a heart or two hearts has its origins in conspiracy. The classic central formula of amorous conspiracies and spells postulates a fusion and unification of hearts: 'May the heart of this servant [woman's name] fuse and adhere to this servant [man's name] so that they become one...'. The text of an 'amorous' tattoo may be equated by its author with an 'event', an accomplished fact. It is not simply the word acting on life, it is life itself. The composition of a text 'about love' is perceived as the act of 'creating' love. Such texts can be found in graffiti as well as tattoos: 'I love Marina!' – followed by a response in a different script: 'Love her in your heart and not on the wall, Cupid', followed by: 'Fuck off'.[10] The various images of hearts pierced by an arrow, intersecting or drawn one inside the other, are texts of sexual magic which are intended to act on the object of love through the mediation of a 'different' world. The human body begins to resemble a magic idol when this 'creation' of love takes place on its surface: it is transformed into inanimate material for the act of creation.

When men tattoo the name of the woman they love on their bodies, in the eyes of the woman this 'ritual act' proves the sincerity of her partner's feelings: the act is equated with the act of love. The recording of the name of a woman on one's body, on a stone or in a passport confirms certain social relations. It is a curious fact that the veneration of 'a stamp in the passport' (under the heading 'marital status') is also derived from a 'magical' attitude to the text.

Thieves' tattoos which are often regarded as erotic, amorous or even pornographic are in fact only indirectly related to eroticism. For instance,

images of copulation are tattooed on the body of a thief who fails to pay his debts at cards. These tattoos are a punishment, they deprive the person concerned of any status in the world of thieves. This is 'degradation', 'obliteration', social execution, but not eroticism. For instance, a tattoo with the inscription: 'Even devils love whores and oral sex' shows a girl engaging in oral sex with a devil. The image metaphorically equates the loser at cards with a prostitute or whore. And when the word *blyad* (whore) is applied to a man, in the world of thieves, it is one of the worst possible insults. To regard this kind of tattoo as pornography is equivalent to suggesting that *Playboy* should publish a photograph of a naked female corpse. The only feeling such tattoos arouse in inhabitants of the zone is horror. Everyone shuns a man with such a tattoo, they avoid him like the plague, because any contact with him could mean social death. All the tattoos with devils, negroes and Georgians raping girls are conventional symbols entirely devoid of any erotic subtext.

Tattoos that are actually related to the sexual lives of thieves are entirely non-erotic in appearance. Such a tattoo might simply be an image of a crown with the suit of hearts. A man wearing one of these hearts really is an erotic object, because he plays the role of a 'woman' in the zone (and since he plays the role of woman, it is not entirely correct to call him a homosexual). Similarly a *mokhnoryly* (shaggy face) or *mokhnaty vor* (shaggy thief) is a sexual tattoo that imparts female characteristics to a man (*mokhnatka*, literally a 'furry mitten', meaning the vagina). Other erotic signs, of which there are many, include dots applied to specific areas of the body, and images of shoes. These tattoos are also in effect social stigmata, assigning their wearer to an erotic role in the world of thieves (they literally transfer him from the role of male to female). Diamonds, the other 'red suit' in cards, are known as the *kumovskaya mast* (chummy suit). The diamond is the forcibly applied symbol of the *stukach* (stool pigeon). It also deprives its wearer of all status and may lead to sexual violence and rape.

In this context pornographic tattoos in the literal sense are impossible. Manifestations of sexuality and a serious attitude to love are not encouraged in the world of thieves. Sexually obsessed convicts are even forcibly marked with a tattoo of a hare, which lowers their social status. Such a man can no longer wield any authority among thieves. In one sense the world of thieves is asexual, the sexual act here is often one element in a political struggle, an act of *opuskanie* (lowering). As a rule, the literal depiction of the sexual act in a tattoo is also devoid of any sexual subtext and possesses a quite different symbolic meaning.

A distinct group of erotic tattoos consists of drawings on the bodies of prostitutes. These include a naked woman drawn on the stomach, inscriptions such as 'I never hold anything heavier than a glass or a prick in my hand', images of a woman's head in a crown surrounded by roses, and butterflies and hearts. These tattoos should also be regarded as less

pornographic than social in substance, defining the woman's status as a prostitute, assigning her to this 'job' and creating a specific 'social position' for her in the world of thieves. A genuine social position, because no one has any right to force a prostitute to work, or even to perform any unpleasant act that does not correspond to her 'professional' status. In the world of thieves a tattoo like this also protects her.

'Whiskers', 'beads' and 'tulips'

The objectification and reification of the thief's body, the perception of it as inanimate matter, is accompanied by its symbolic death. The *kol'shchik* (pricker), the tattooer, is a like a priest who performs a function similar to that of an executioner. The process of tattooing as an act that transforms the body into a symbolic corpse is specifically related to torture and execution. It is no accident that a 'legitimate thief' is often represented as a skeleton or a skull, or that the process of tattooing, like torture, is often employed coercively as a means of forcing the body to tell the truth. In addition, not only are tattoos often applied with cruel intent, the process is also accompanied by *shramovanie* (scarring), *rubtsevanie* (seaming) and *kleimovanie* (branding), so that a kind of bas-relief of three-dimensional images is created on the human body. These sculptural elements indicate that the body has not merely been transformed into an object, but that it has become 'formless' matter. This is the ultimate ritual 'dehumanisation' of the body and the creation of a 'new' man.

The symbolic operations that may be performed on the human body in the world of thieves are not limited to tattoos. In order to sexually 'improve' a thief's body, small beads are sewn into his foreskin and 'whiskers' or 'bracelets' are set into it; the head of his penis is cut into four parts and becomes a 'tulip'. Similar operations transform certain parts of a thief's body into instruments of execution and in this way the entire sexual sphere of his life mutates into the action of an executioner enacting a ritual of violent rape on his victim. This is the nature of the relationships with subordinates and *fraera* (outsiders). Thieves have an array of symbolic actions which are intended to mutilate the body. These include traditional ritual ways of severing an ear, or putting out an eye and removing the scalp together with the skin. In the course of such operations the body is transformed, its meanings and functions are changed. The traces left by the removal of tattoos and the scars and deformations resulting from torture acquire quite specific meanings. They are symbols of the same kind as the tattoos. In thieves' argot the word *raspisnoi* (decorated) is used not only for a man covered in tattoos, but also for one with a large number of significant scars. Danzig Baldaev gives both of these meanings in his dictionary.

In this social space the notion of the self, the individual, is broken down. The thief does not belong to himself, he belongs to the world of

thieves. The life of one man is not important where the struggle for the immortality of the law of thieves is being waged. Here the body is only a part of the language of thieves, the language of tattoos, scars, ritual gestures and tortures. And torture is only one kind of question asked of the body, it is simply the language of a thing, for instance the language of a 'pen' (knife) addressing the body. Only the body can be trusted here, only the body does not lie, only the body can be forced to speak the voice of truth.

In thieves' culture the body is the traditional focus for the performance of various social rites. It ceases to be static and the act of its creation continues without interruption. In this context the *glavny pakhan* (head boss) naturally acquires the features of a Demiurge and Creator. But all of these operations on the body, including torture, are regarded here as 'speech acts', as communication in the true, sacral language of thieves. The signs of this language – the tattoos – protect the body, for they are the signs of the divine speech of the *demiurge-pakhan*. A thief's tattoo indicating that the body concerned belongs to the world of *vory v zakone* (legitimate thieves) also renders it unavailable for any social involvement not sanctioned by the law of thieves. Tattoos are also a political problem because of the way they politicise the body.

All of these processes are typical of the world of thieves, which long ago became the model for our society as a whole. It is fashionable, prestigious and profitable to be part of the world of thieves. It is a fine and noble thing to take an interest in this world. Our popular entertainers sing songs in criminal jargon, authors write entire novels in it, thousands of films are made about the criminal world, in which noble bandits 'bump off' ignoble ones by the dozen, or vice-versa. The myth of the mafia society and state is actively propagated, with texts about thieves playing an important part in the process. But if our entire country is one immense gang led by a *pakhan* (criminal boss), why shouldn't we accept *blatnaya fenya* (criminal spiel) as our normal form of speech? To *botat' po fene* (reel the spiel) is fashionable and chic. A dictionary of thieves' jargon and an album of convict tattoos are becoming chic accessories, like a sailor's striped vest over bare skin. The language of thieves is becoming the language of the reader, linguistic self-awareness is criminalised. Language is turned inside out in the reader's mind, reinterpreted, it is mutating into 'newspeech'.

The world of thieves is attempting to absorb and subjugate all social space. Meanwhile the guardians of linguistic purity have long been complaining about the rapid infiltration of standard speech by all sorts of 'bad' words, in particular from thieves' jargon. But the actual scale of the infiltration of thieves' culture into life is greater than anyone can imagine. And this infiltration occurs via a different route. It is not the penetration of culture by mafia practices that is expanding and growing, it is our awareness of this infiltration. It is the mind that is infiltrated,

not life. And then we begin to see all of our life in terms of thieves'
culture. The collection of tattoos published in this book gives some idea
of the breadth of the front along which the world of thieves is advancing
on mass consciousness. And if we look around we shall see that not only
'legitimate thieves' but also millions of perfectly honest, upright citizens
are covered with these tattoos. Simply because every fifth inhabitant of
our country has passed through the camps, and every second has been
through the army 'zones'. And we honest, upright philistines and law-
abiding petty bourgeois have long ago become used to seeing ourselves
in the role of noble bandits, downtrodden victims and fearless inhabitants
of tattooed slums.

1   'A Dictionary of Prison and Camp Jargon' (*Slovar tiuremno lagerno blatnogo zhargona*)
(Moscow, 1992)

2   M. Demin, 'Convict' (*Blatnye*) (Moscow: Panorama, 1991)

3   'Capital' (*Stolitsa*) (No.1, 1991)

4   D.S. Baldaev, 'A Dictionary of Criminals' and Thieves' Jargon' (*Slovar blatnogo vorovskogo
zhargona*) (2nd Edition, Moscow, 1997)

5   A. A. Medyntseva, 'Old Russian inscriptions in Novgorod's St. Sophia Cathedral'
(*Drevnerusskie nadpisi novgorodskogo Sofiiskogo sobora*) (p.149, Moscow, 1978)

6   ibid. p.149

7   ibid. p.194

8   ibid. p.195

9   L.A. Milyanenkov, 'On the Other Side of the Law' (St. Petersburg, 1992)

10   Block 2, 13 Pulkovo Chaussee, St. Petersburg. 1994

Photographs. Section One

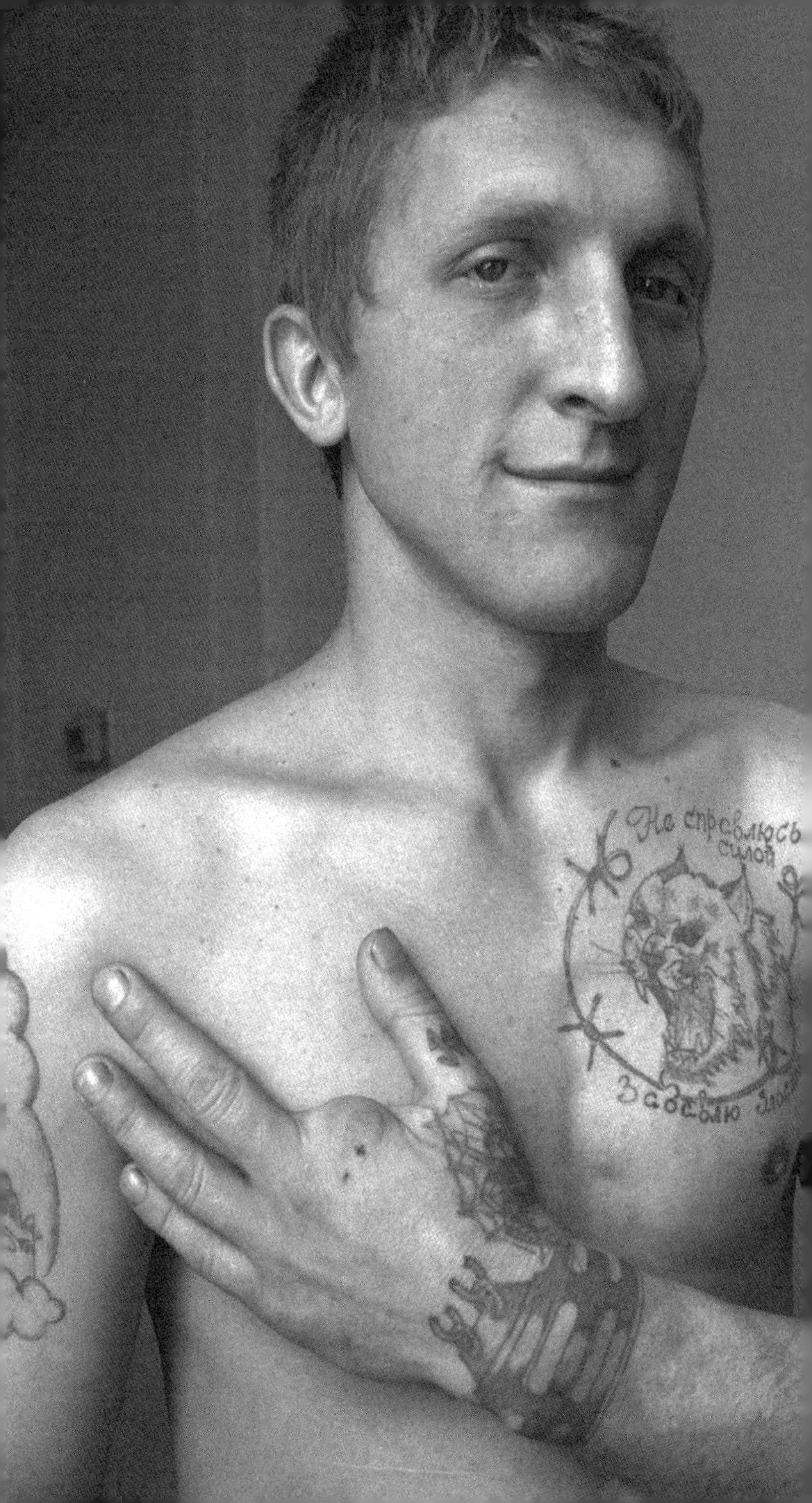

Не спасёшь силой
Забрыю зло

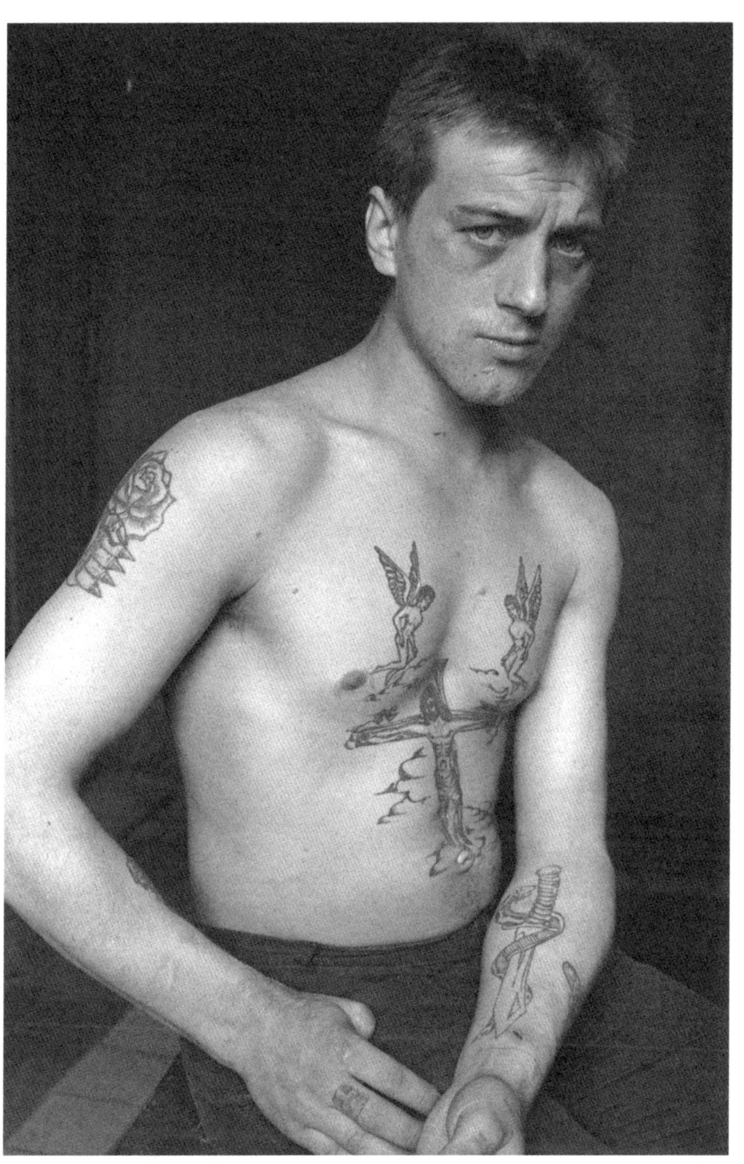

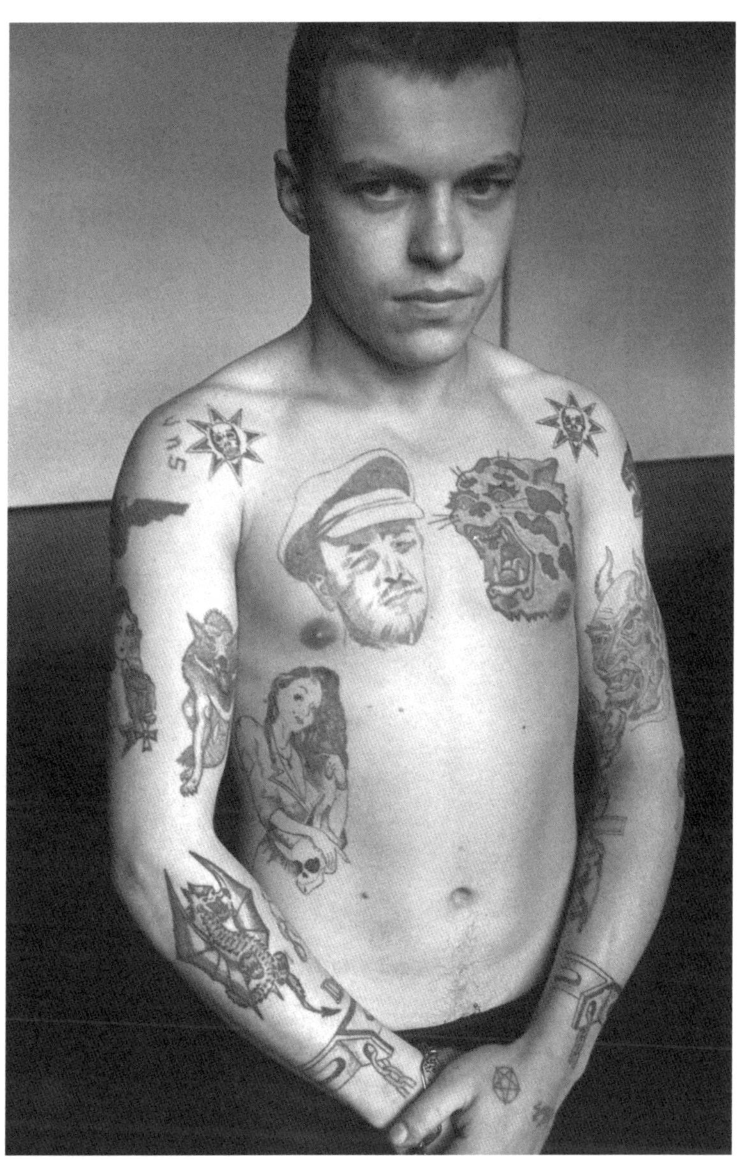

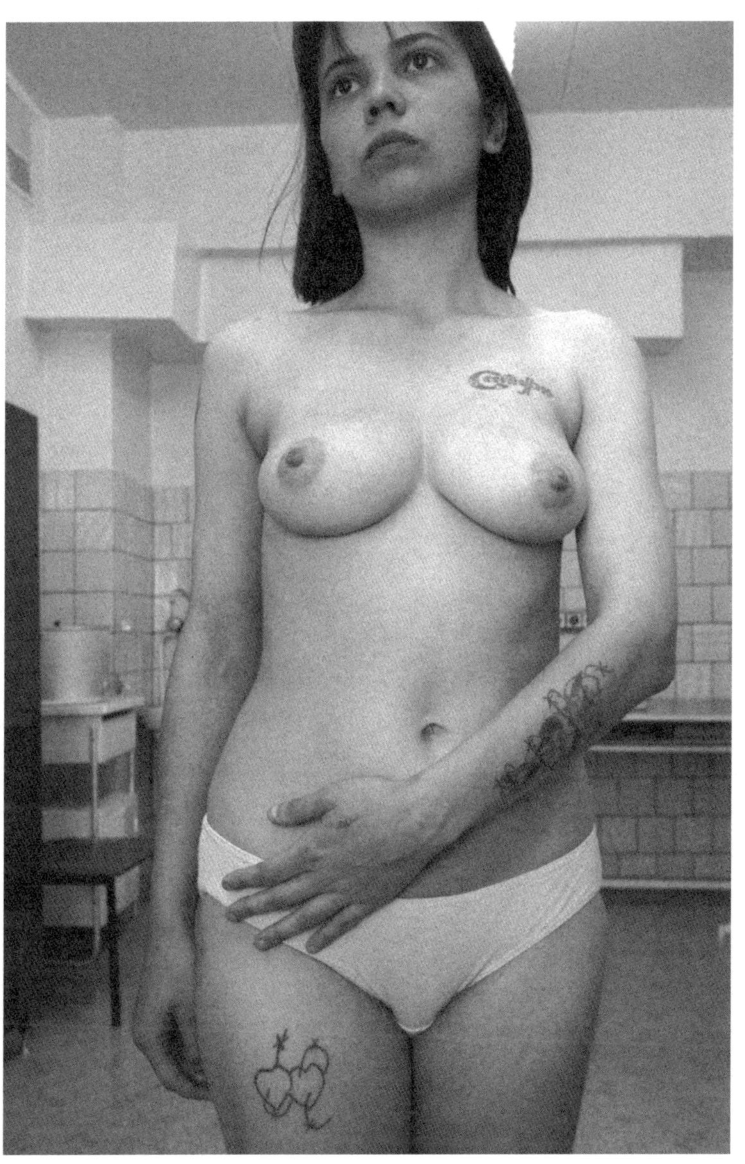

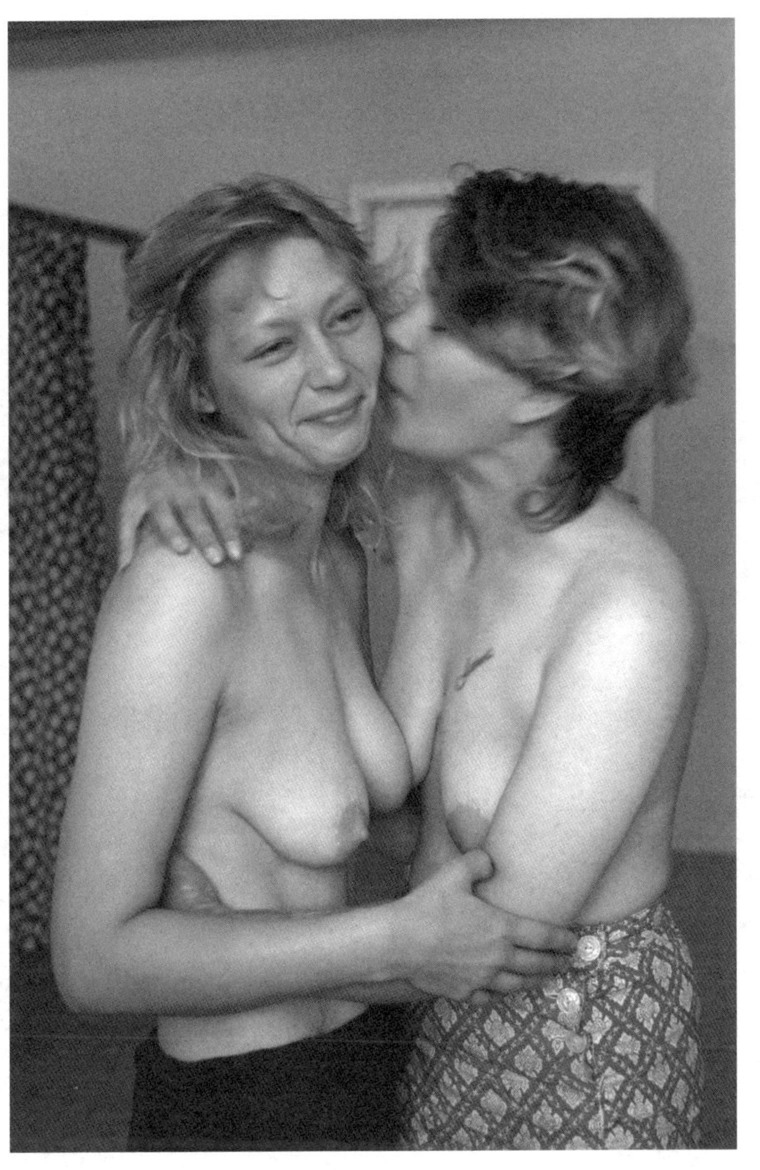

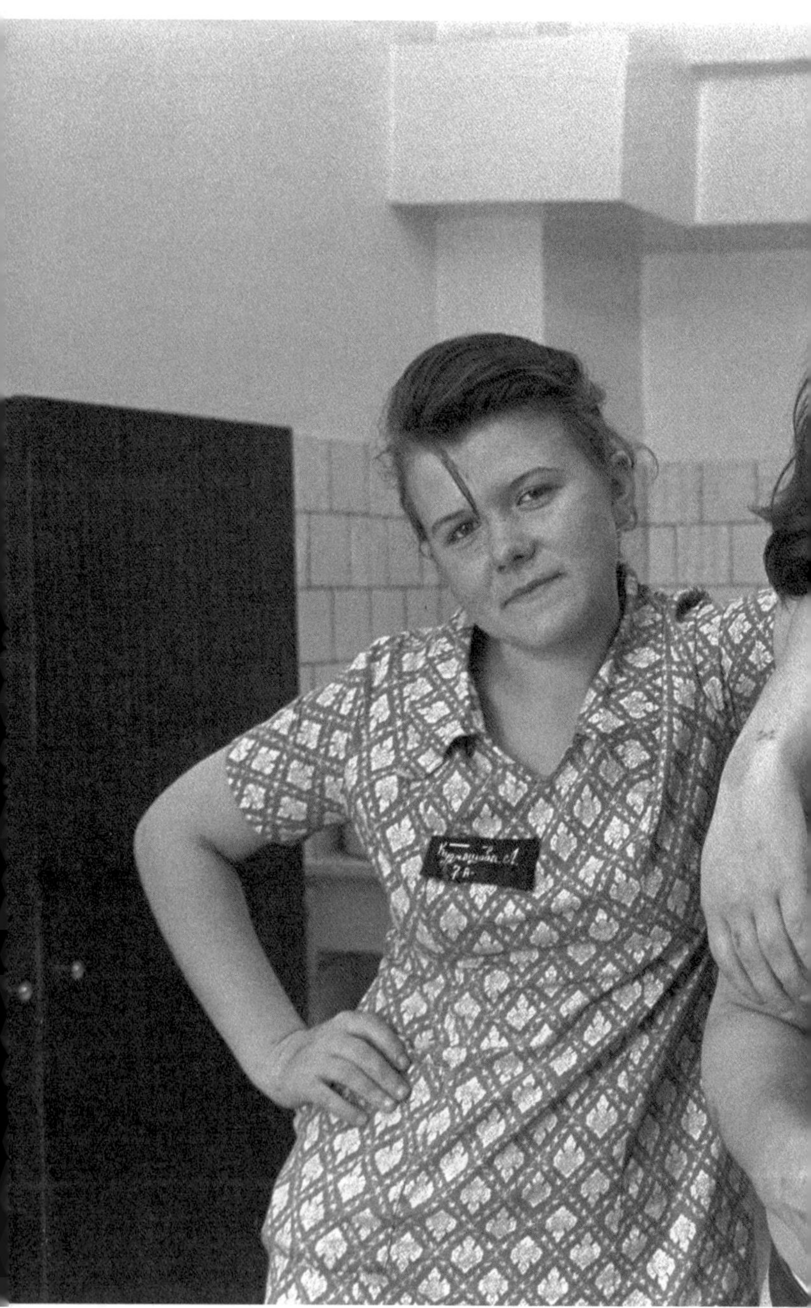

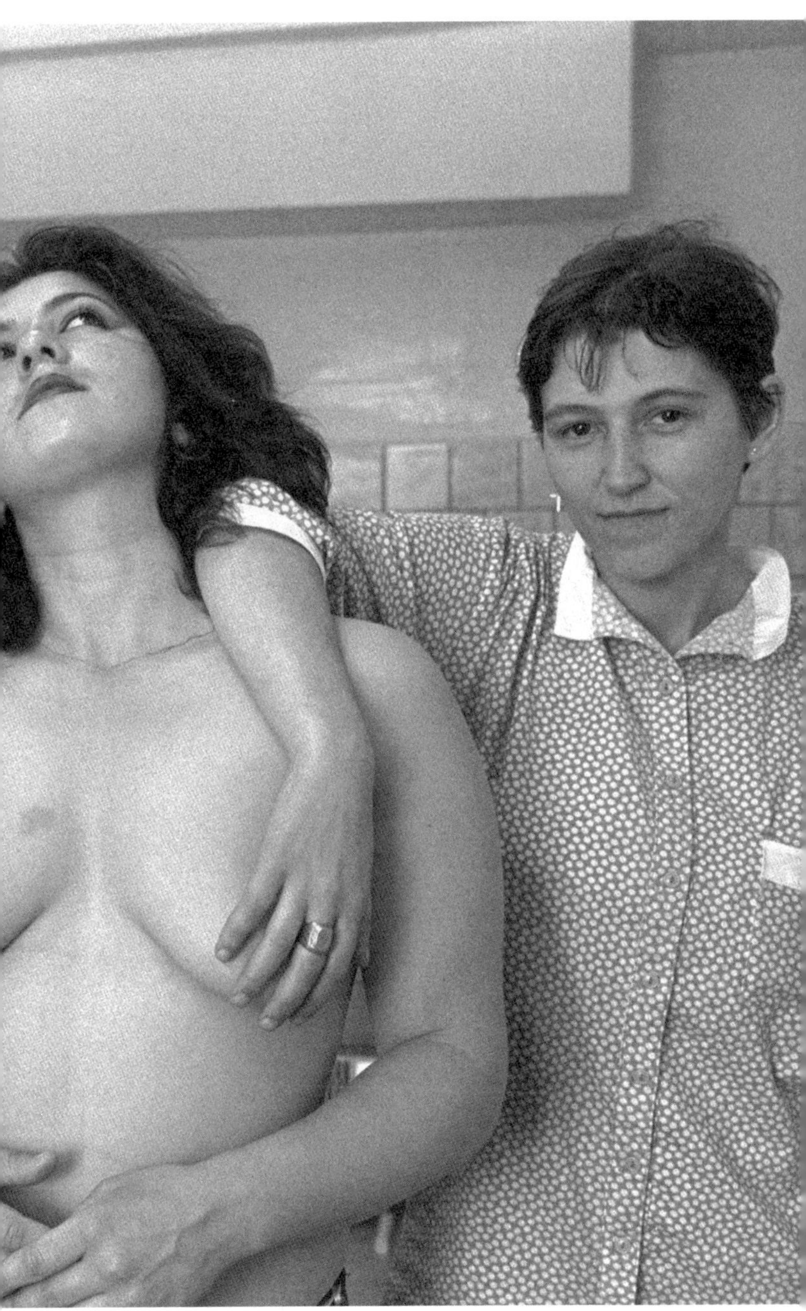

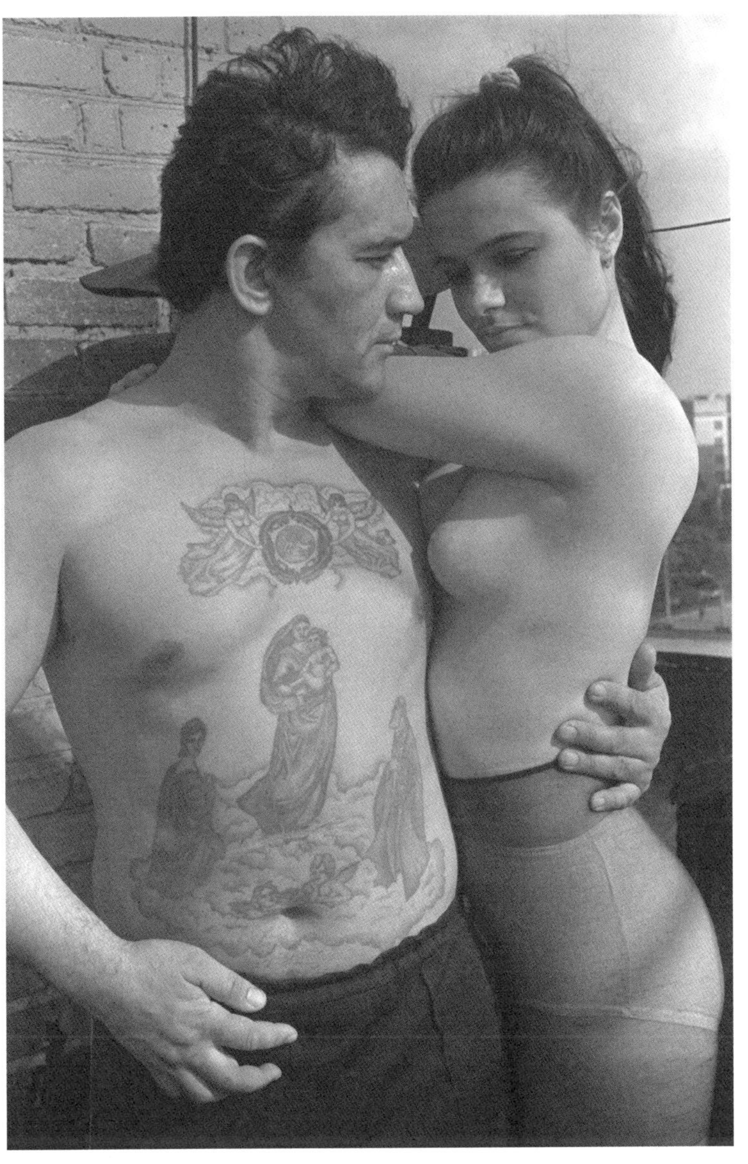

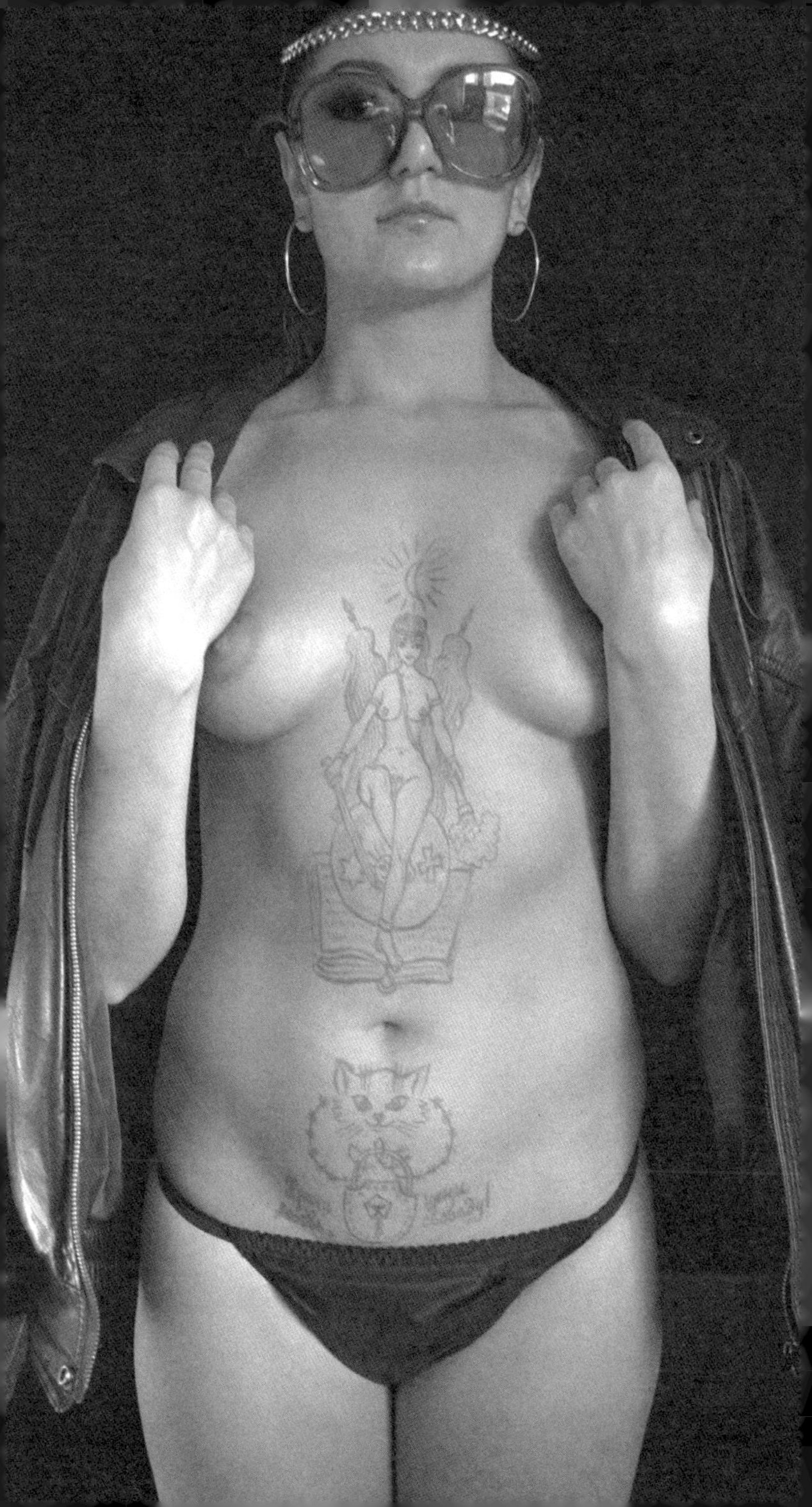

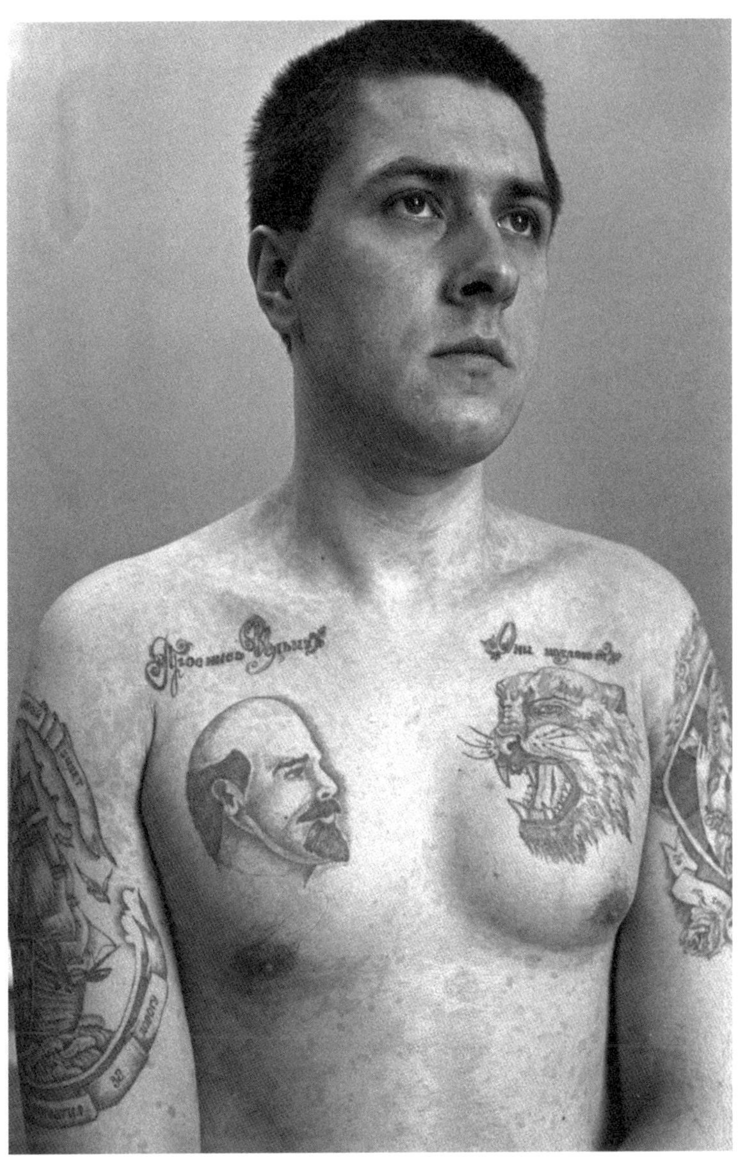

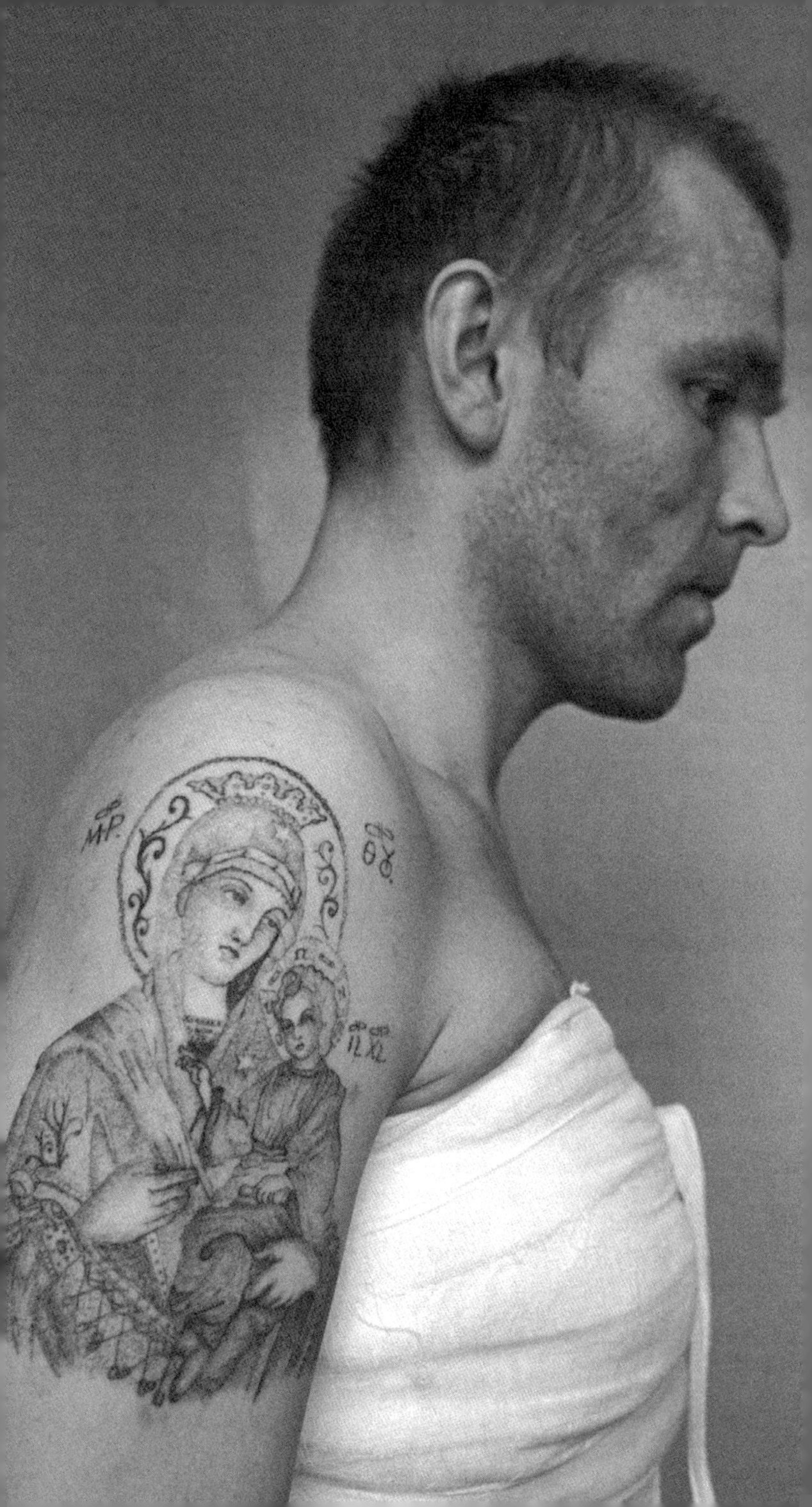
МР ΘΥ
ΙС ХС

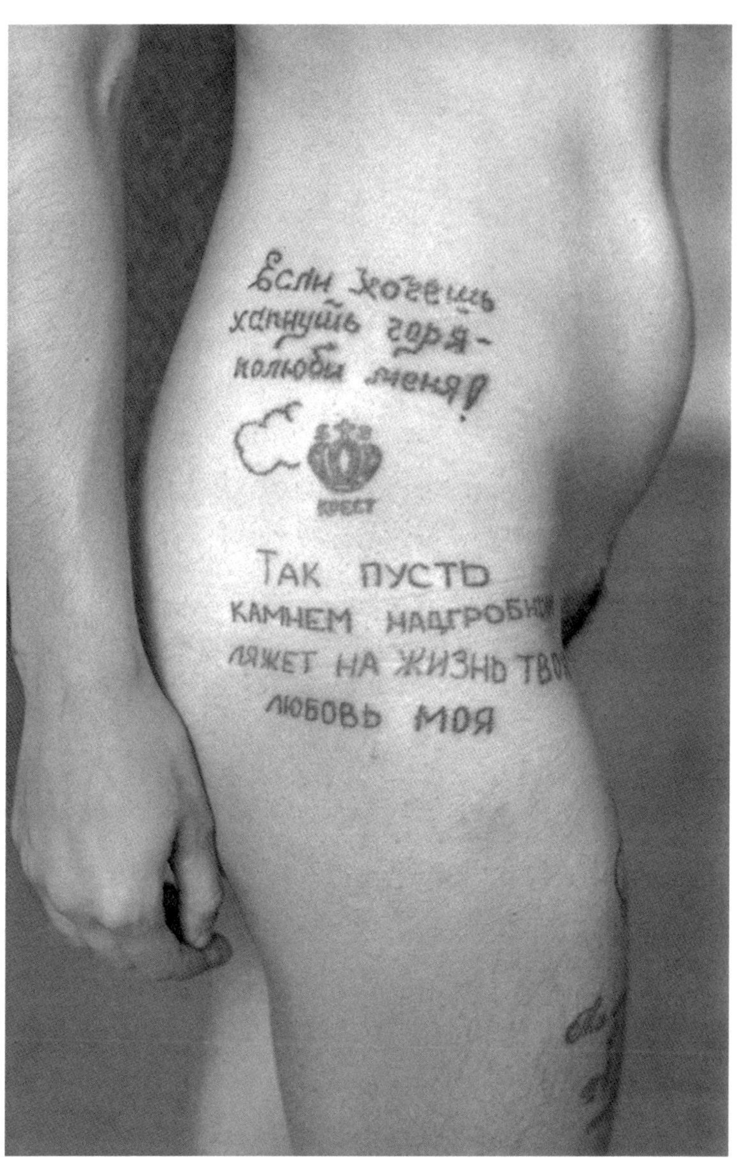
Если хочешь
хапнуйь горя -
полюби меня!
КРЕСТ
Так пусть
камнем надгробной
ляжет на жизнь твою
любовь моя

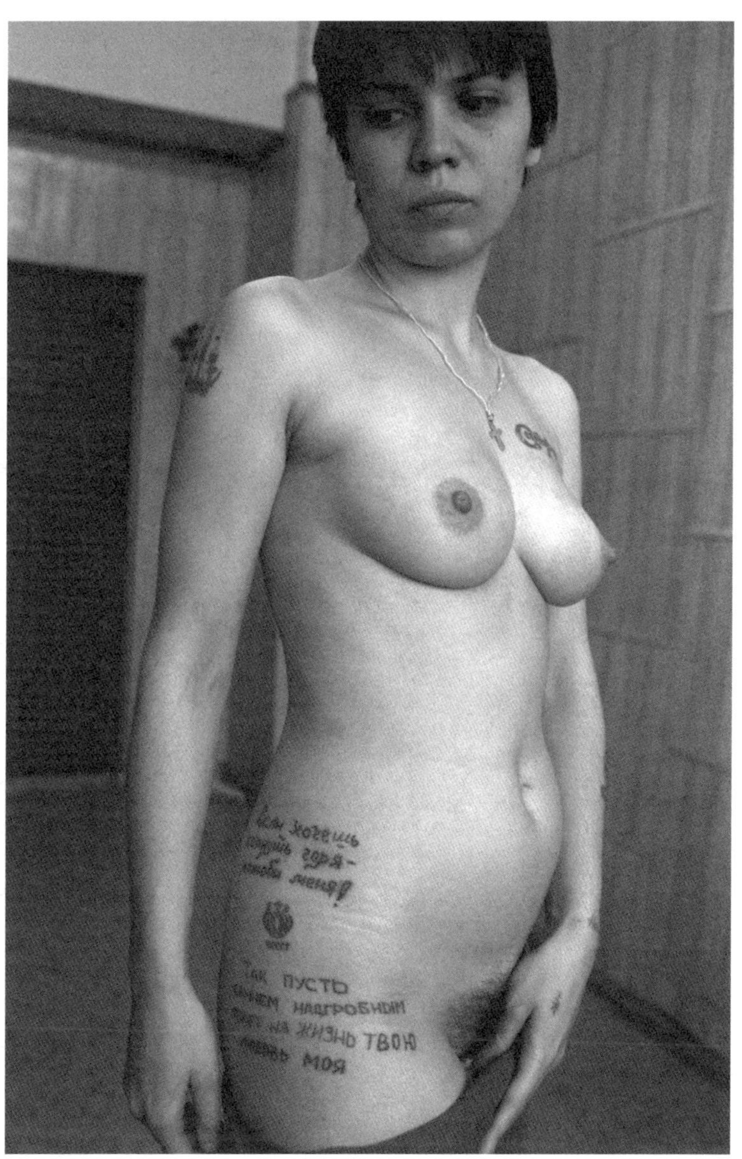

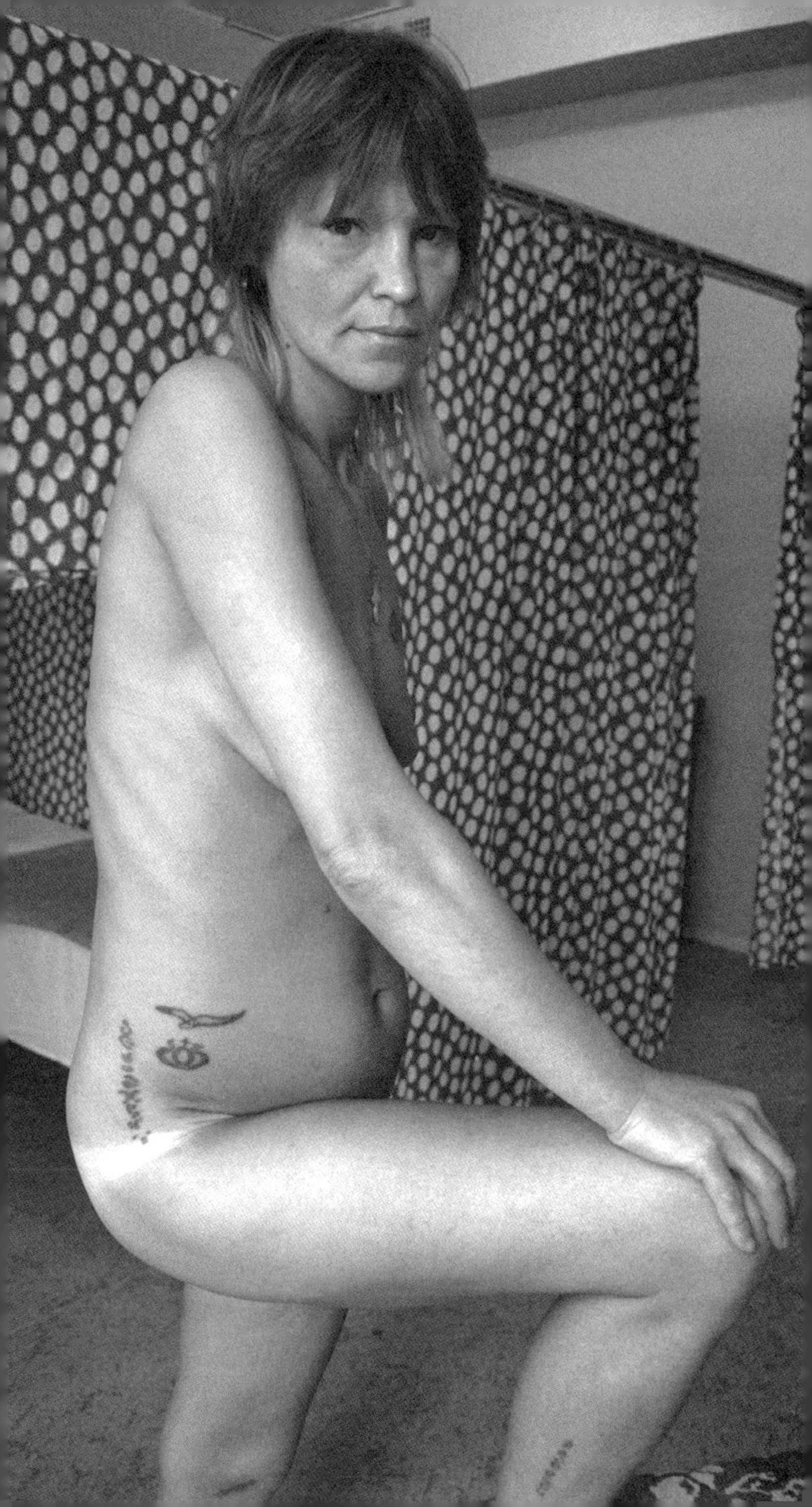

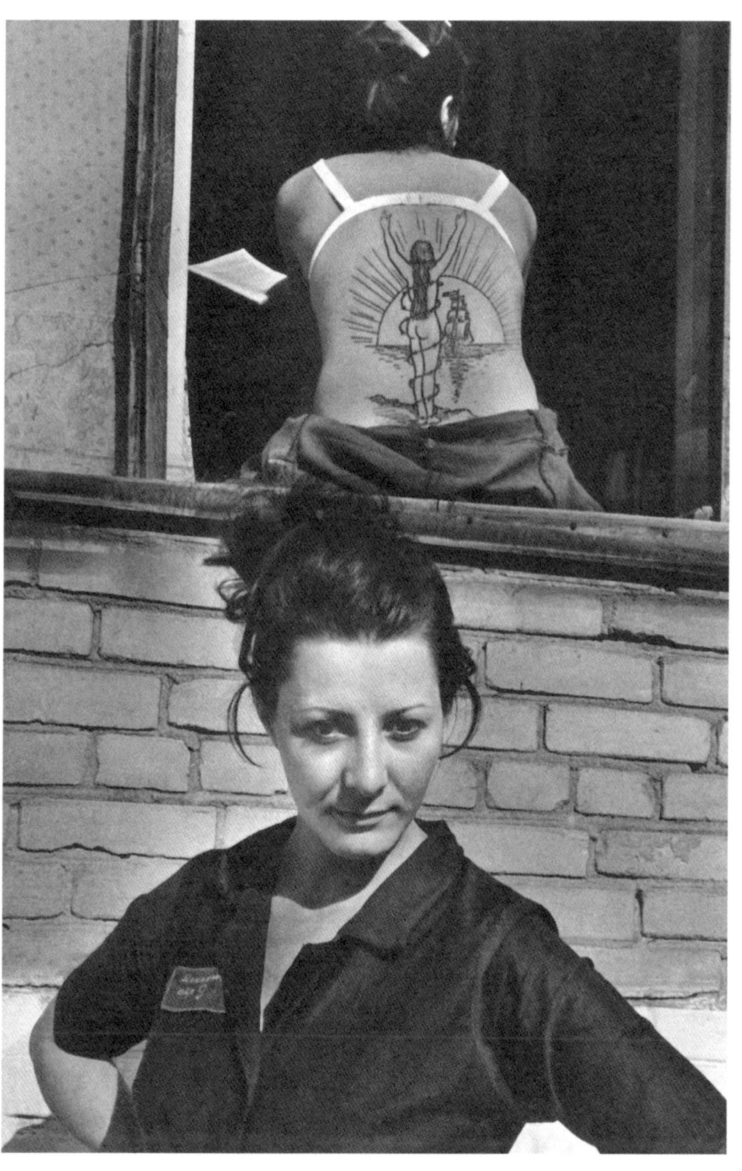

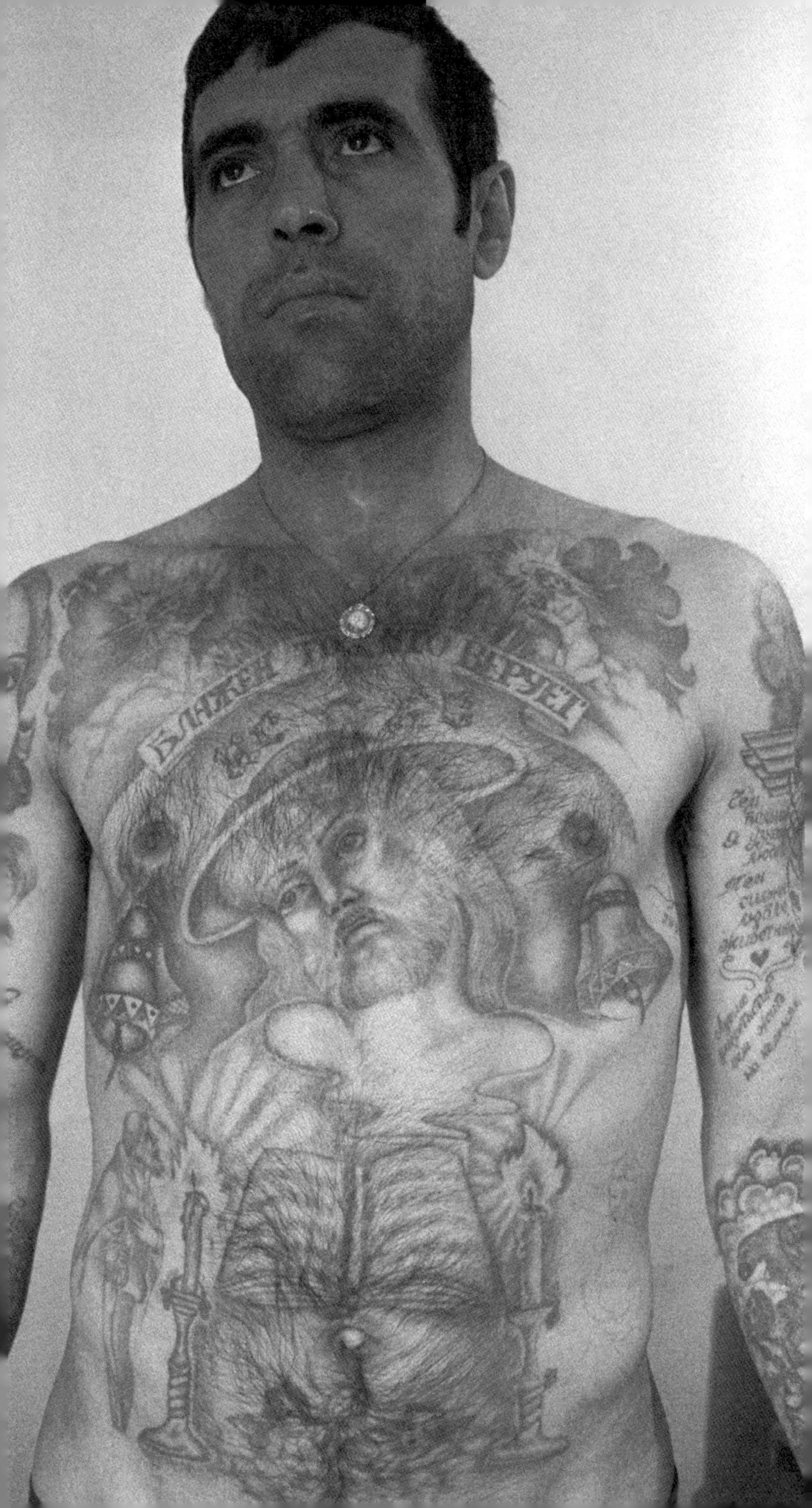

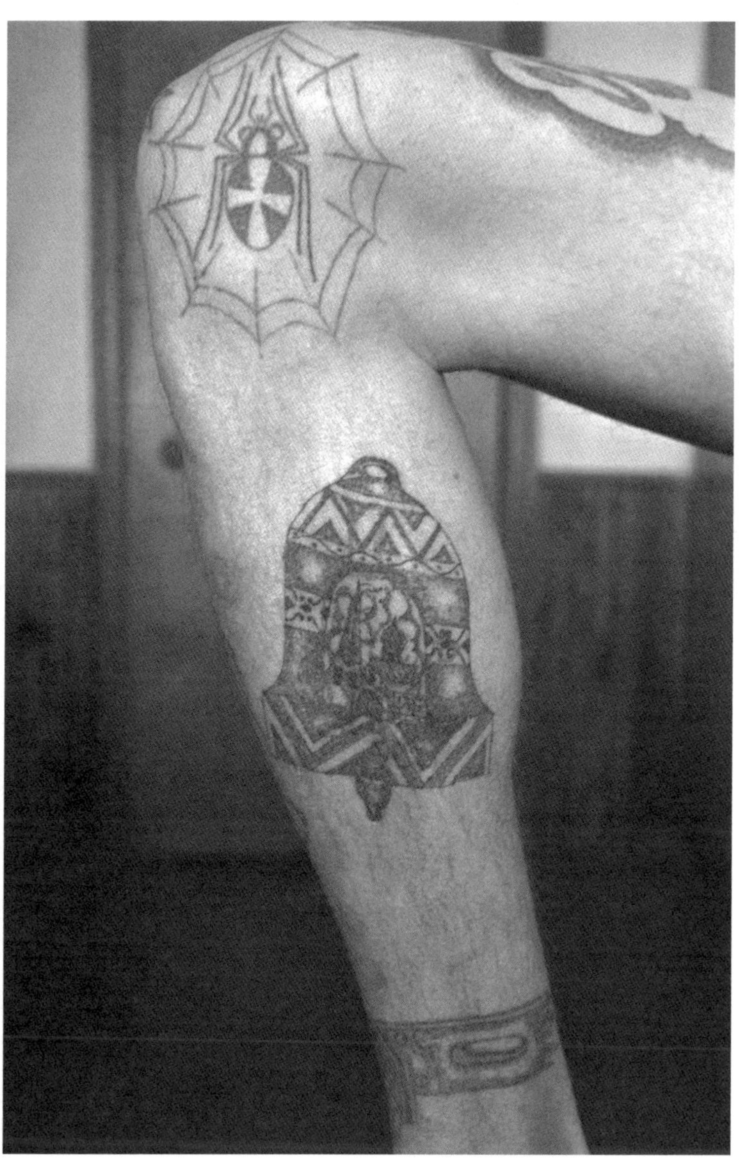

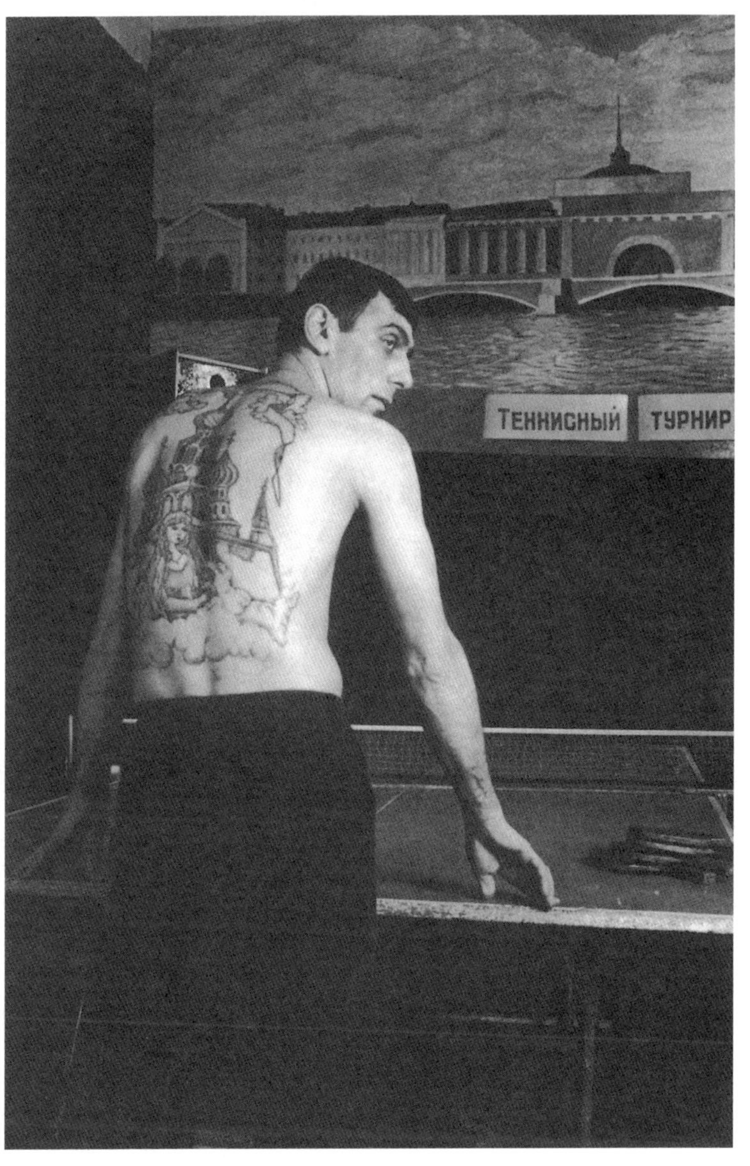
ТЕННИСНЫЙ ТУРНИР

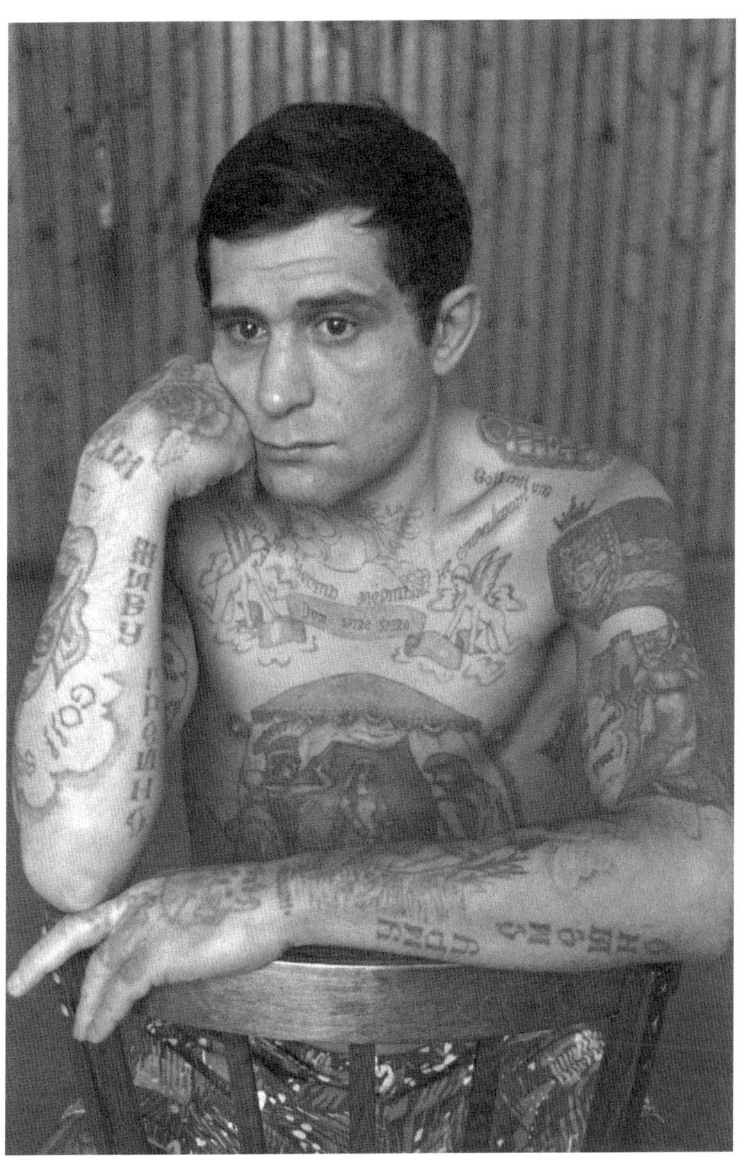

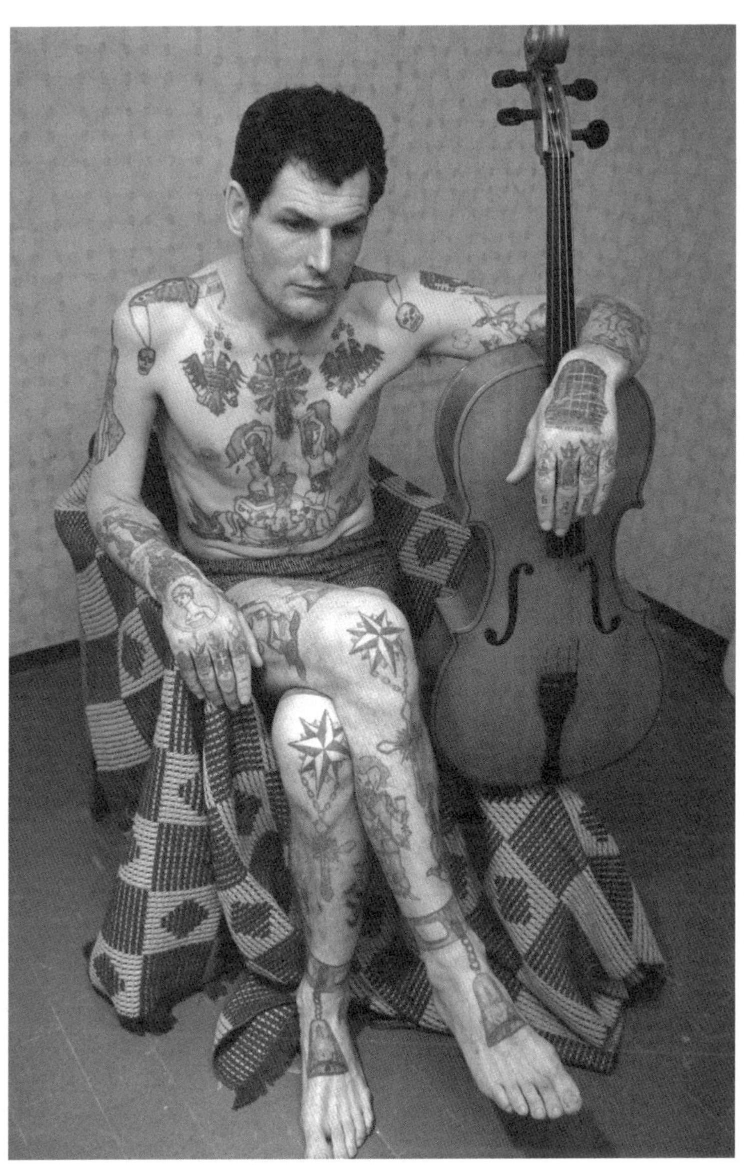

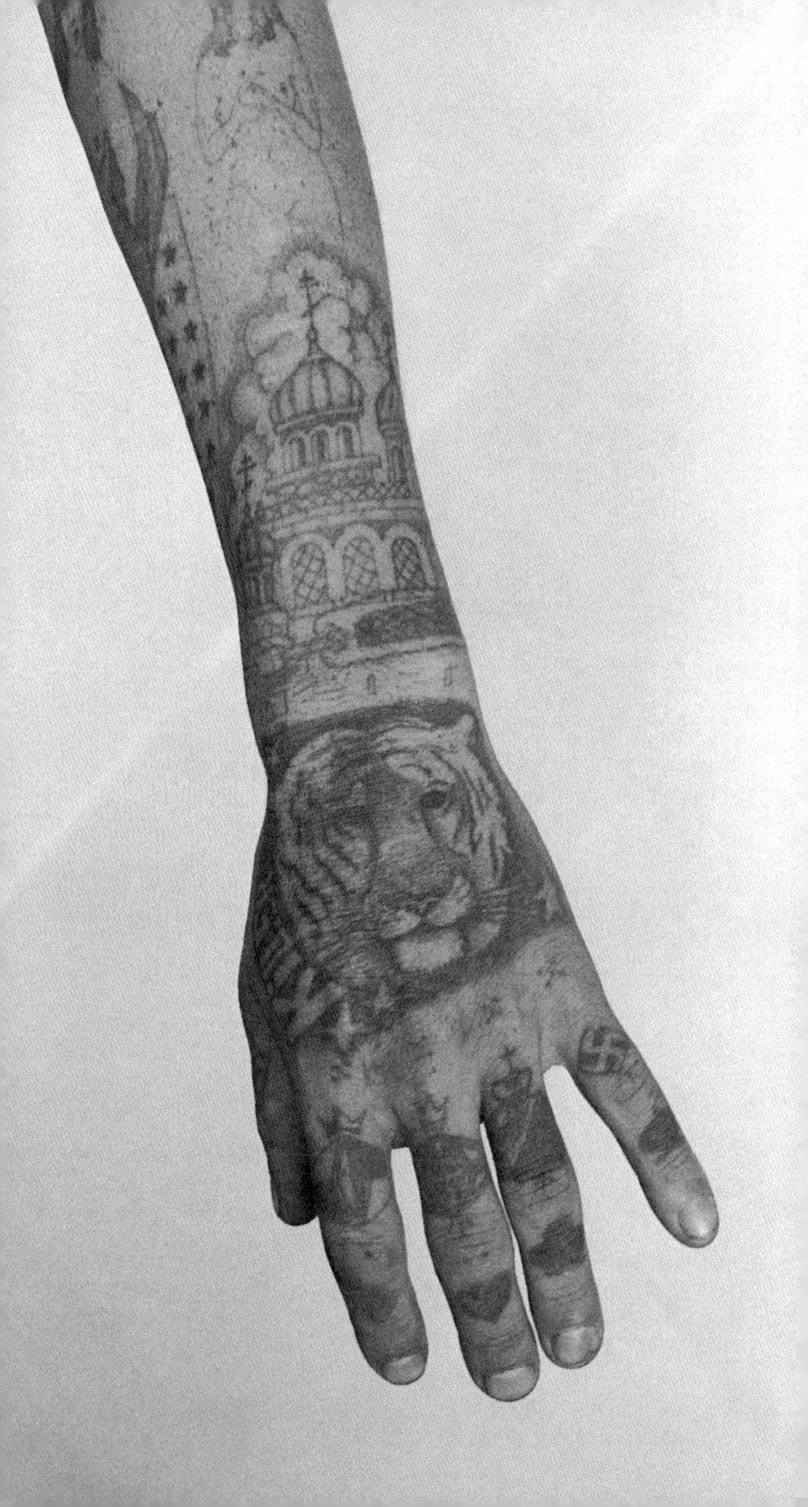

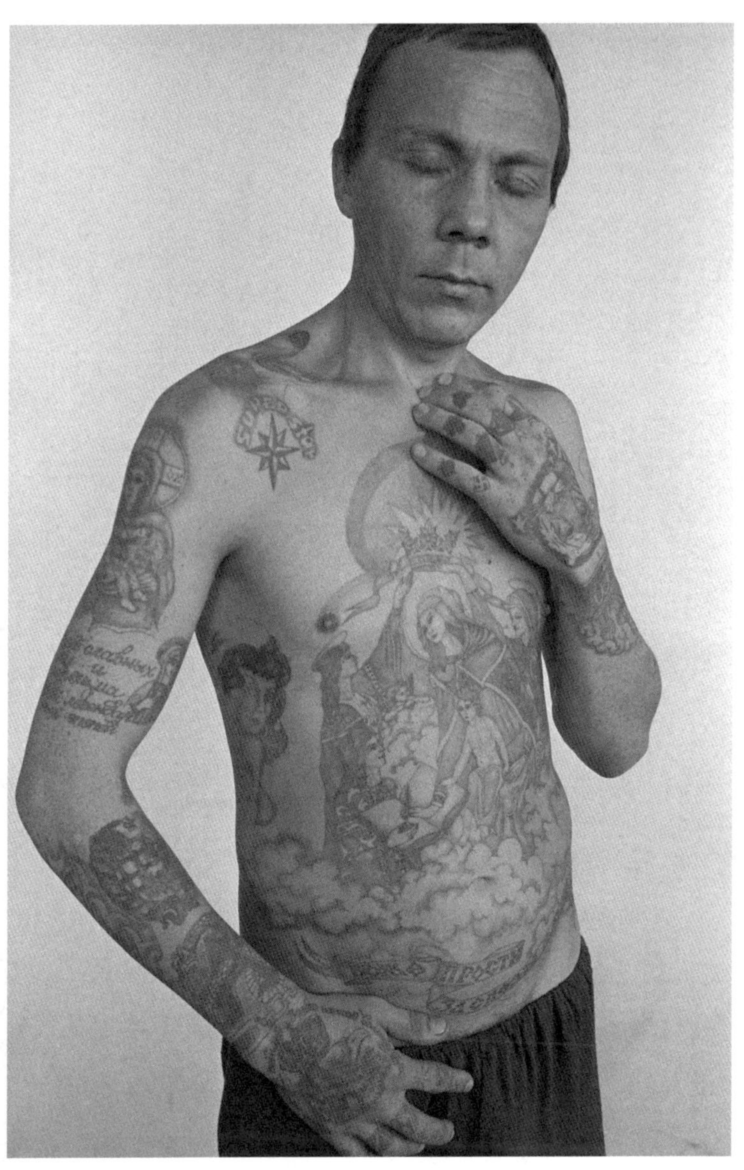

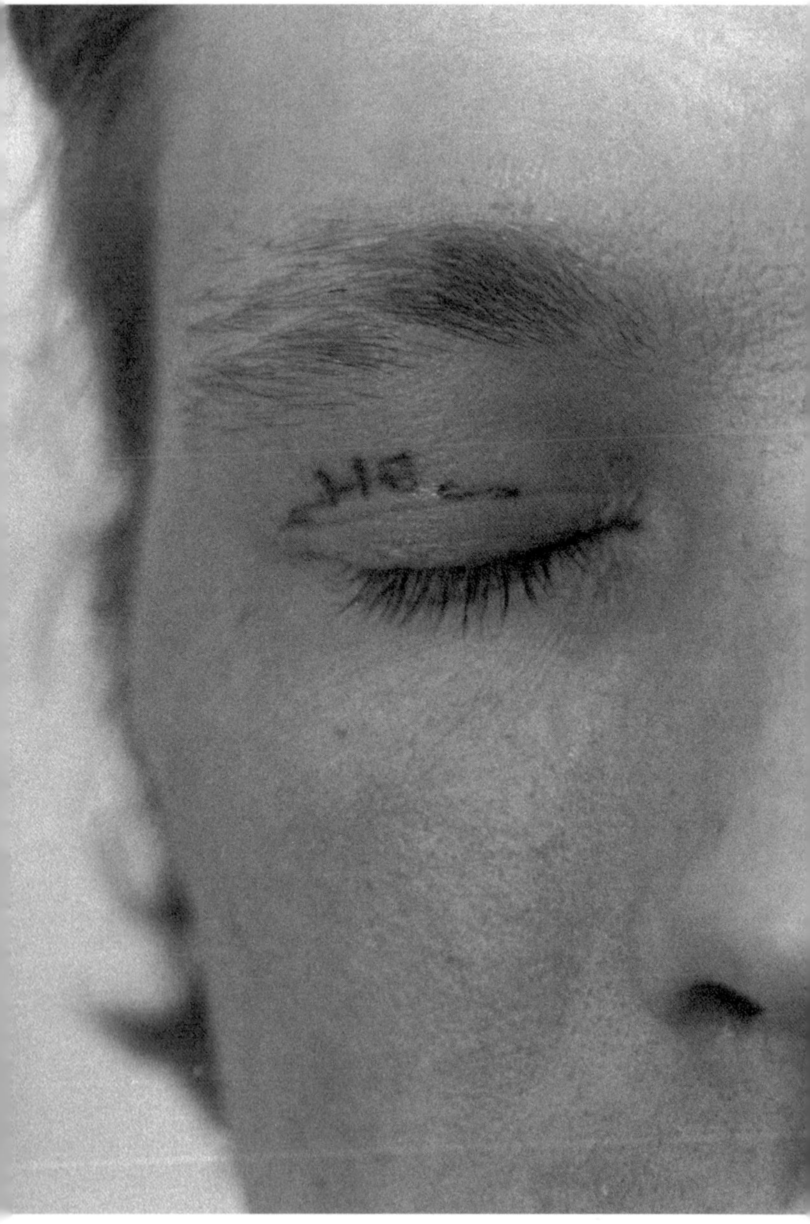

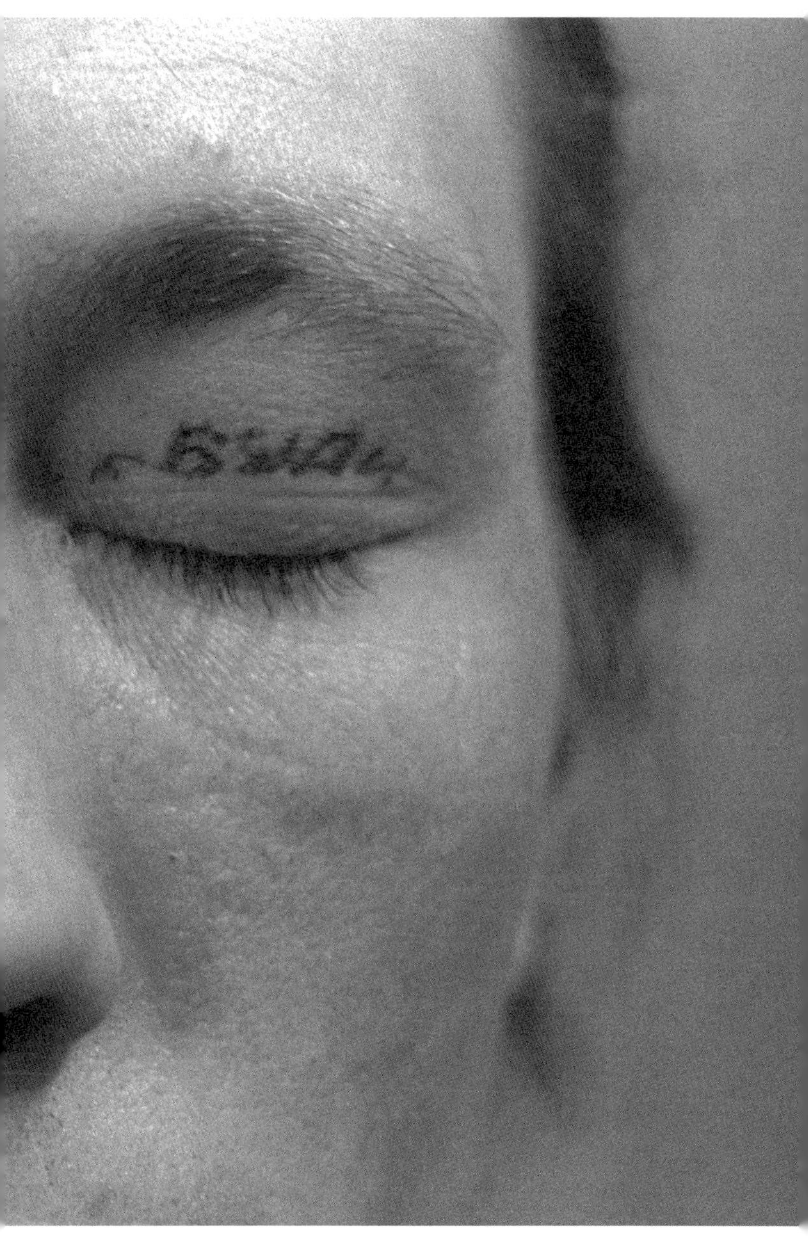

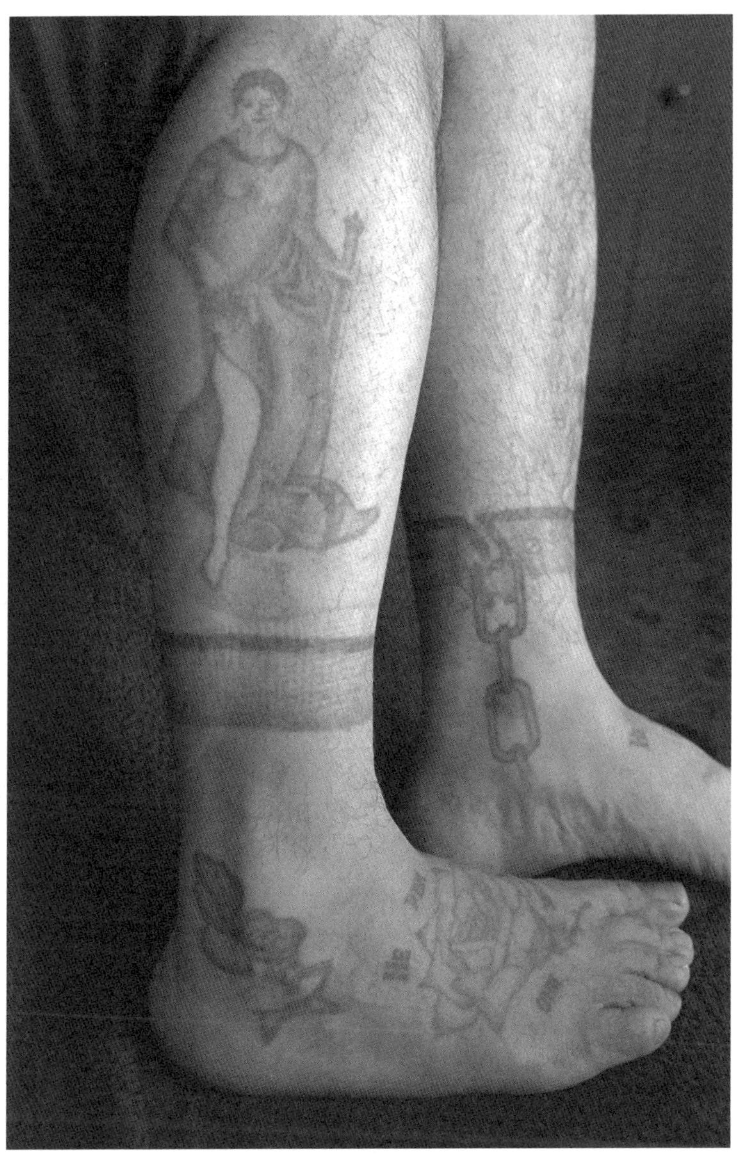

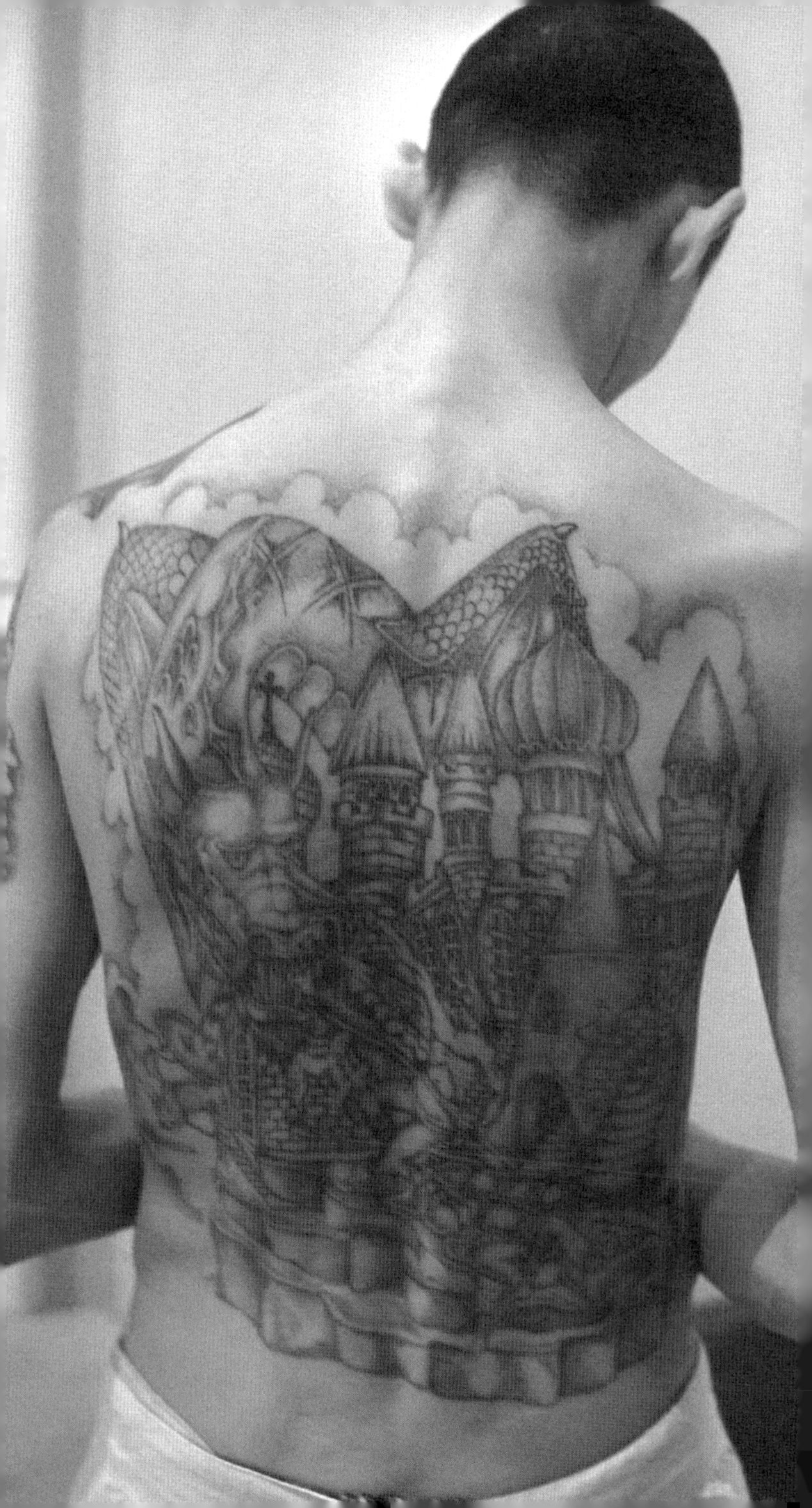

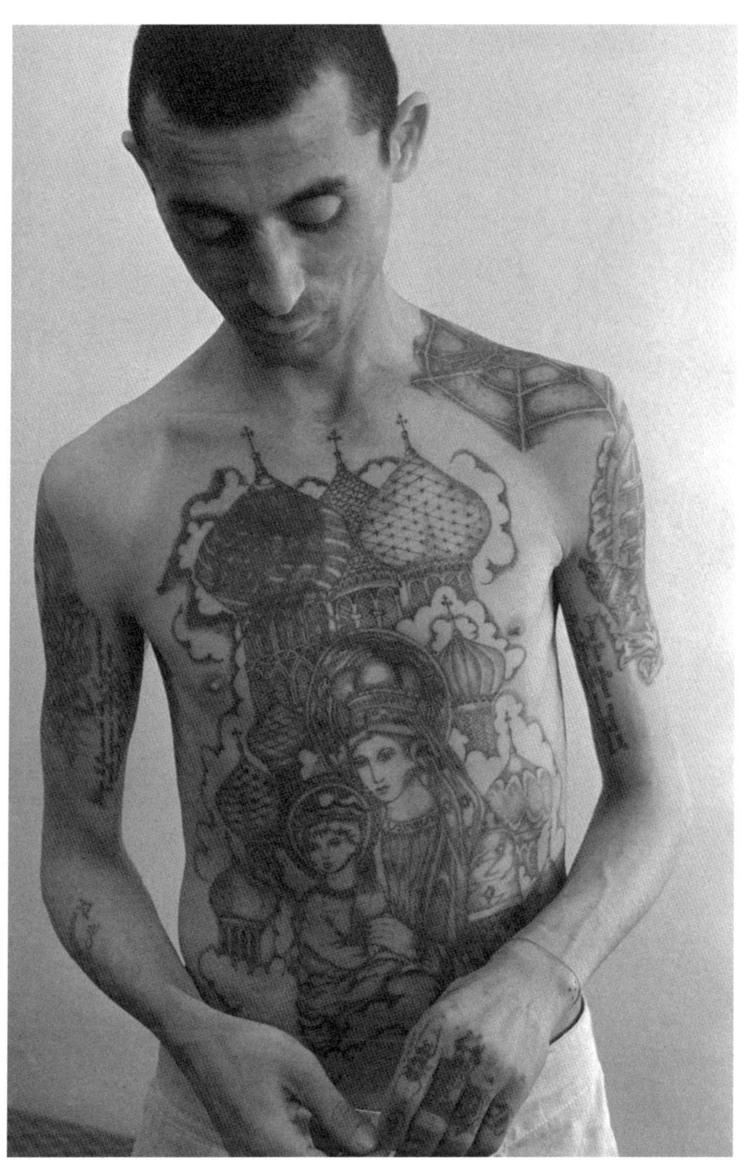

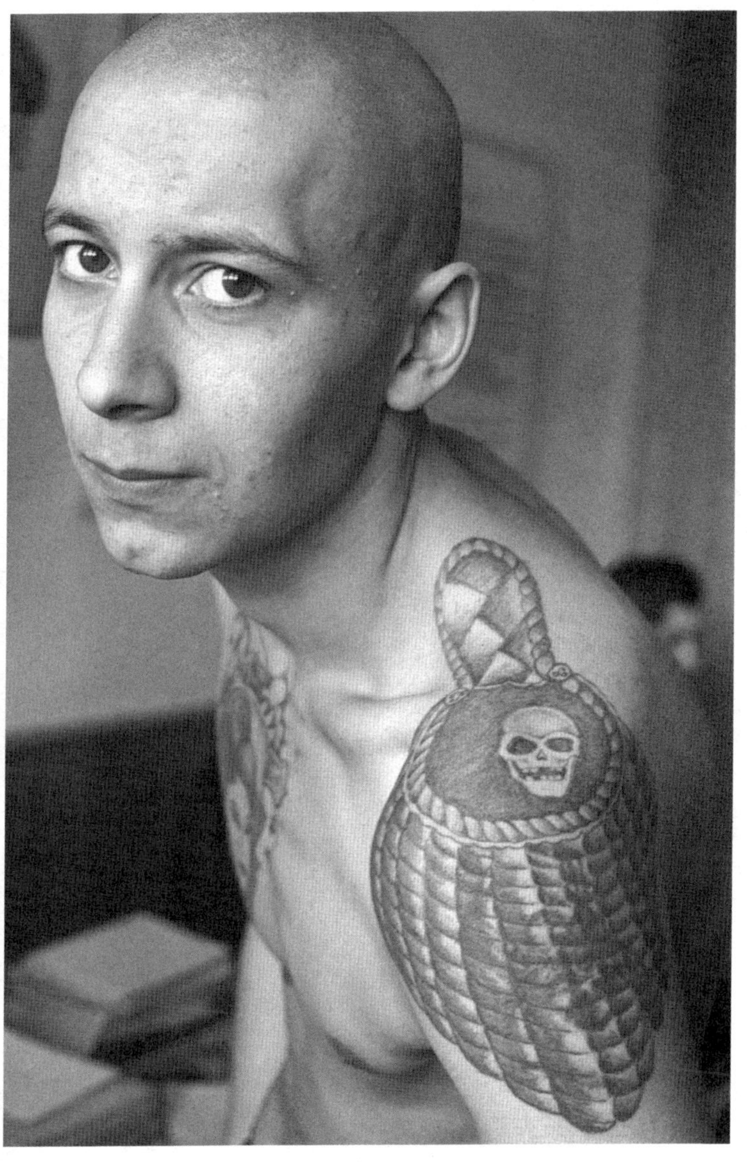

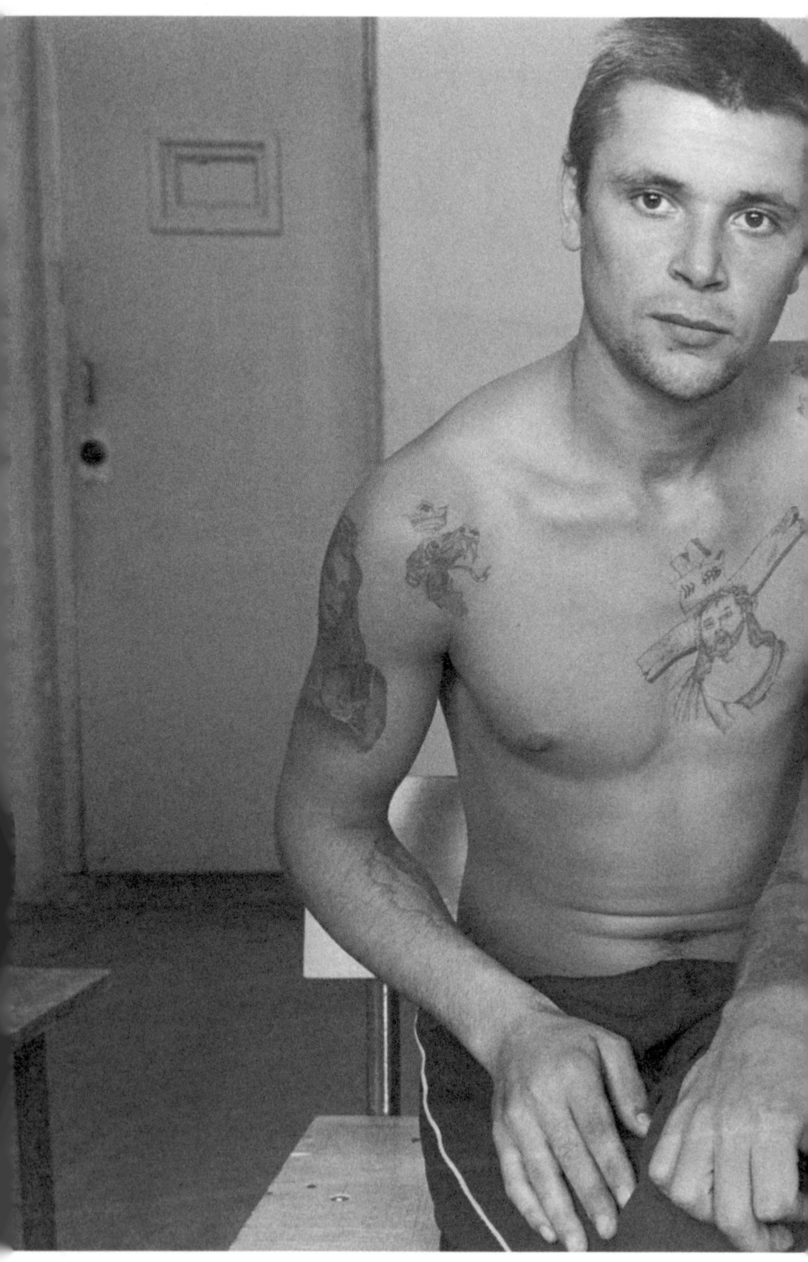

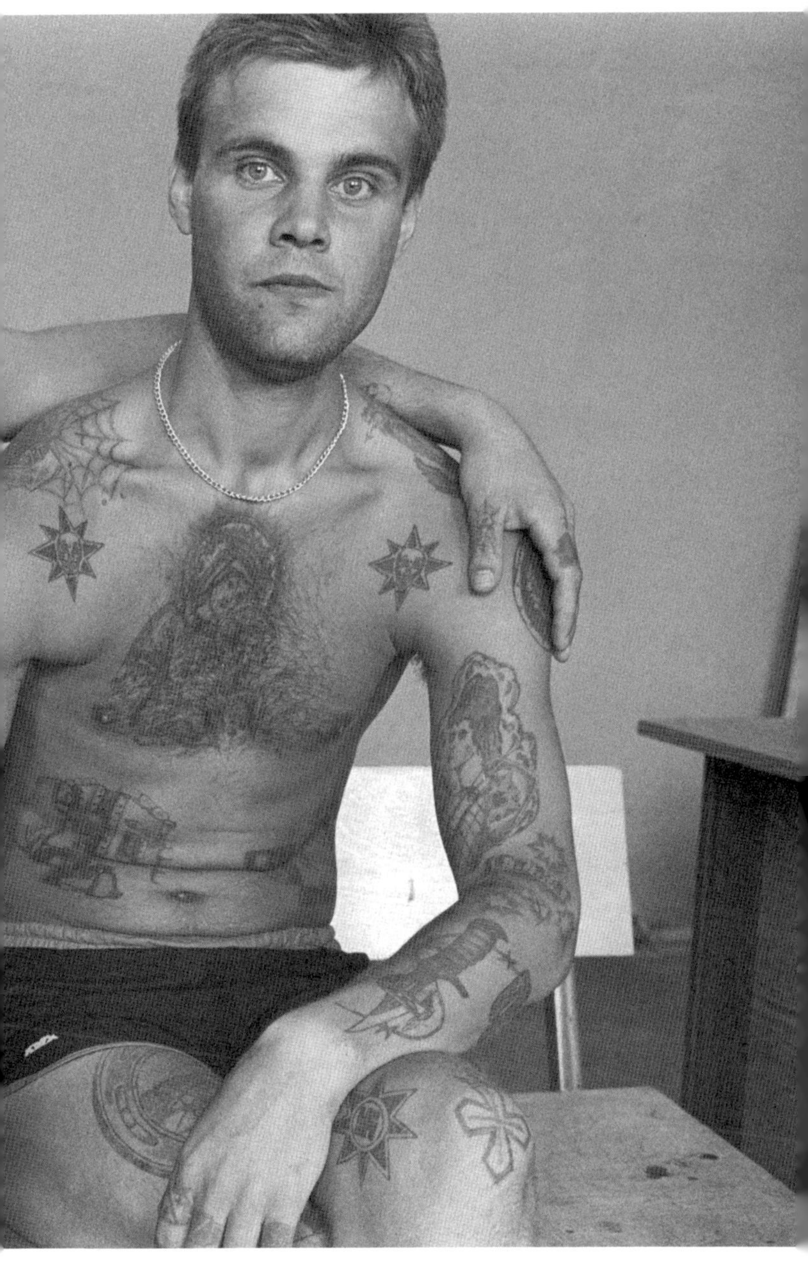

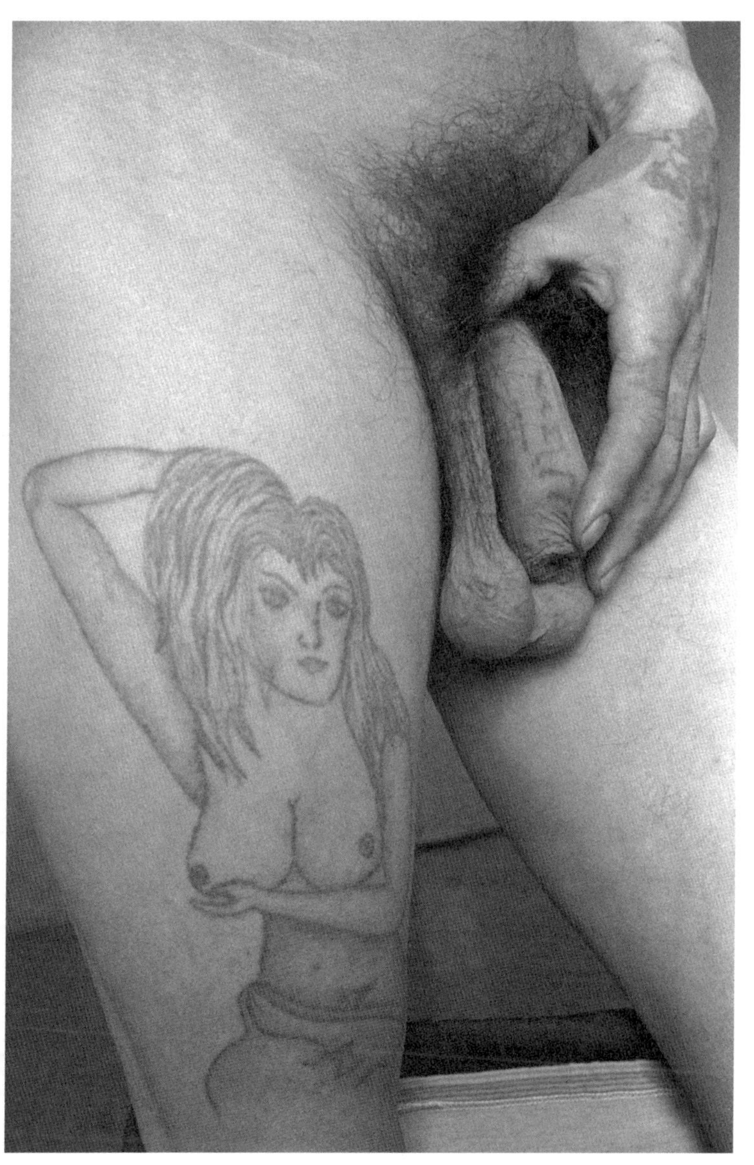

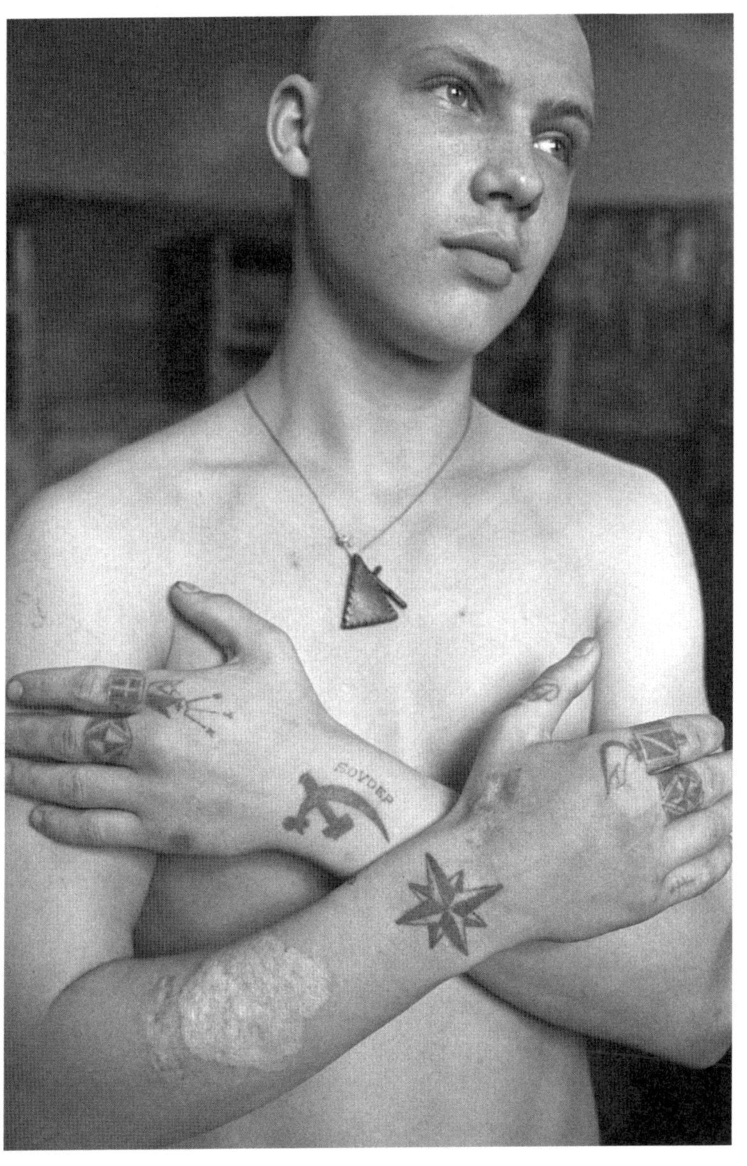

Drawings. Male Tattoos

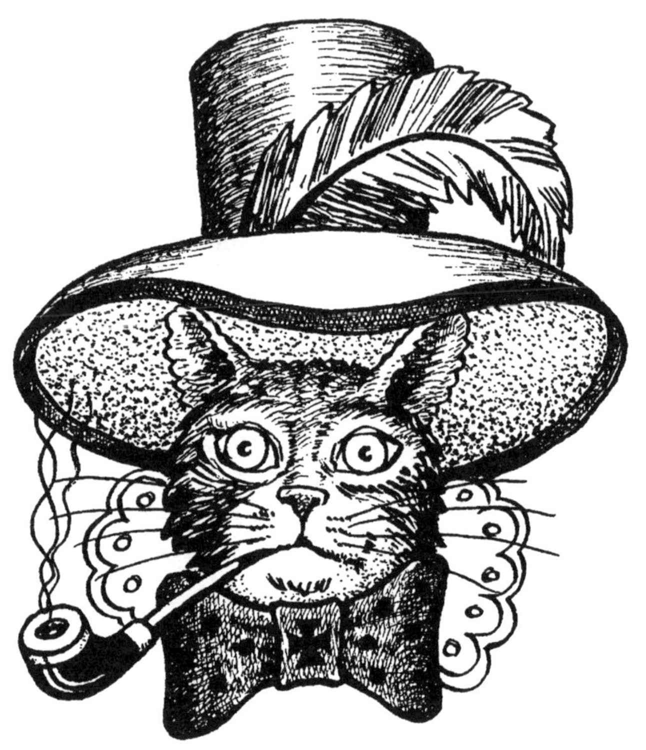

A convict's tattoo signifying 'I am a recidivist convict. I have no resources to support a conscience'.

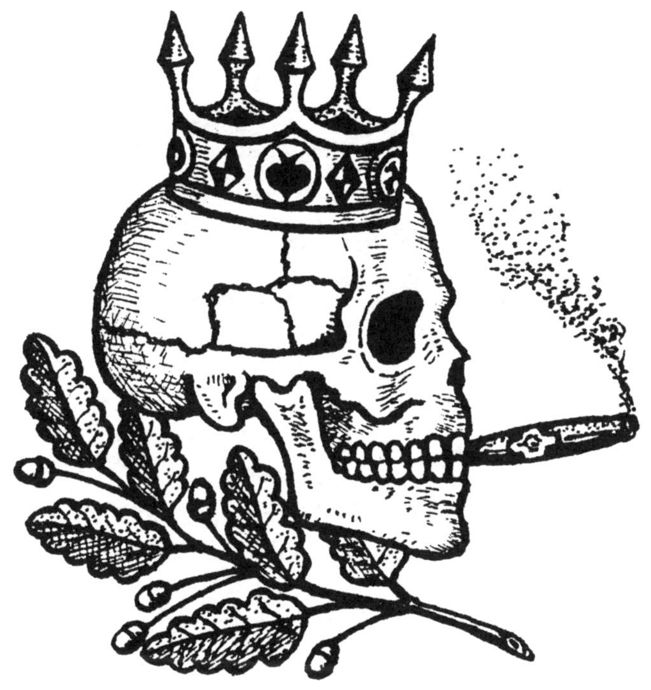

The tattoo of a criminal 'authority', first recorded in 1954. It was later widespread in the corrective labour institutions of the Urals.

'I live one a day at a time. Death is always close – it is a release from earthly suffering. A thief is not afraid of death.'

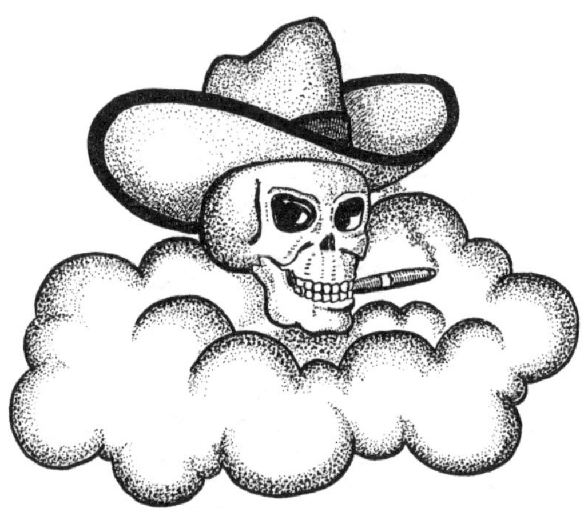

Subclavicular

A thief's subclavicular tattoo.

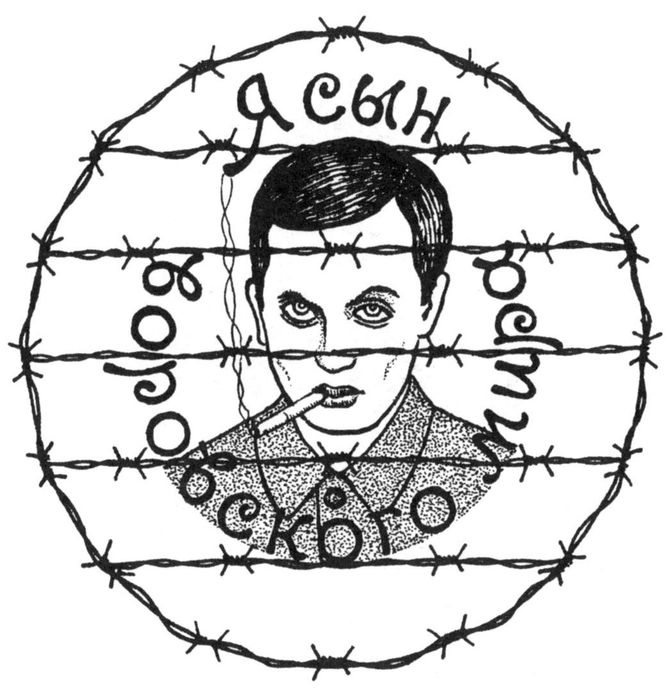

Konyashin Hospital Morgue, 104 Moscow Prospect, Leningrad. 1966. Right side of chest.

A rare specimen of a tattoo with a portrait. The wearer of this tattoo was killed in an attack on a militiaman (policeman). On 18th July 1966 at about three o'clock in the morning, beside the House of Culture on Moscow Prospect, a ferocious attack was launched on a militiaman on point duty, in an attempt to steal his official issue weapon. The attacker, I. Tikhonov, had several previous convictions for theft. He failed to react to a warning shot from militiaman Stepanov of the Moscow District Militia, and in the ensuing struggle he attacked Stepanov with a knife. He was killed by the second shot from Stepanov's gun.

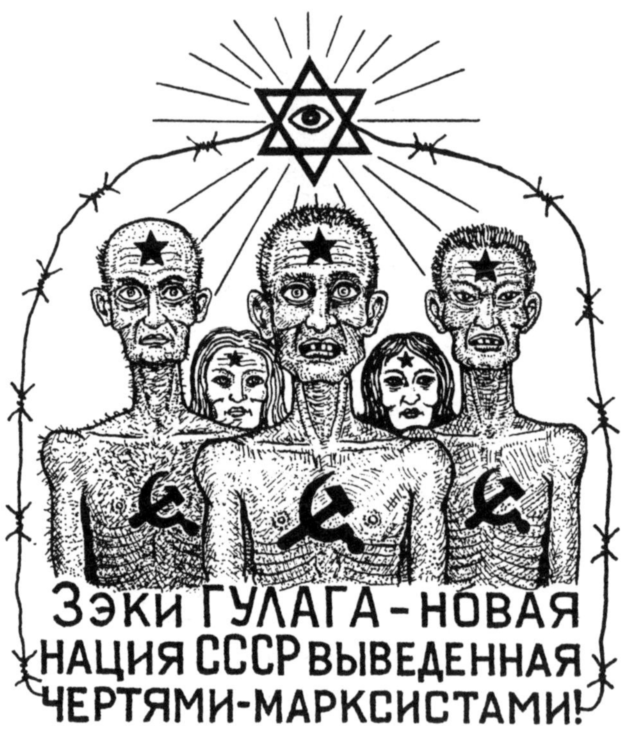

State Office of Internal Affairs, 25 Voinov Street, Leningrad. 1963.

An anti-Soviet tattoo, from a prisoner arrested for petty hooliganism. Drawn in a corrective labour camp in the Pechora camp system in 1952, during a six-year sentence for theft under the decree of the Supreme Soviet Presidium of 4th June 1947. The tattoo was copied at the technical support centre of the Leningrad Region State office of Internal Affairs at 25 Voinov Street, where people under administrative arrest worked.

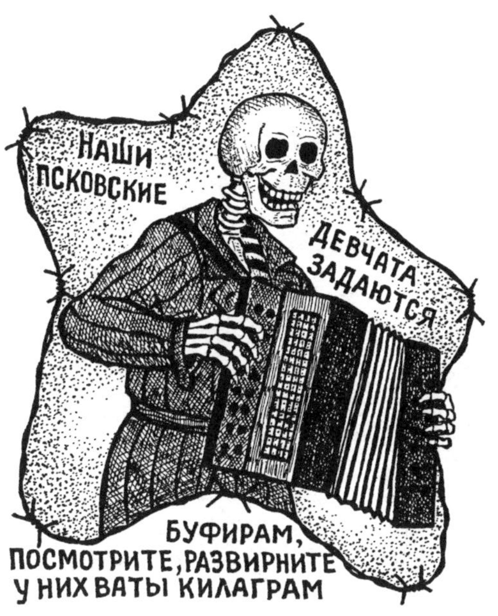

1961. Hip.

A tattoo drawn from the rapist and murderer Tikhomirov. On 13th June 1961 the body of a woman was discovered along the Warsaw railway line close to the track. Her skull had been smashed in and a garrotte made of nylon stockings was deeply embedded in her neck. She wore only a blouse. A tracker located the dead woman's bra 200 metres from the body. The tracker's dog led the operations group to a residential building close by and attacked railway worker Tikhomirov. When his room was searched traces of blood still remained on the floor, walls and furniture, despite his attempts to clean up. The weapon, a heavy spanner, was also found. Further investigation of the site by the tracker dog revealed the victim's shoes and bloody clothing buried in the ground. The victim was a milkmaid from the Pulkovo state farm. When the woman had resisted his attempt to rape her she was killed and then raped. When night fell Tikhomirov had removed her clothing, made the garrotte from her stockings and used it to drag the body into the exclusion zone alongside the railway line. It was later discovered by people gathering mushrooms.

'I'm an angel! Right, let's have all of you who aren't happy with Soviet power and who'd like some prison rations!!! Rostov-on-Don 23.II.1958'. The text on the club reads 'Additional rations for convicts from the Ministry of the Interior'.

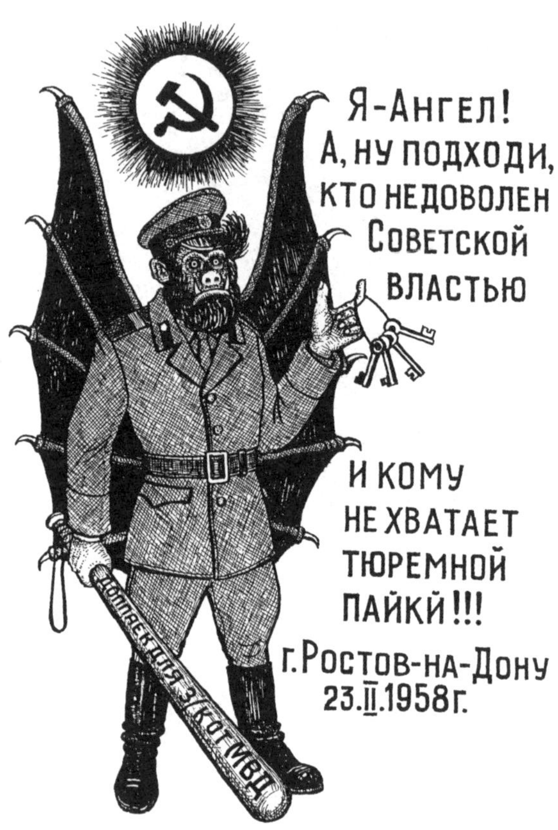

Corrective Labour Colony, Nalchika, Kabardino-Balkarsk Autonomous Soviet Socialist Republic. 1958. Stomach.

A 'grin' depicting a 'filth' and 'screw', the head warder of the cell block in Rostov prison. The wearer was convicted under the Supreme Soviet Presidium decree of 4th June 1947. He was given ten years.

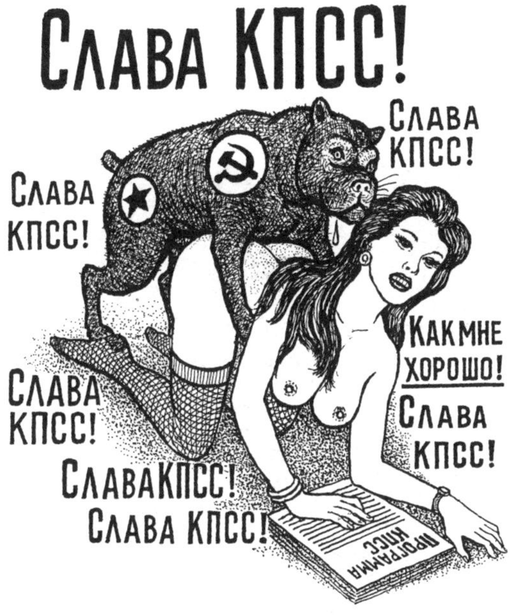

Ministry of the Interior Inter-Regional Hospital. 1992. Hip.

According to the wearer, this rare 'anti-social grin' is called 'the state or Party husband on duty'. He claimed that at one time the CPSU employed young men for 'special duties', which included satisfying the sexual demands of the wives of party bureaucrats while their husbands were 'playing at love' with 'state prostitutes' in secret dachas and special residences guarded by the KGB. These 'dogs' weddings' were kept a strict secret by the Party nomenklature husbands and their wives. The 'Party husband' or 'husband from the Party' was usually summoned by phone to join his high-ranking client for cognac, champagne and fine hors d'oeuvres at the Party's expense.

'Granny, take more commies than there are in the plan away to their bright future: the head of the colony, his administration and production deputies and all his cronies from the operations section... I'd be glad to go with you!...'. The barbed-wire letters read **'CPSU'**. The hem of death's robe reads **'Resolutions of Lord God. The plan will be ful[filled] at any price'.**

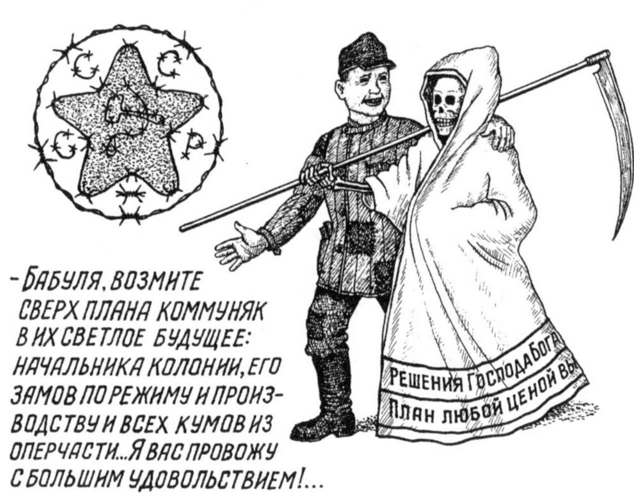

Ministry of the Interior Inter-Regional Hospital. 1987. Hip.

The tattoo of a male 'anti-social' – a criminal hostile to the administration of the Corrective Labour Colony.

‘Greetings from the Vorkuta Camps! 1947-1963. In the **USSR** labour is a matter of honour, prowess and glory! Shelyabozh, Eletsky, Izhma, Kozhma, Khalmer-South’

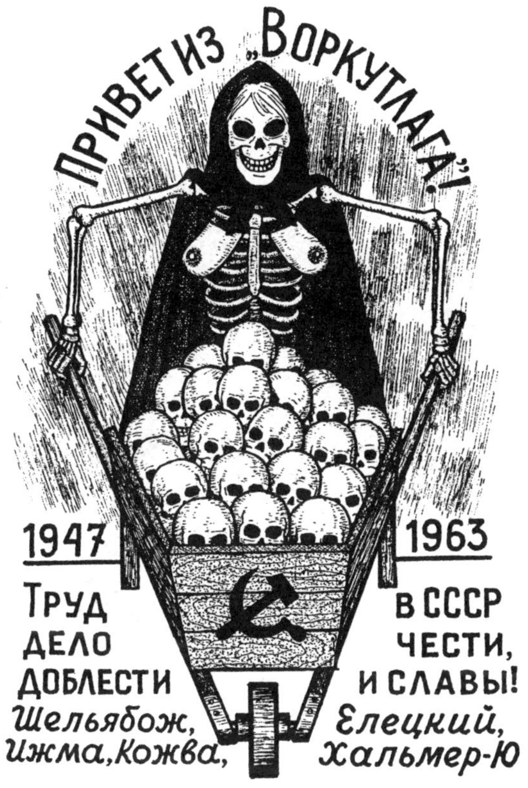

Ilich Lane Bathhouse, Leningrad. 1964.

A 'grin' tattoo worn by a convict from the Vorkuta Camps. The wearer evidently passed through five corrective labour colonies from 1947 to 1963. The tattoo was made in 1962, a year before he was released.

The acronym signfies **'Wherever I see you, I'll rape you on the spot and strangle you!'**.

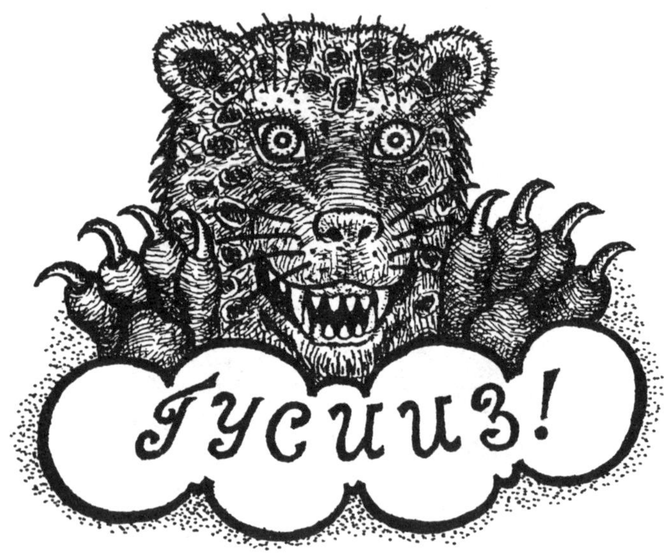

A 'grin' tattoo. A woman was possibly responsible for the wearer of the tattoo being imprisoned, 1960s-1970s.

'Don't believe in the new red Democuntfuckracy and its lying wankers!'

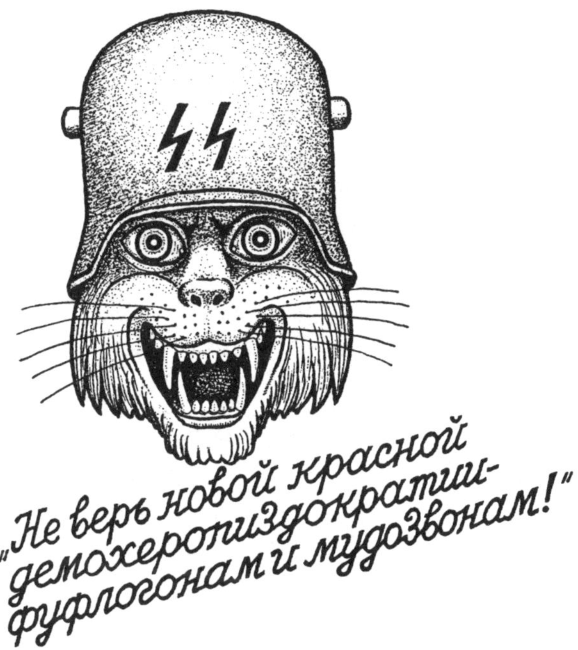

Brick factory reservoir, Kupchino, St. Petersburg. 1997.

A typical 'grin', from a prisoner convicted for hooliganism under article
206 of the Criminal Code of the RSFSR.

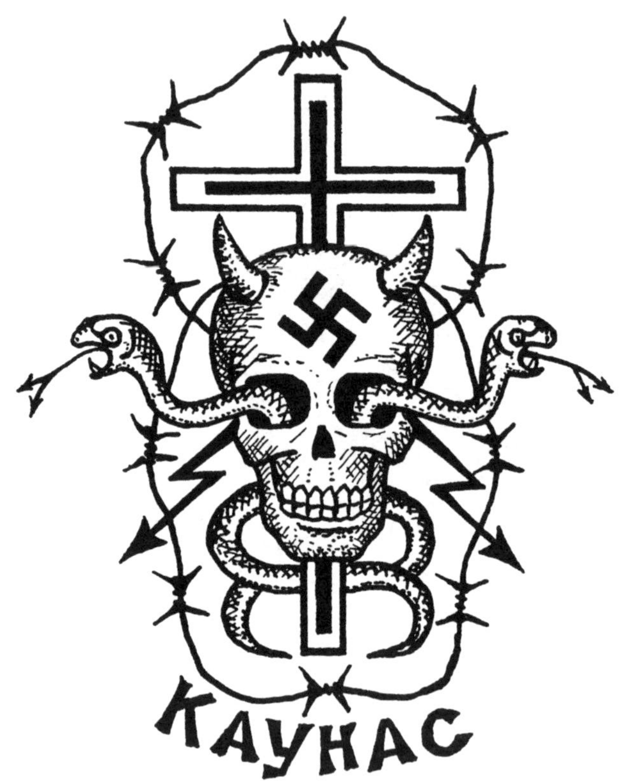

The Baltics. Chest, stomach, hip.

The tattoo of a criminal boss or 'authority'.

'Peter (St. Petersburg) – **village of Gorelovo'.** The text on the dagger and shackles reads **'Art**[icle] **146, Corrective Labour Colony 9, 1960'.**

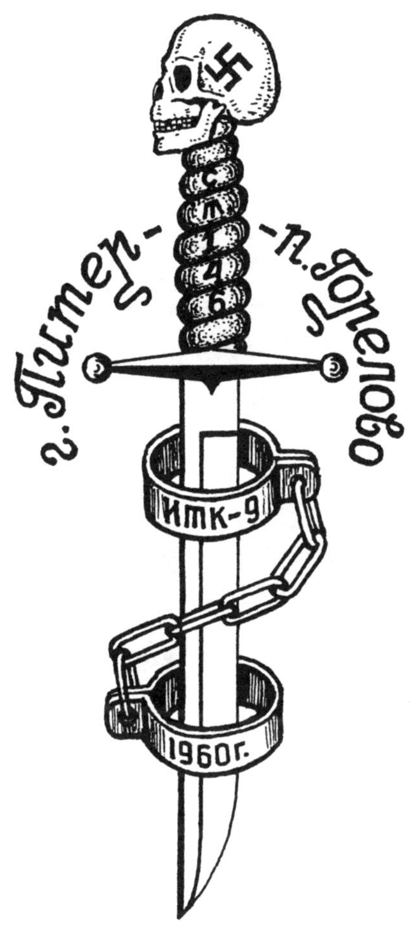

Corrective Labour Colony No.9. Shoulder, hip, stomach.

The wearer was convicted for brigandage under article 146 of the Criminal Code of the RSFSR.

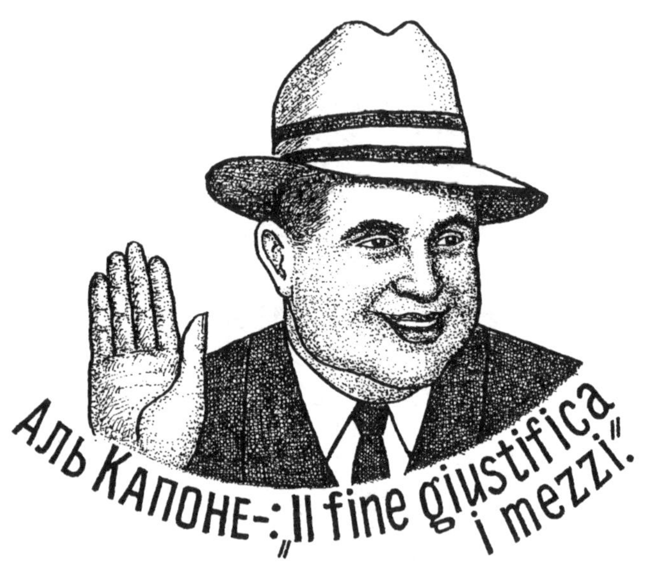

Morgue at Obukhov Hospital, Zagorodny Prospect, Leningrad. 1962.

The tattoo of a young convict. He had been murdered in his flat at 22 Pravda Street (Leningrad) by drug addicts – he'd added ashes to the 'dose' when he was dealing in hash. After striking him several times on the head with an iron, they then strangled him with an electric flex. The dead man also had a common tattoo on the right side of his chest: the head of Jesus Christ in a crown of thorns.

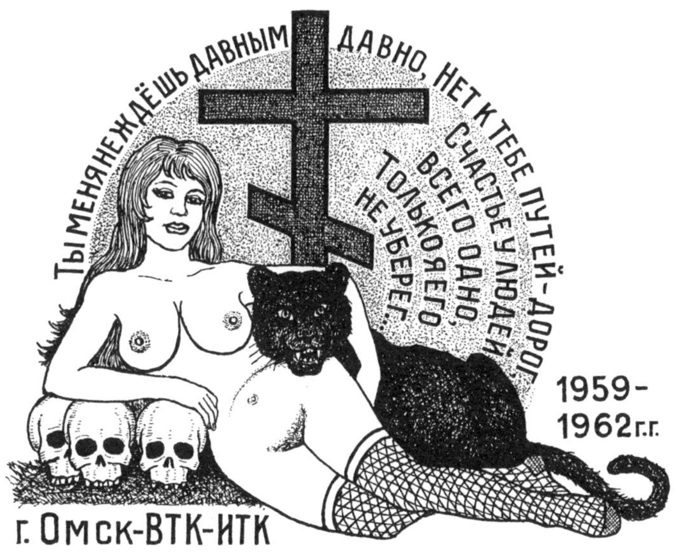

Copied in Isolation Cell Block No.1. 1982. Left side of chest.

A so-called 'lyrical tattoo', containing an extract from the words of a criminals' song. The woman, the black panther and the skulls are symbols of devotion, fearlessness and cruelty. The wearer was twice convicted of theft under article 144 of the Criminal Code of the USSR. The dates 1959-1962 refer to time spent in the Omsk Corrective Labour Colony.

Widespread criminal finger-ring tattoos. Male.

From the top:
Five dots: four watchtowers and a convict.
Devil's head: 'Grin'. 'I hold a grudge against the authorities'.
Single Dot: 'I escaped'.
'SLON' – an acronym that spells the Russian word for elephant but which stands for, 'From my early years nothing but misery'.
Crosses on knuckles: 'Trips to the zone'. 'I've been in prison three times'.
Thumb: 'I'm following in my father's footsteps'.
Forefinger: 'Anti-social' – an inveterate transgressor of the prison regime who refuses to work.
Middle finger: A criminal boss or 'authority'.
Third finger: 'I was condemned by Soviet power'.
Little finger: 'Anarchist'.
Date of birth: **1973**.

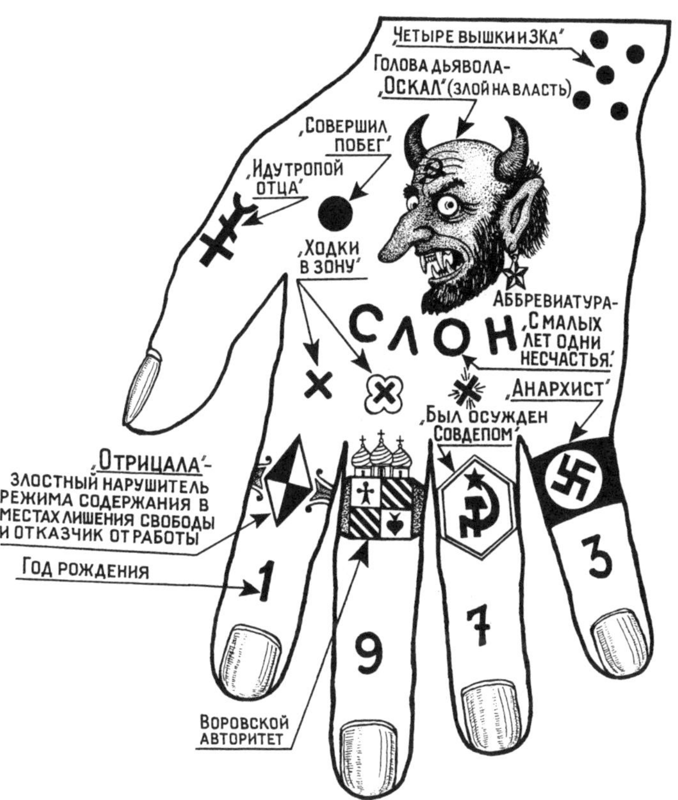
„ЧЕТЫРЕ ВЫШКИ И ЗКА"
ГОЛОВА ДЬЯВОЛА-
„ОСКАЛ"(ЗЛОЙ НА ВЛАСТЬ)
„СОВЕРШИЛ ПОБЕГ"
„ИДУТ РОПОЙ ОТЦА"
„ХОДКИ В ЗОНУ"
АББРЕВИАТУРА-
„С МАЛЫХ ЛЕТ ОДНИ НЕСЧАСТЬЯ."
СЛОН
„АНАРХИСТ"
„БЫЛ ОСУЖДЕН СОВДЕПОМ"
„ОТРИЦАЛА"-
ЗЛОСТНЫЙ НАРУШИТЕЛЬ
РЕЖИМА СОДЕРЖАНИЯ В
МЕСТАХ ЛИШЕНИЯ СВОБОДЫ
И ОТКАЗЧИК ОТ РАБОТЫ
ГОД РОЖДЕНИЯ
ВОРОВСКОЙ АВТОРИТЕТ

i An 'anti-social' convict – one hostile to the legal authorities and law-enforcement agencies, who rejects the prison regime and refuses to work. Until fairly recently 'anti-socials' would be driven into 'pressing-huts', where the 'pressers' – specially selected criminals – 'applied the method of Leninist physical persuasion', beating and raping them until they were 'completely broken'. The 'pressers' were well-fed from other prisoners' food parcels and not made to do any work. If after his release a 'presser' offended again and ended up in a part of the zone where his former activities were known, his life was made a living hell. He would not usually survive for very long.

ii This is an old tattoo worn by a criminal boss or 'authority' – an experienced 'legitimate thief' who possesses undisputed authority among other prisoners. In the past the commands of a criminal boss or 'authority' were obeyed without question by lower-ranking thieves and other convicts. He was surrounded by a group of 'outrunners' or bodyguards and 'sixers' or lackeys.

iii 'I resent the sentence'. The acronym spells the Russian word for God, but it stands for 'I was condemned by the State'. A tattoo widespread among young convicts in the 1960s and 1970s.

iv & v An 'anarchist' convict – one who rejects the prison regime and refuses to recognise prison camp laws, rules and etiquette. In some places in the west, the laws of prison and camp life ceased to be observed and the influence of the caste of 'legitimate thieves' was weakened. In places of detention in the far north of Siberia, the 'black thieves' zones', there are no 'anarchists', since the entire camp can make such convicts 'bunkless outcasts'; their arrogance is quickly beaten out of them and they 'keep their horns down' to avoid a 'battering'.

vi 'I was in a closed jail'. A corrective labour colony with a special prison regime for particularly dangerous prisoners, known for attacking overseers and administrators in the prison camp system. Men wearing this tattoo possess status among other convicts. As models of endurance and loyalty to the criminal world, they are an example to be imitated by the young.

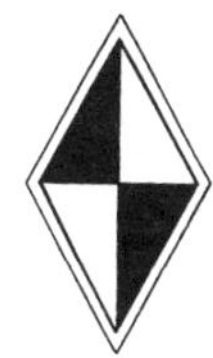

i

ii

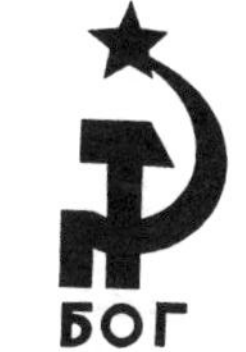

iii

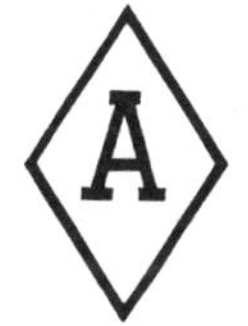

iv

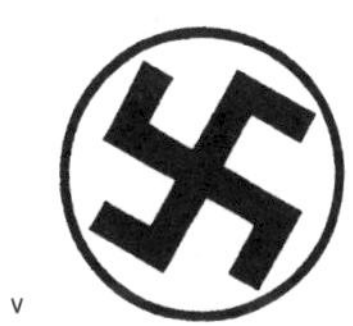

v

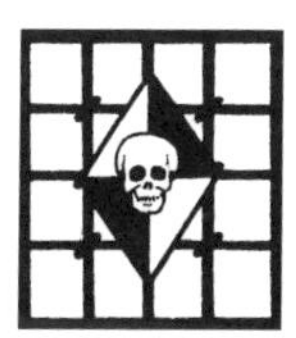

vi

vii An 'apartment thief' (a specialist thief) – a 'housebreaker', 'cat-burglar', 'plumber'.

viii A murderer on the orders of the administration of a corrective labour institution, usually of political prisoners. Attached to the third internal operations unit of a remote camp site, corrective labour colony or corrective labour camp of the department of state political administration. An 'executioner', 'wet-jobber', 'hit man', 'gravedigger of the proletariat', 'red angel'.

ix 'I'm registered in the zone', 'The mark of fate', 'Prison gave me my name'. This tattoo may be drawn on the forearm with the date of the 'first trip' (first conviction), the nickname conferred and the relevant article of the Criminal Code. It became widespread among young convicts in the 1970s.

x 'I cut loose in the zone' – committed a crime in places of detention.

xi 'I've been through a special purpose prison.' Special purpose prisons were primarily intended for political prisoners. They had an extremely severe regime in which the overseers were strictly forbidden to talk with the convicts. Some people who survived to be released from special purpose prisons were unaware that the Second World War had started and ended. Especially dangerous criminals were kept in special purpose prisons during the 1940s and 1950s.

xii 'Never renounce prison and poverty', 'Prison's always waiting for me'. A youth tattoo that became widespread in the 1960s and 1970s.

xiii 'I don't want to graft and I won't.' A convict who refuses to work in places of detention.

xiv 'I ended up in the zone as a kid and was promoted to the grown-ups.' A youth tattoo that first appeared in the 1960s-1970s.

xv 'I was born in prison', 'My fate is the sky in big squares'. An old tattoo.

vii

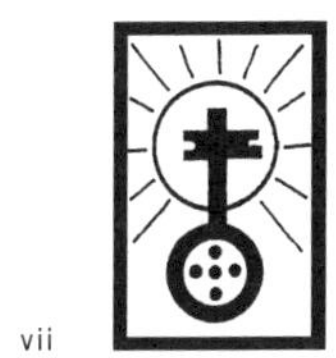

viii

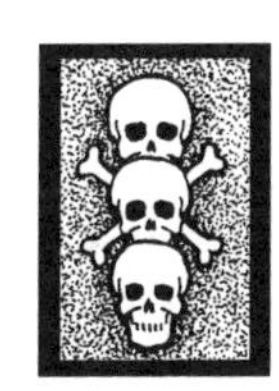

ix

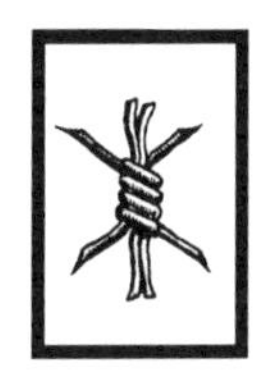

x

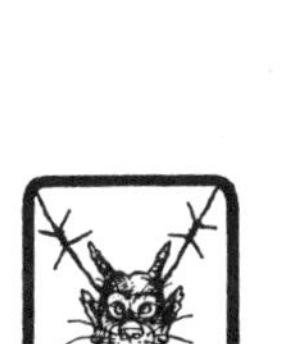
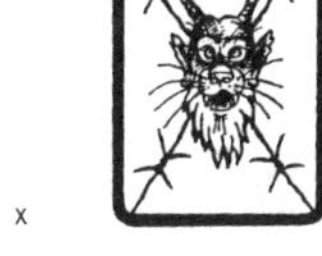

xi

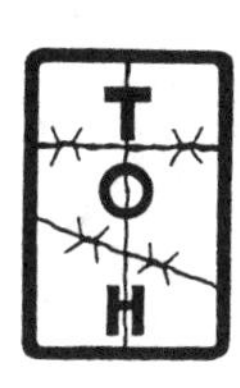

xii

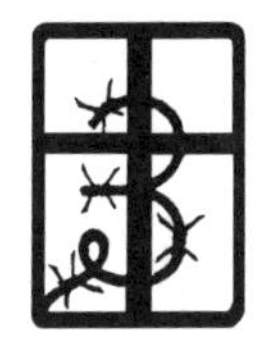

xiii

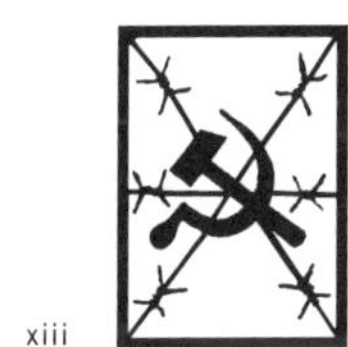

xiv

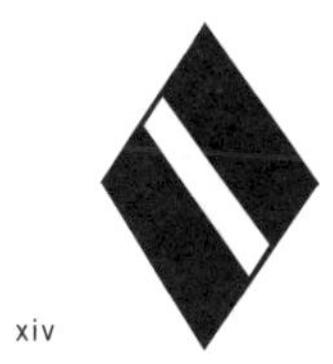

xv

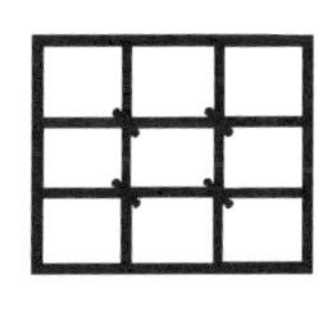

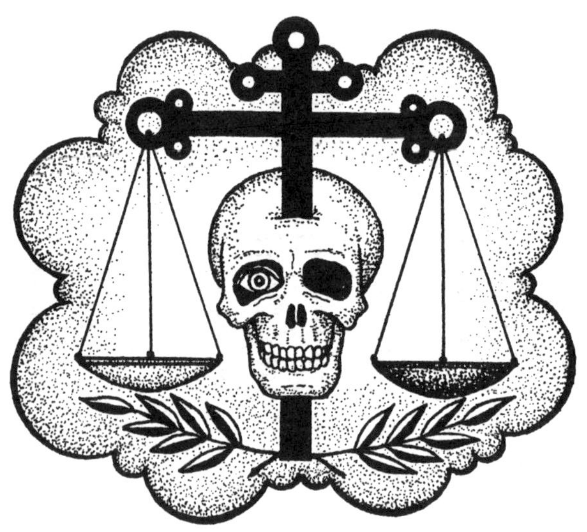

Chita jail. 1950s. Shoulder, occasionally other places.

This convict tattoo represents an 'orthodox' – a thief who has never transgressed the convicts' laws and rules. He acts as a judge in settling accounts between thieves in prisons and camps, and also in the outside world.

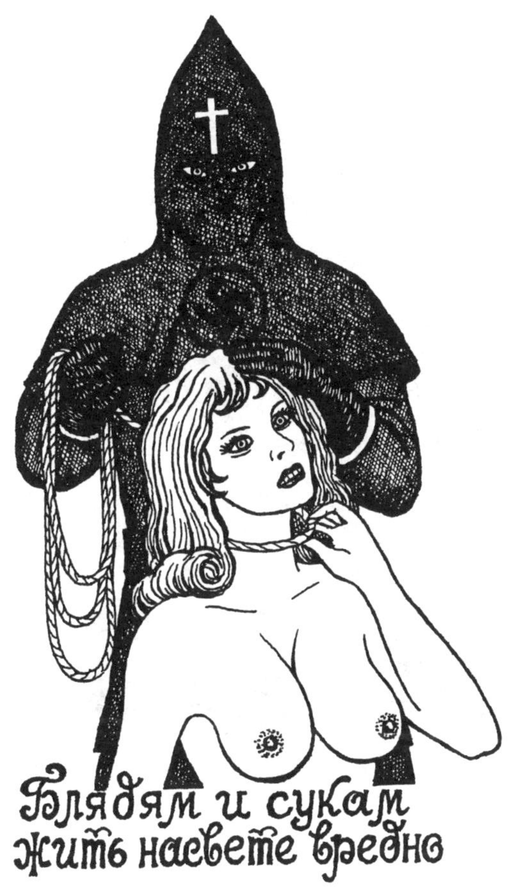

Corrective Labour Colony No.7. 1960s. Stomach, hip.

A youth tattoo symbolising implacable cruelty.

Latin text reads **'Crush the arrogance of the rebellious!'**.

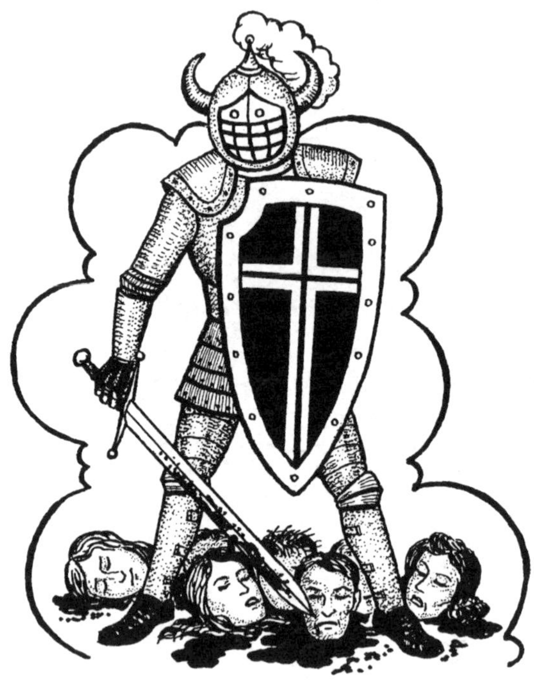

Corrective Labour Colony No.6. 1988. Hip.

A youth tattoo, widespread in the 1970s and 1980s among 'anti-socials' or inveterate transgressors of the prison regime in places of detention, who taunted and insulted other prisoners. They carried out reprisals against convicts without status.

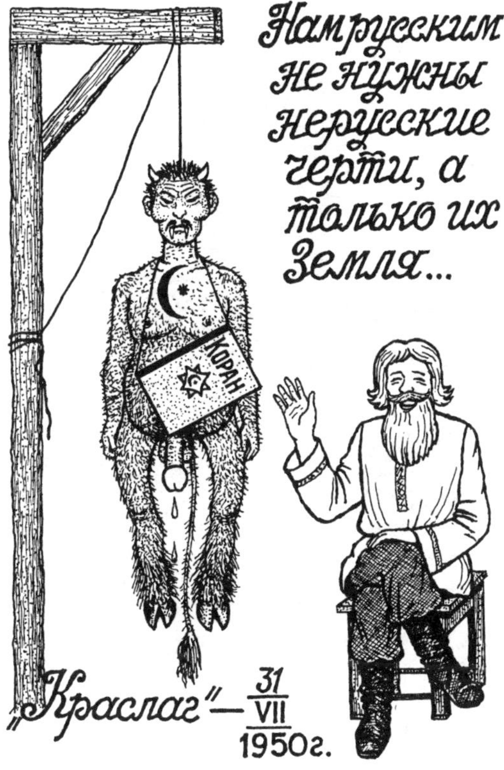

'Stroikrasmasha' Corrective Labour Colony, Enisei Settlement, Krasnoyarsk Territory. 1950s. Stomach.

A 'nationalist' tattoo from an 'Old Believer' convict. This is an example of an extreme nationalist tattoo that expresses the bloodthirsty attitude of devotees of the 'Great Russian Idea' towards all non-Russians. Typical for 'warriors', 'hitmen' and 'wet-jobbers'.

'President, you have no teeth! We are everywhere! Cede power to us – we will impose order in Russia and the CIS!' The word on the figure's chest is '**Mafia**'.

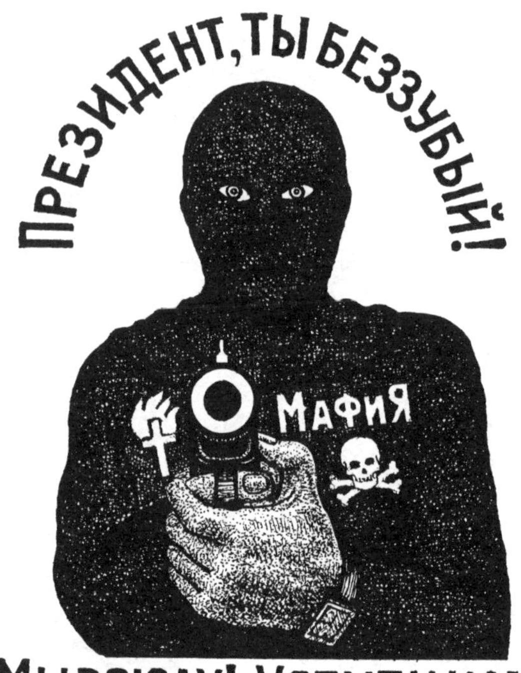

Swimming pool, 70 Glory Prospect, St. Petersburg. Hip.

A youth tattoo of the so-called 'bandit grin' at the authorities. The wearer of this tattoo had been convicted under article 146 of the Criminal Code of the RSFSR (banditry), and first served time in an educational labour colony for juvenile offenders and later in Corrective Labour Colony No.5, where he had the tattoo made.

'**Take out bitches, stool-pigeons and traitors!**' The acronym '**MIR**' spells the word for peace and stands for '**Shooting will reform me**'.

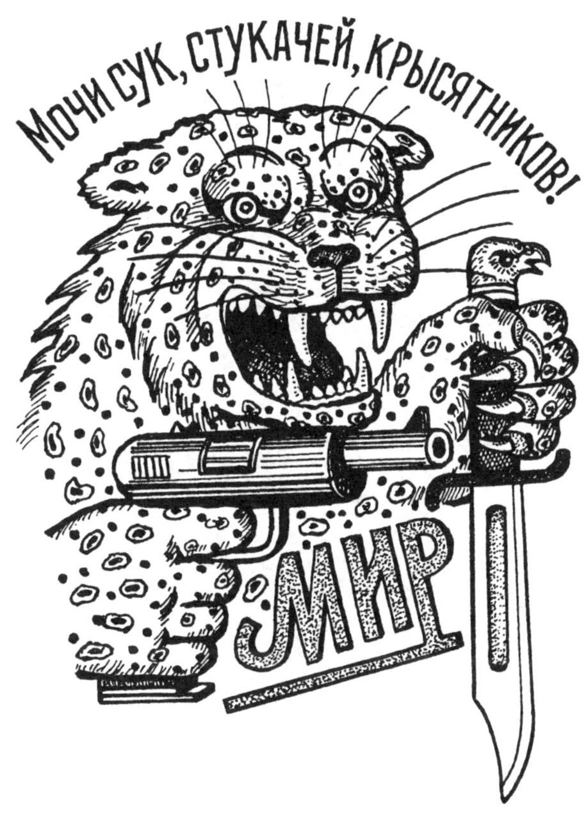

A 'warrior's grin'.

'**Art**[icle] **89** (three times) **of the Criminal Code. US-20/9**'.

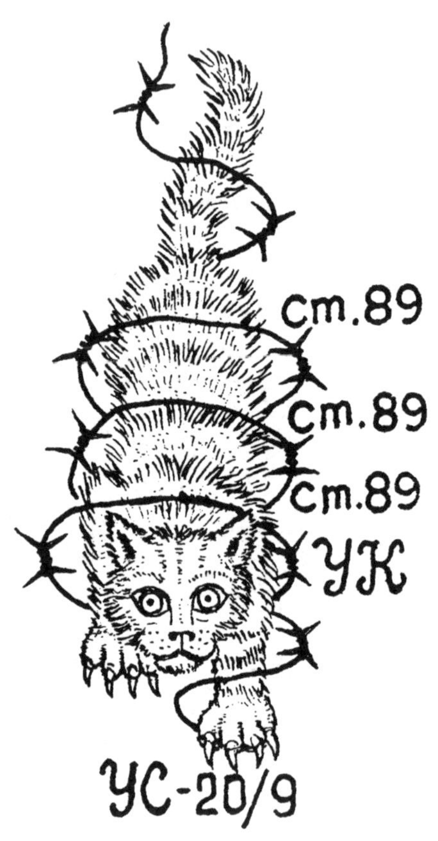

Morgue, 10 Ekaterinsky Prospect, Leningrad. 1988. Hip.

This tattoo is from a criminal boss or 'authority' and recidivist thief who was convicted three times under article 89 of the criminal Code of the RSFSR, 1960. This criminal 'authority' died from loss of blood due to knife wounds suffered during a settling of accounts between thieves on Shkapin Street.

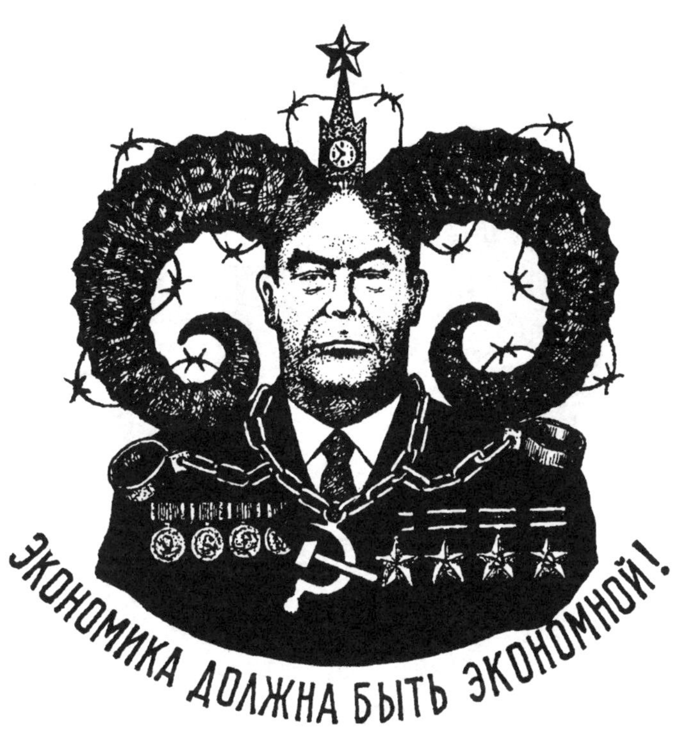

202 Ligovsky Prospect, Leningrad. 1970s.

An anti-communist caricature tattoo. The wearer had been convicted for illegal foreign exchange dealing under article 88 of the Criminal Code of the RSFSR.

The acronym under Lenin's head spells **'THIEF'**. It stands for **'Leader of the October Revolution'**.

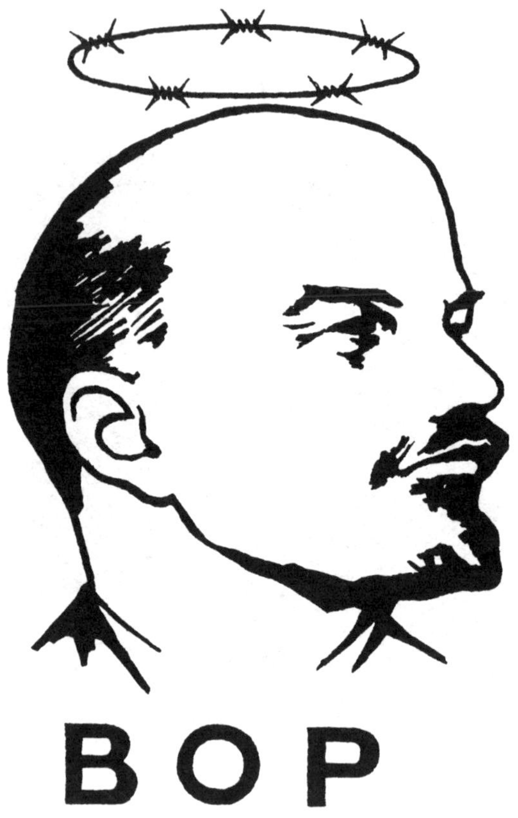

Corrective Labour Colony, Ulan-Ude, Buryat Autonomous Soviet Socialist Republic. 1960s. Chest.

The criminal 'authority' who wore this tattoo was nicknamed 'Chebak'. He was convicted under article 89 of the Criminal Code of the RSFSR for theft of state and public property.

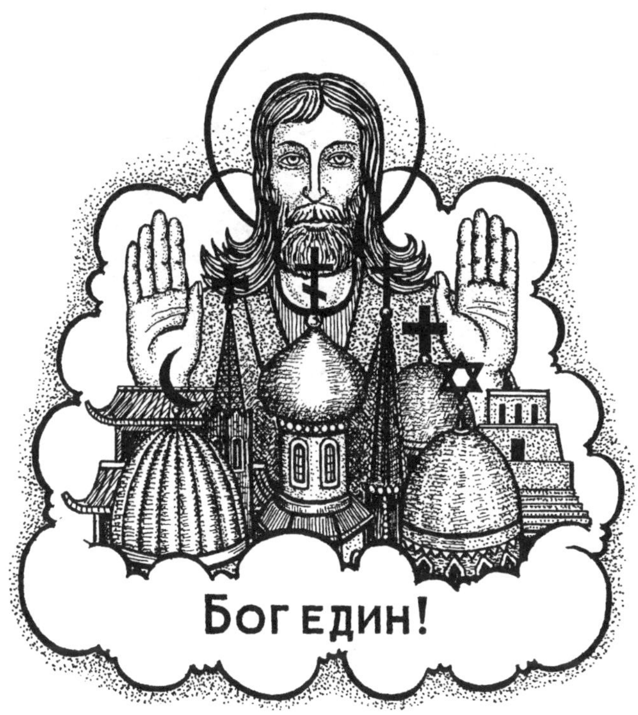

1980s. Chest, stomach.

A 'talisman'.

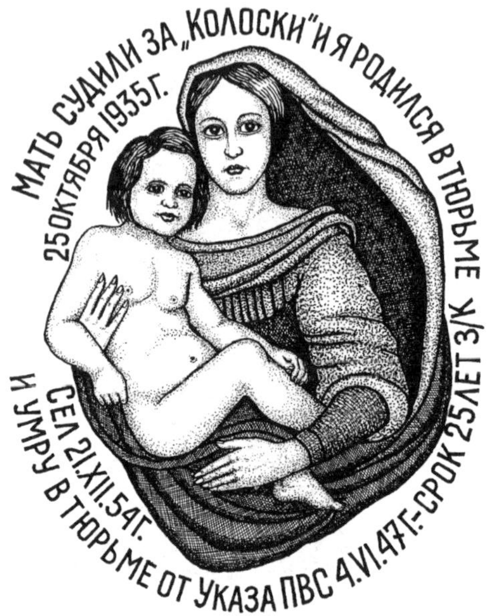

Corrective Labour Colony, Ulan-Ude, Buryat Autonomous Soviet Socialist Republic. 1960s. Chest.

This thieves' 'talisman', based on Raphael's 'Madonna from the Sistine Chapel', was worn by a convict sentenced to twenty-five years for the group theft of food products from a military depot in the town of Irkutsk. He was known as 'Bely' (White). According to 'Bely', his mother was convicted under a decree of the Council of People's Commissars from 7th August 1935, for gleaning ears of grain after the harvest had been collected. A canvas sack containing about three kilograms of grain was confiscated from her in the collective farm fields of the Nizheudinsk district, Irkutsk region. She had collected it to feed her two daughters, aged five and seven. She was sentenced to five years imprisonment. She gave birth to 'Bely' in one of the Taishet camps. He did not know his father, who was drowned in 1935 while tying together log-rafts for the timber enterprise he worked for. While his mother was in prison his sisters were sent to a children's home, from which she collected them when she was released in 1940. A little later she collected her son, then scarcely alive, from a home for the children of convicted female criminals.

Ukrainian text reads **'Long live red Ukraine!'**.

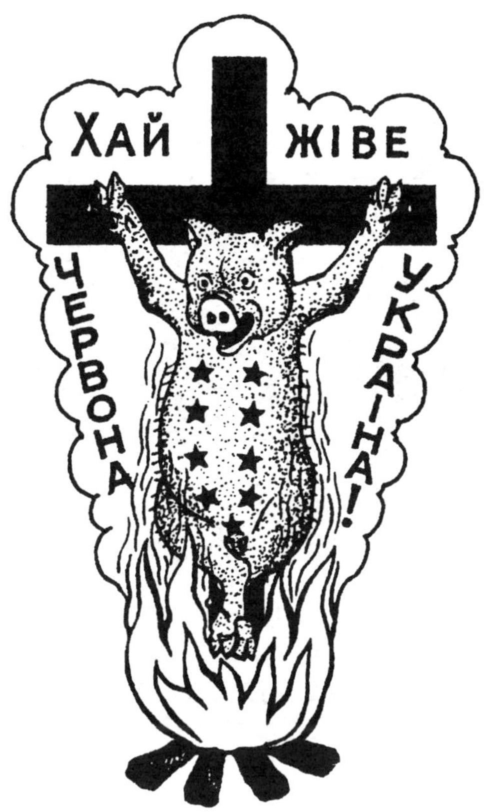

Municipal Militia Department of Nadvornaya, Ivano-Frankovsk region, Ukrainian Soviet Socialist Republic. 1969. Right hip.

An anti-Ukrainian tattoo from a Russian nationalist.

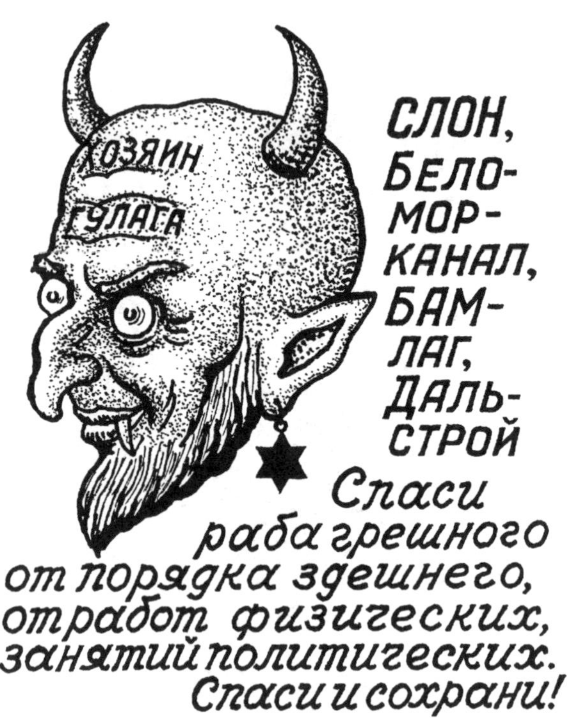

Corrective Labour Colony, Ulan-Ude, Buryat Autonomous Soviet Socialist Republic. 1960s. Chest.

A tattoo worn by a 'Boss of the GULAG', and found in almost all the detention centres of the former USSR from the 1930s to the 1980s. The text accompanying the image varies, but it is generally anti-Soviet in content.

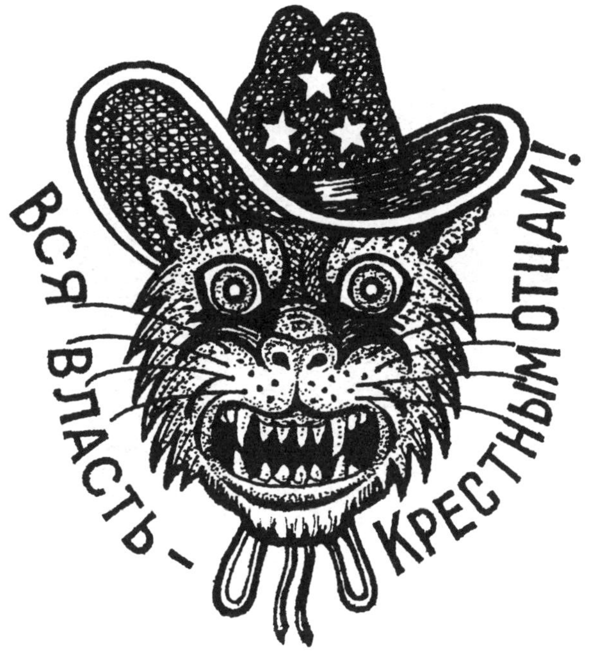

1980s.

A rare tattoo of a cat wearing a cowboy hat.

The acronym stands for **'And separation is hell when you're not beside me'**.

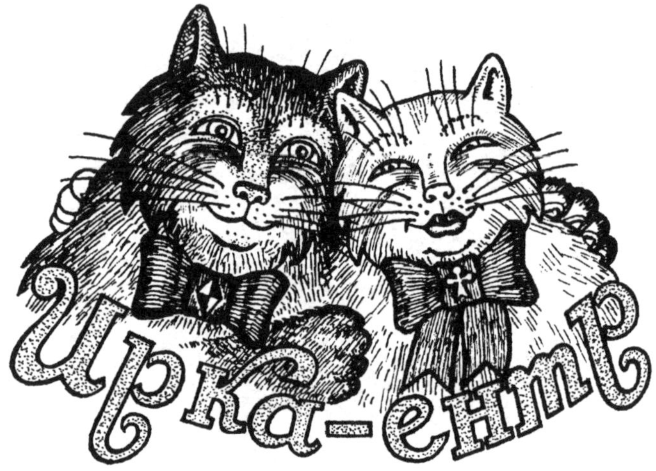

Stomach, hip.

This tattoo means, 'Husband and wife are a family of thieves'.

'**Art**[icle] **17-91**'.

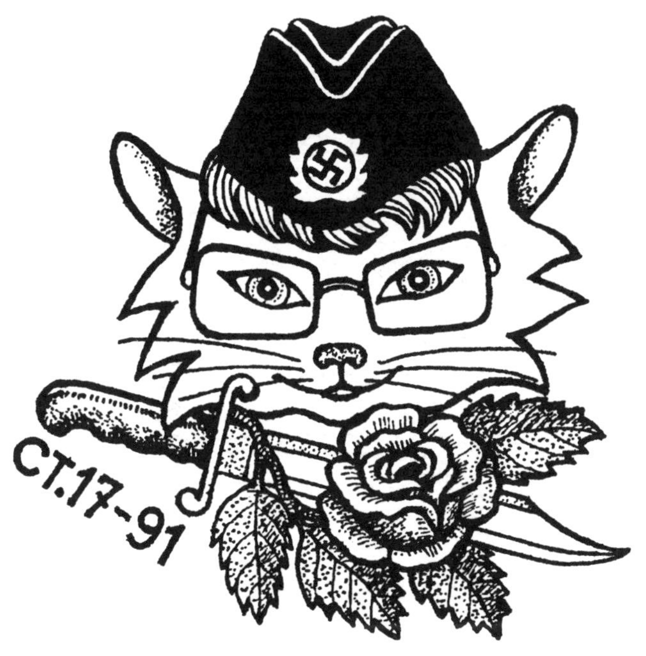

An 'SS' tattoo which means, 'I turned eighteen in prison, convicted as an accomplice to brigandage (article 17-91 of the Criminal Code of the RSFSR).'

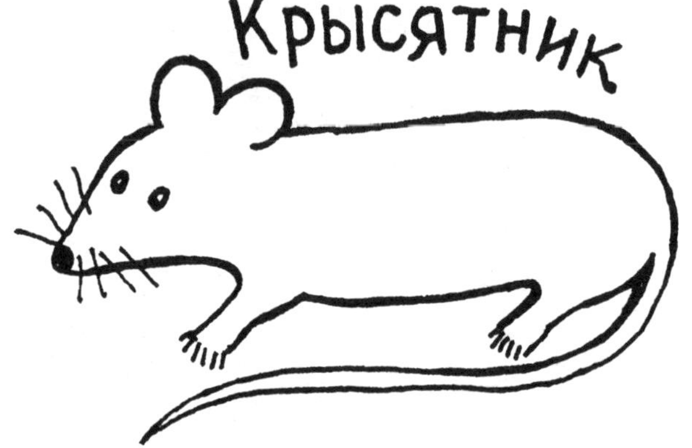

Stomach, hip.

'Rat-thief' is camp slang for a petty criminal who steals from other thieves.

'Count Taburetkin'

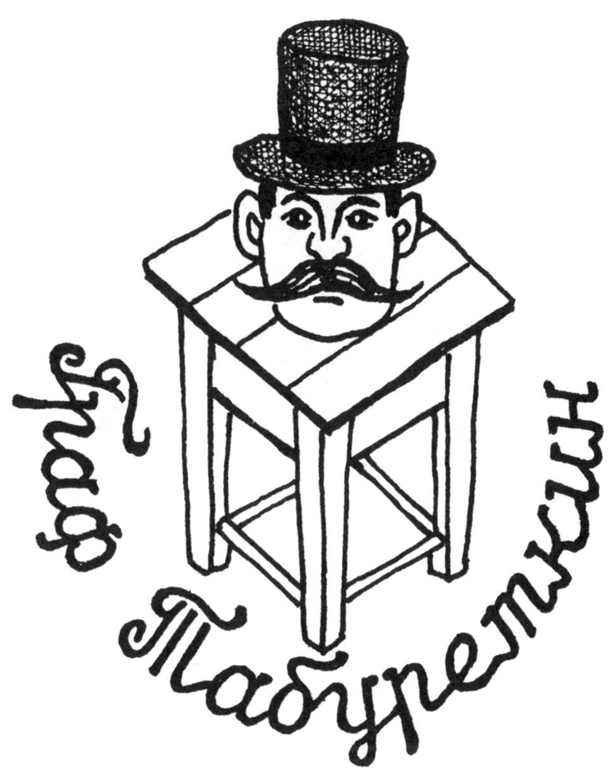

Khabarovsk Invalid Corrective Labour Camp, State Camp Administration of the USSR Ministry of the Interior. 1950.

A rare old tattoo from a man convicted for depravity. 'Count Taburetkin' was a name taken from the Russian word for 'stool'. The wearer of this 'humiliating' tattoo was convicted four times under article 152 (depravity), and article 192-a (infringements of the passport regime, vagrancy), of the 1926 Criminal Code of the RSFSR.

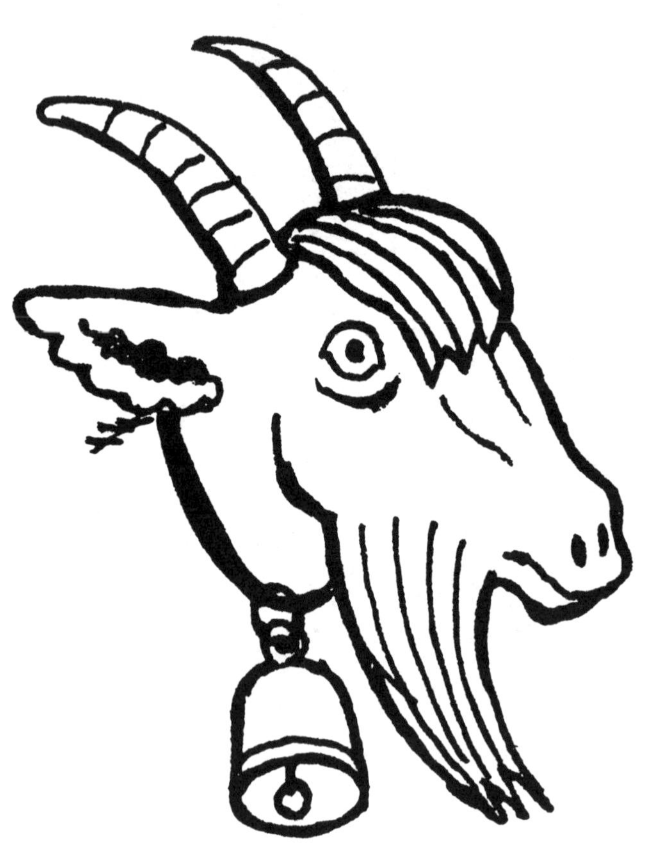

Example of a tattoo forcibly applied to a male 'untouchable'.

'Novozybkovo Corrective Labour Colony – General Barracks 21 1991.'

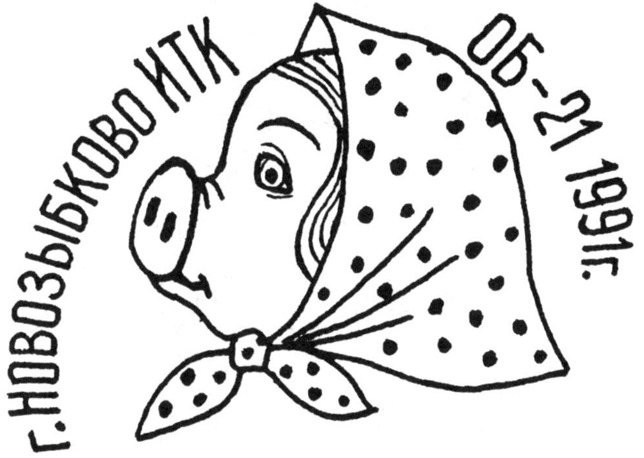

Female 'untouchable' tattoo.

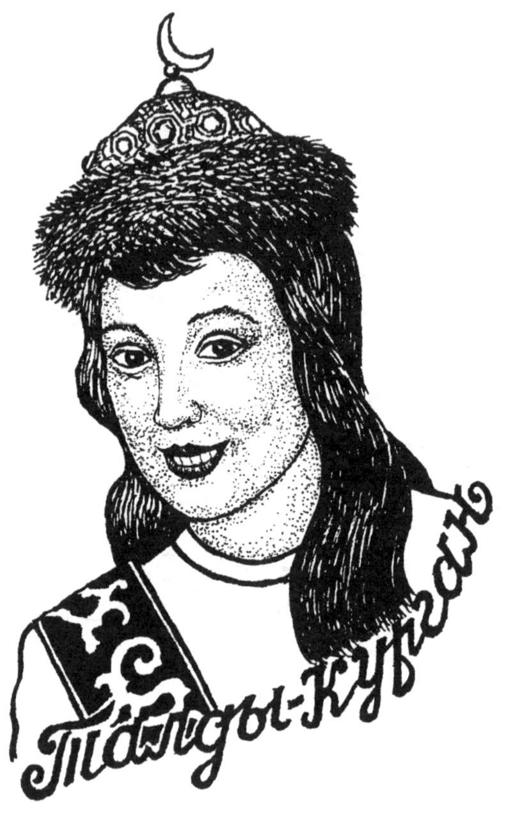

A portrait of a loved one, a Kazakh girl. In prison and camp conditions this type of portrait tattoo is expensive.

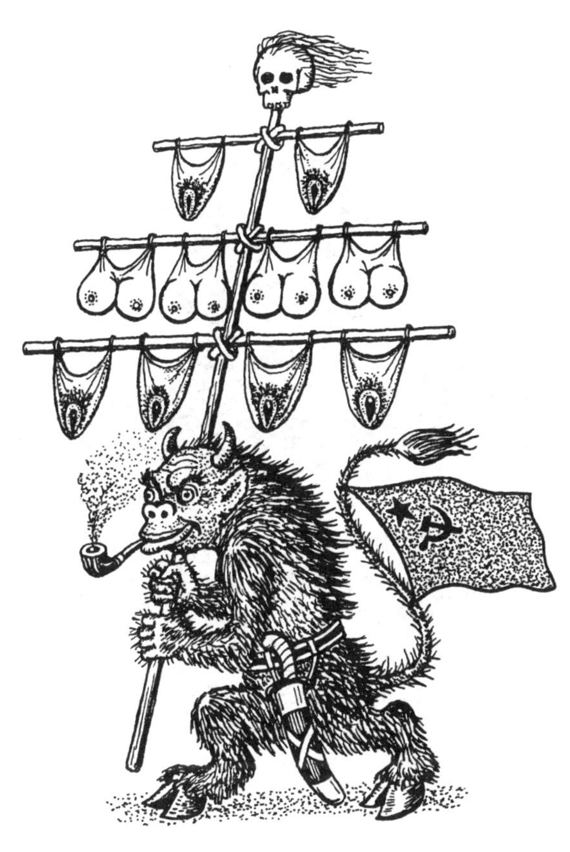

Intricate tattoo from convict imprisoned 'because of a woman'.

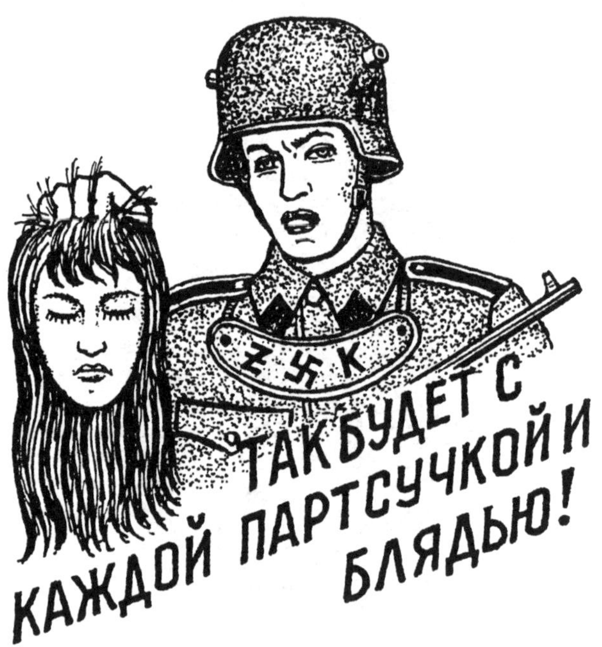

1980s. Stomach, hip, shoulder.

Tattoo drawn from the same prisoner as page 159.

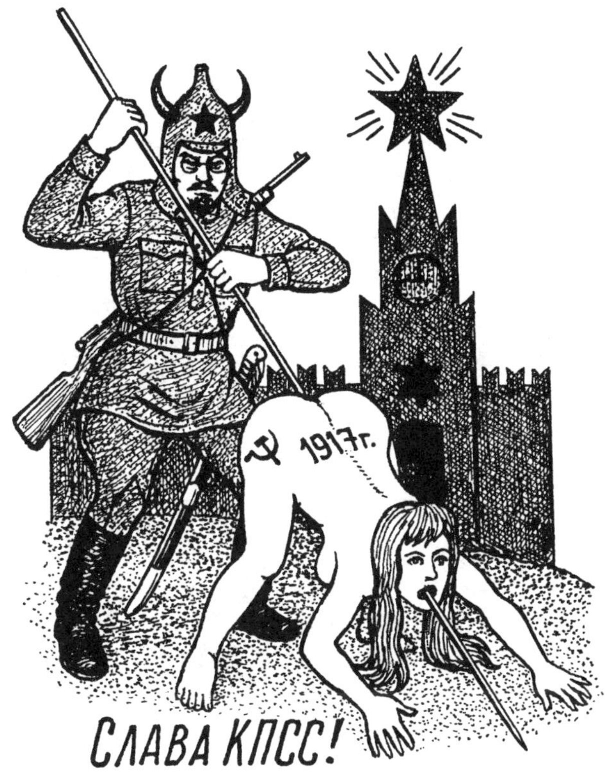

The Ministry of the Interior Inter-Regional Hospital, Leningrad. Late 1980s.
Stomach.

An anti-Soviet youth tattoo. A 'grin' at the authorities.

'Men, don't trust whores, they can drown you in their cunt!'

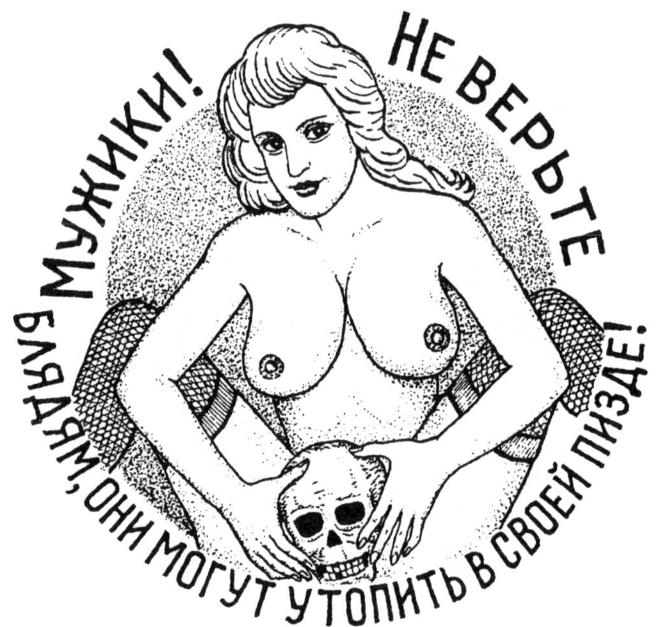

Corrective Labour Colony No.9. 1981. Stomach.

Convicted of burglary under article 144 of the 1960 Criminal Code of the RSFSR, this prisoner kept the things he stole at his mistress's home. She later became afraid of her involvement, and together with her mother and sister betrayed him to the militia.

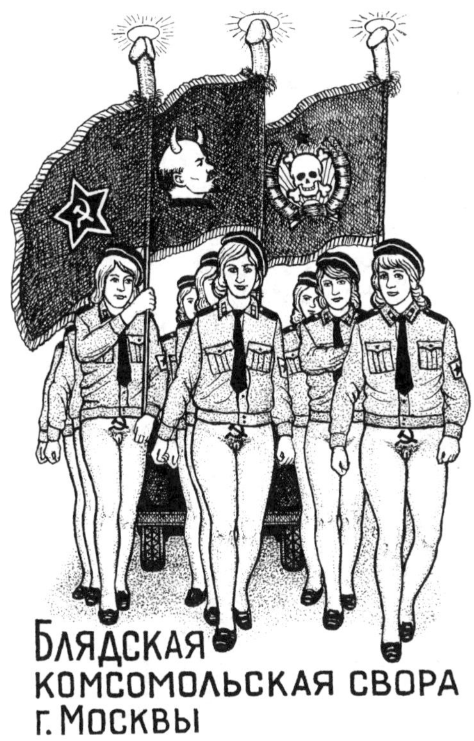

Ministry of the Interior Inter-Regional Hospital, Leningrad. 1986. Stomach.

This rare anti-Soviet hooligan tattoo was applied in the Tula Corrective Labour Colony in 1968 and recorded in 1986. Cynically anti-Soviet, it came from a prisoner twice convicted under articles 206 and 109 of the 1960 Criminal Code of the RSFSR. In 1962, when he was drunk, he violently resisted a Komsomol patrol, and was subsequently sentenced to three years imprisonment. In 1967 he was apprehended by a Komsomol patrol for drinking hard liquor in a public canteen. Again he was violent when resisting arrest. He was taken to the 17th precinct militia station on Petrovka Street in Moscow, prosecuted under articles 109, 191 and 206 of the Criminal Code of the RSFSR, and sentenced to five years imprisonment.

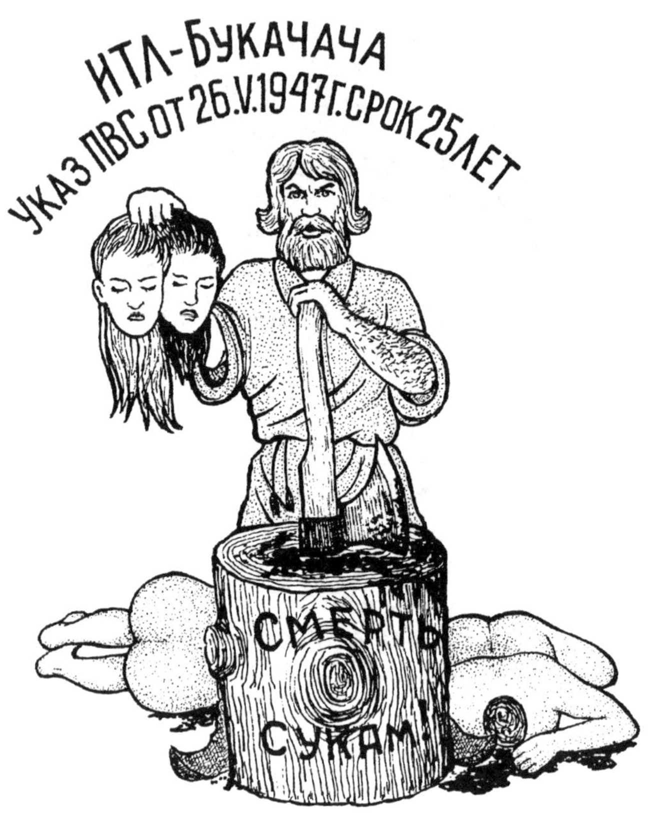

Medical Unit, Corrective Labour Camp, Bukachacha, Chita Region. 1950s.

This tattoo was worn by a convict nicknamed ‘Mukhorty’ (Puny). He was imprisoned for a double murder, he had killed his neighbours in revenge for their hostility. Under the Supreme Soviet Presidium decree of 26th May 1947 Mukhorty's death sentence was commuted to twenty-five years imprisonment.

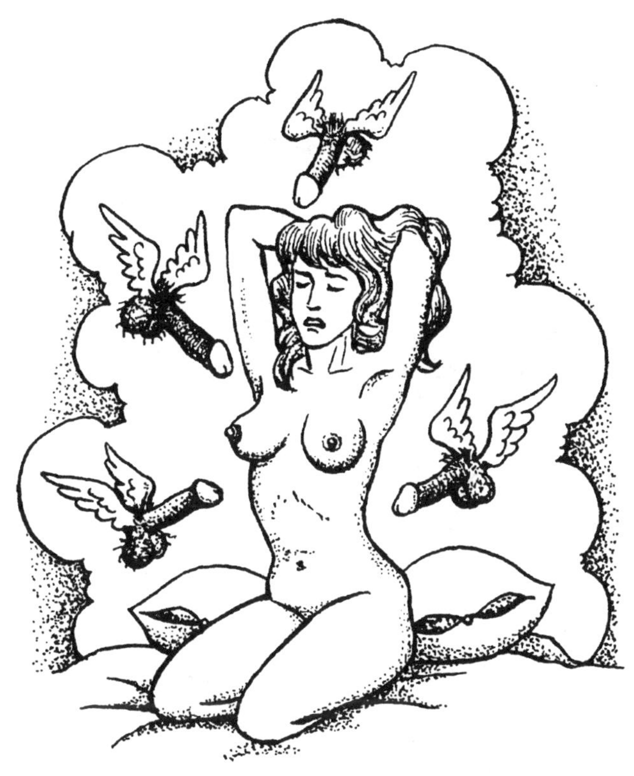

Maintenance Unit, Isolation Cell, Block No.1. 1960s.

This tattoo is widespread among male convicts who hold a grudge against their sexual partners. Among prisoners it is known as 'A whore's dreams'.

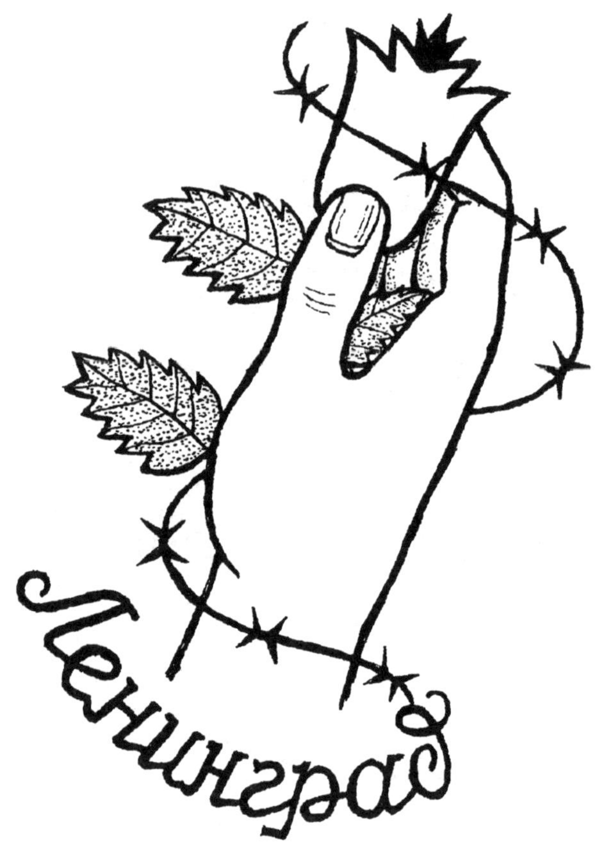

Educational Labour Colony for Juvenile Criminals, Kolpino District, Leningrad Region. Summer 1990.

This is a variation on a tattoo with a tulip which signifies, 'I was convicted for theft and robbery when underage, and when I reached eighteen I was transferred to Corrective Labour Colony No.5 to serve out the rest of my sentence (three years)'.

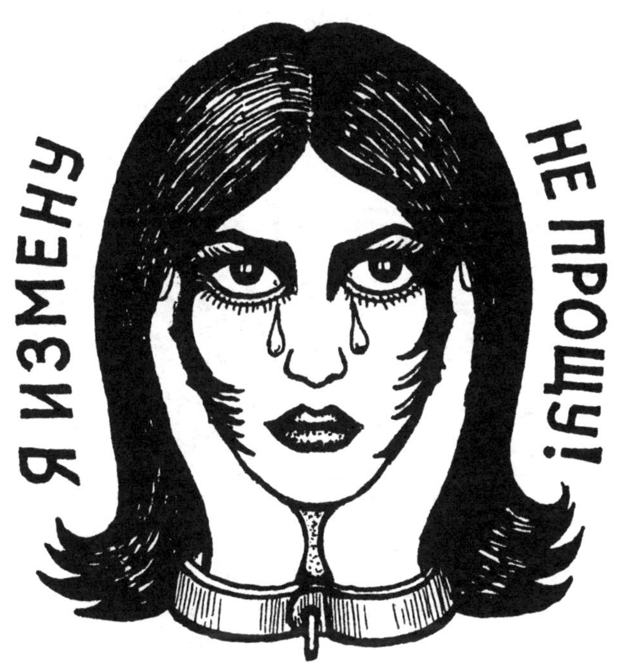

Special Reception Centre, 10 Bakunin Street, Leningrad. 1960s. Shoulder, forearm.

A male or female 'gypsy' youth tattoo.

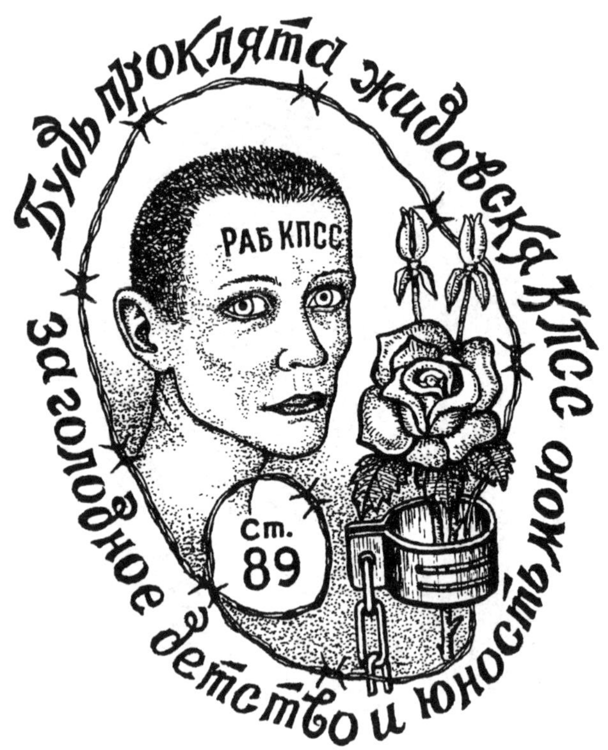

Corrective Labour Colony No.9. 1970s.

The tattoo of a prisoner convicted under article 89 of the criminal Code of the RSFSR for theft of state or public property. The number of spikes on the barbed wire may indicate the length of the sentence in years. Portrait tattoos from photographs are considered elite items in the camp zone, as they can only be made by genuine craftsman.

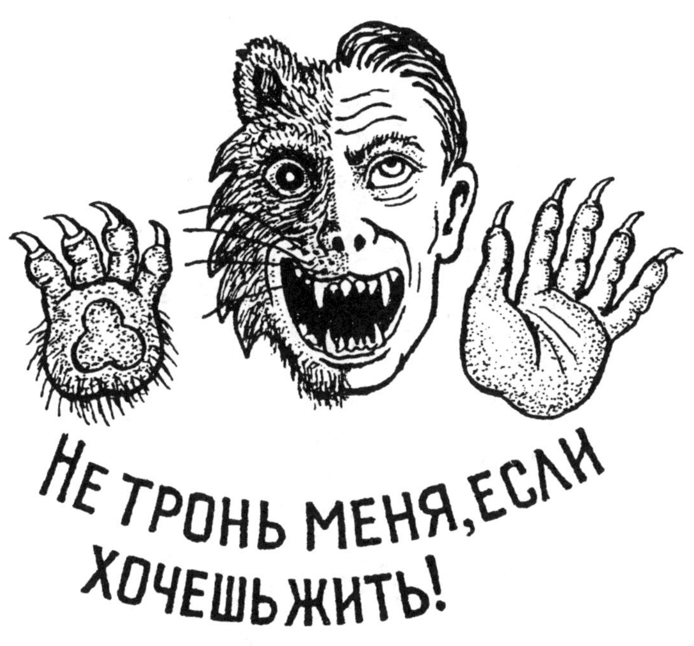

Remote Camp Site, Lesosibirsk, Krasnoyarsk Camp Zone. 1950s-1960s. Chest.

A typical 'grin' of a criminal of status. This menacing tattoo depicting a werewolf is usually applied to so-called 'satanists' or 'dunces' – inveterate transgressors of the prison regime. It was widespread in the prison camp system of the former USSR.

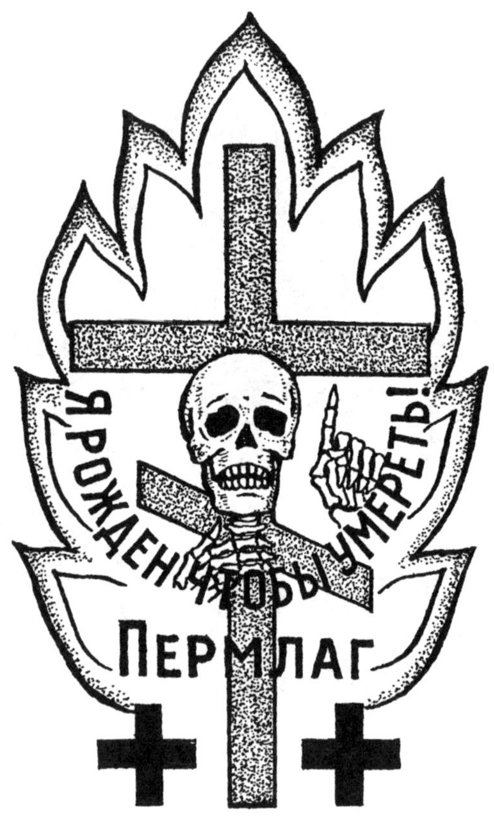

City Morgue, 10 Ekaterinsky Prospect, St. Petersburg. 1997. Left side of chest.

This tattoo was found on the unidentified body of a criminal 'authority'. He was killed by several shots to the head and chest during a settling of scores between rival organised criminal gangs.

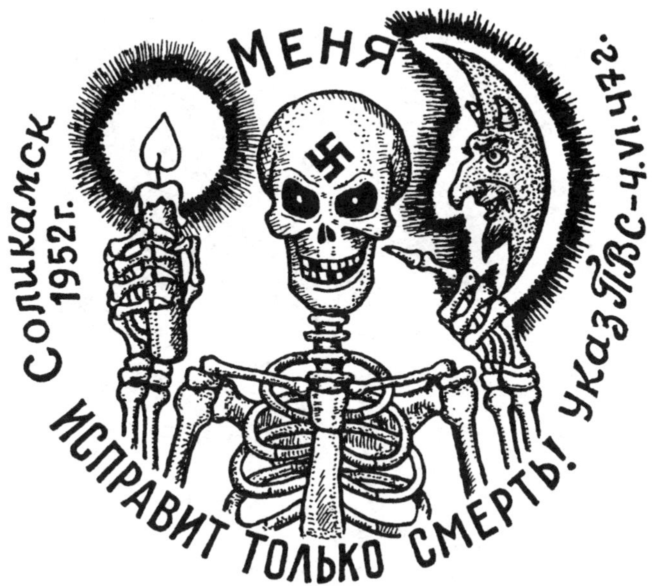

Stomach, hip and occasionally other parts of the body.

The tattoo of a criminal 'authority' and 'legitimate thief' among convicts.

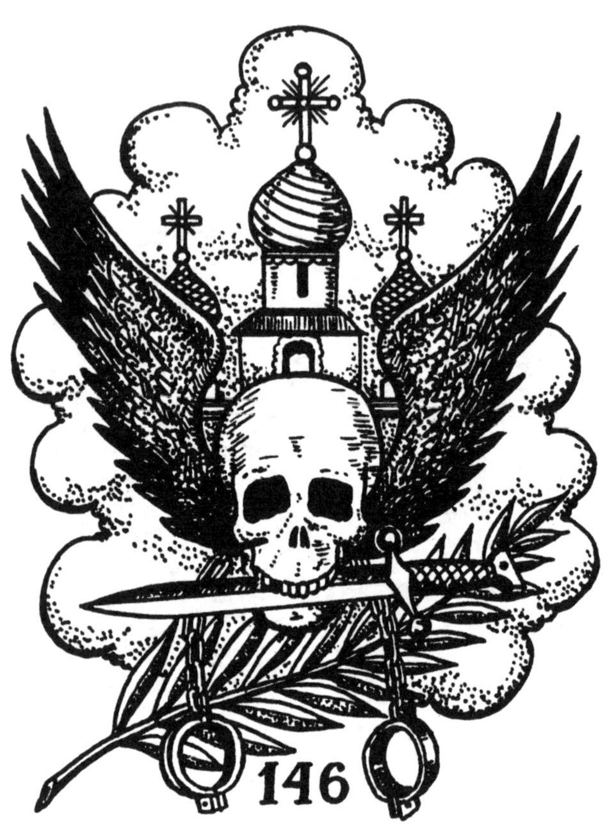

Zima Corrective Labour Colony, Irkutsk Region. 1960s. Right side of the chest.

A tattoo from a criminal boss convicted under article 146 of the 1960 Criminal Code of the RSFSR. In the words of this 'authority', the town of Zima marked the start of an unbroken line of corrective labour camps, corrective labour colonies and educational labour camps, stretching along the Trans-Siberian railway as dense 'as beads strung on a thread', during the period from the 1930s to the 1970s.

Latin text reads **'Remember you will die...'**.

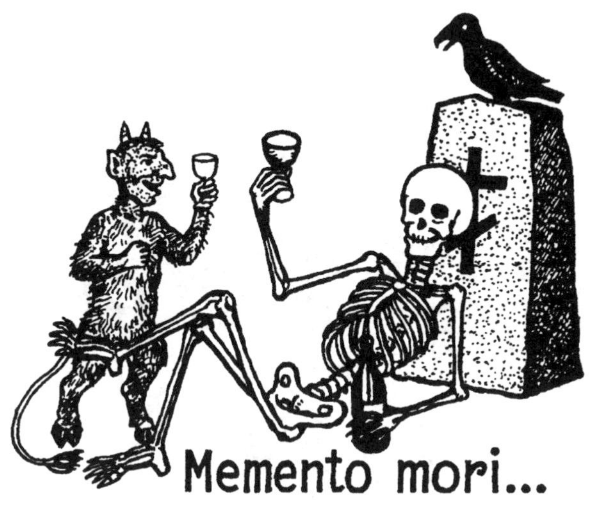

Remote Camp Site, Angara Camp Zone, Bratsk. 1950s. Hip.

This tattoo was worn by a prisoner convicted of the theft of either state or public property under the Supreme Soviet Presidium decree of 4th June 1947. He was sentenced to twenty-five years imprisonment. He explained that in order to improve labour productivity in the remote camp site, a system of so-called 'credits' was introduced, under which any convict who worked intensively for one day without committing any offences against the prison regime was credited with three days. The convicts used to say, 'one day for me, two for the boss'. Under this system a man sentenced to twenty-five years imprisonment could theoretically be released after eight or nine years, but in reality that rarely happened, and the system of 'credits' did not apply to political prisoners.

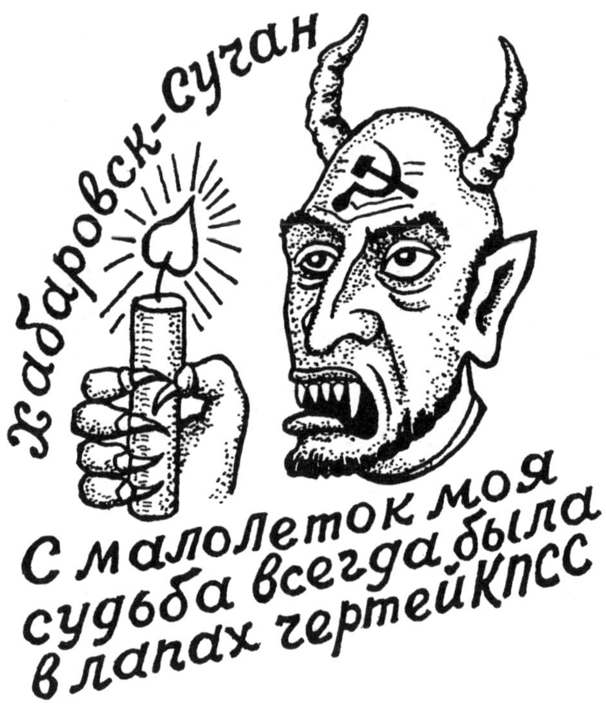

City Morgue, 10 Ekaterinsky Prospect, St. Petersburg. 1997. Left side of chest.

A so-called 'anti-social's grin', worn by inveterate transgressors of prison regime, (permanent residents of solitary cells and other punishment areas).

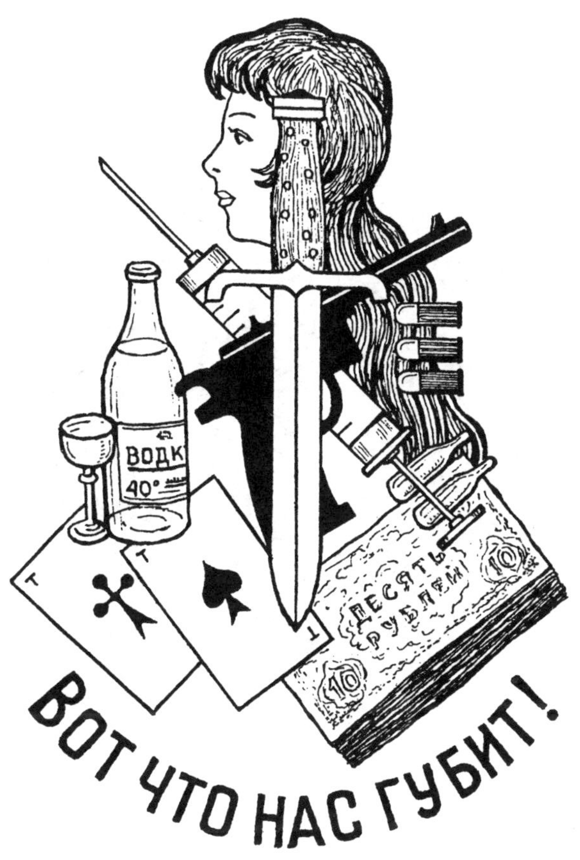

Corrective Labour Colony No.4. Applied to various parts of the body.

This tattoo is widespread in criminal circles. There are several versions, with and without texts.

German text reads **'Don't wait for them to hit you!'** Russian text reads **'White Swan, Perm camp zone'**.

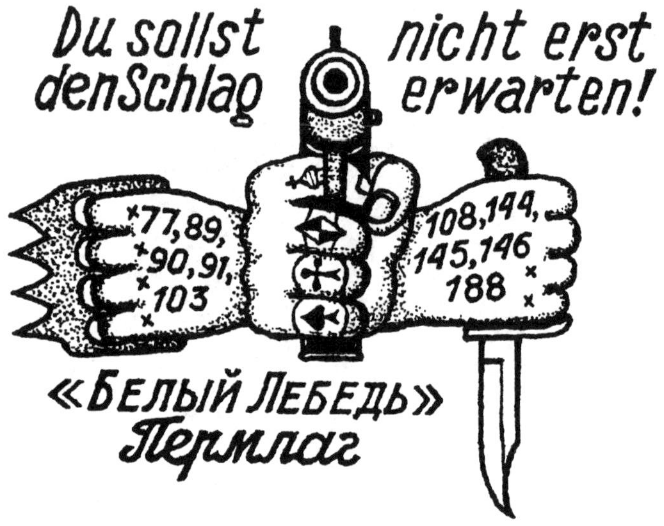

Minister of the Interior Inter-Regional Hospital, Leningrad. 1981.

The so-called 'thief's bouquet', this is a tattoo from a criminal boss or 'authority' nicknamed 'Kudryavy' (Curly) who was completely bald. The numbers are articles of the 1960 Criminal Code of the RSFSR and the design includes an 'authority's' ring tattoo, a knuckle-duster, a pistol and a knife.

'Boss of the Far Eastern construction camps. Curse you, Kolyma Yid construction camps!'

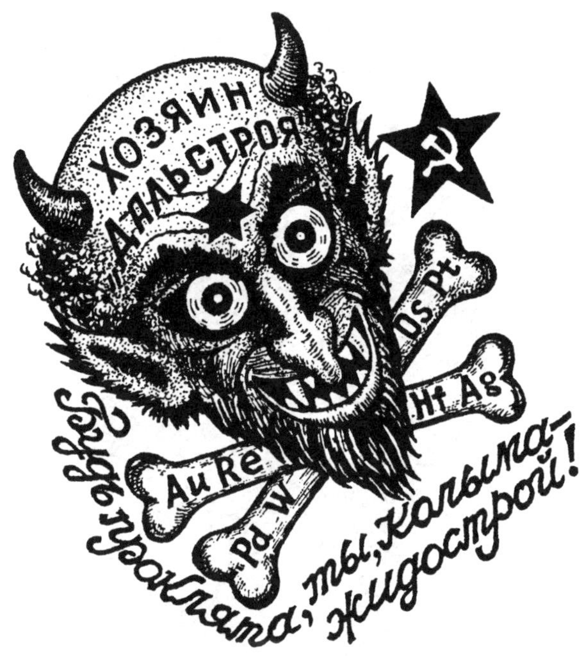

Hospital of the Administration of the North-Eastern Corrective Labour Camps, Khabarovsk. 1950s. Back.

A tattoo forcibly applied to the back of a Jewish prisoner convicted for large-scale embezzlement of state property. After being severely beaten by fellow convicts in a corrective labour camp, the wearer of the tattoo was taken to the North-Eastern Corrective Labour Camp Administration hospital in Khabarovsk. His subsequent fate is unknown.

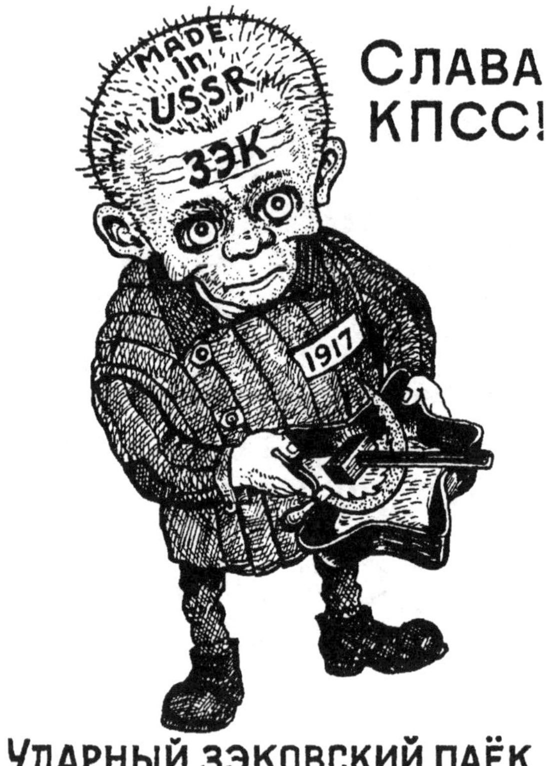

City Morgue, 10 Ekaterinsky Prospect, St. Petersburg. 1997. Left side of chest.

A tattoo from a prisoner convicted under article 206 of the Criminal Code of the RSFSR, for pulling down flags and pennants during the anniversary of the October Revolution celebrations.

'**But in the graveyard everything is peaceful, everything is proper, absolute bliss!'**. Text on the sickle reads **'Glory to the Agricultural State Camp Administration!'**.

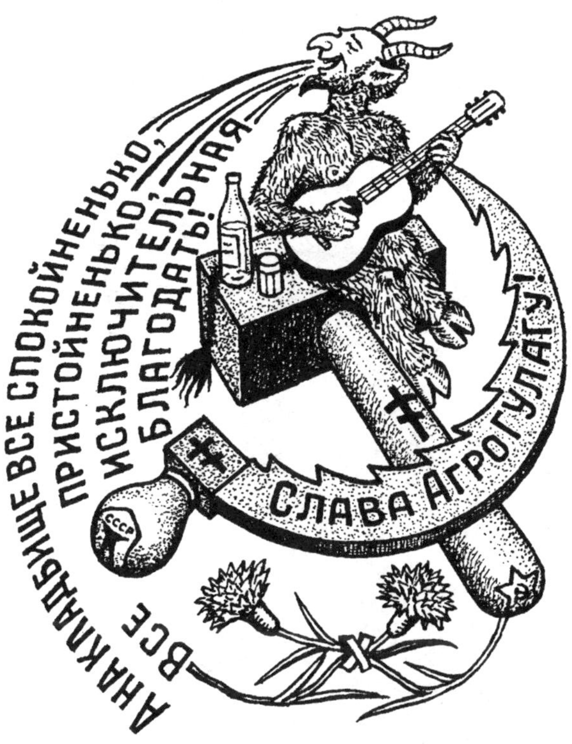

Leningrad. 1989.

The text on the scythe reads **'The banner of communism!'**. Text on the sash reads **'Glory to the CPSU!'**.

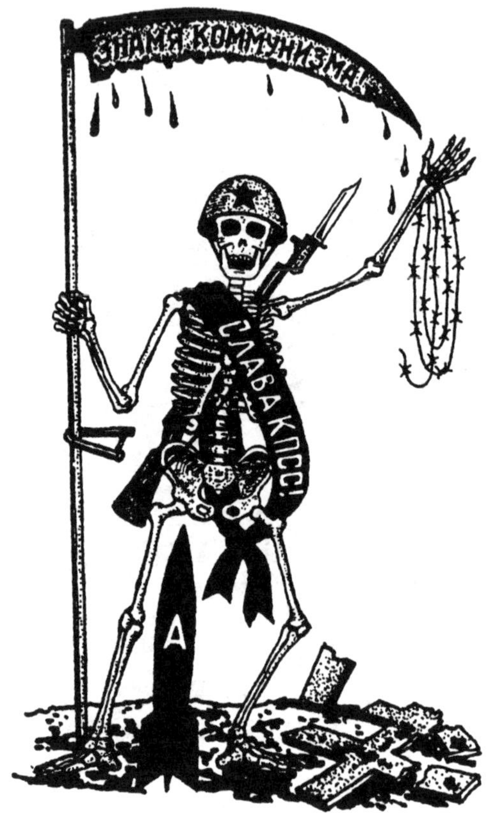

Kashchenko Hospital, Nikolskoe, Leningrad Region. 1970s.

This tattoo was worn by a conscripted soldier convicted for going absent without leave under article 245 of the 1960 Criminal Code of the RSFSR. He was sentenced to two years service in a disciplinary battalion.

'Crush red Jews and bitches!'. Text below reads **'There is nothing in the world more absurd than laws and authority where Marxist communists rule'.**

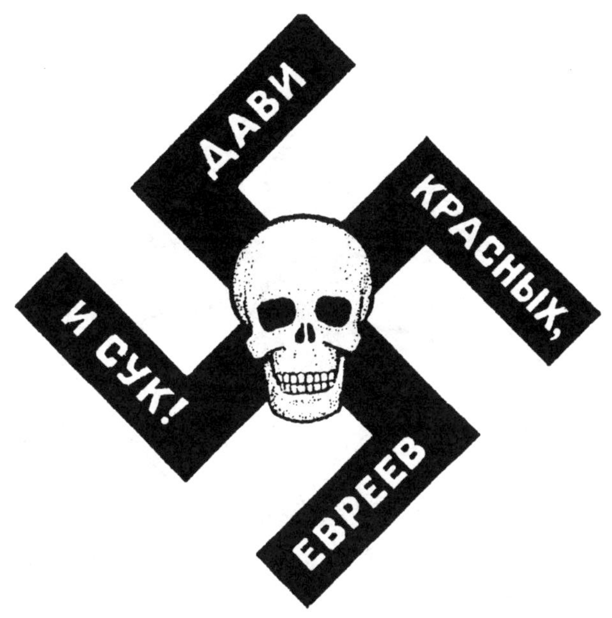

Beach, Peter and Paul Fortress, St. Petersburg. 1993.

A tattoo from a man convicted of hooliganism under article 206 of the Criminal Code of the RSFSR.

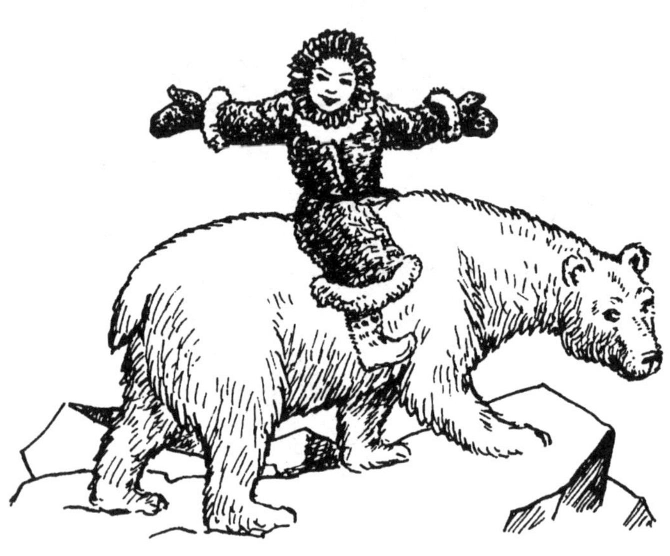

Kashchenko Hospital. 1970s. Hip.

This tattoo was worn by a man who had been convicted under article 250 of the 1960 Criminal Code of the RSFSR. During the period of his service at the marine military base in Murmansk he had 'squandered military property'. His five year sentence was spent in corrective labour colonies at Monchegorsk and Kandalakshi. He was treated for alcoholism in the Kashchenko Hospital.

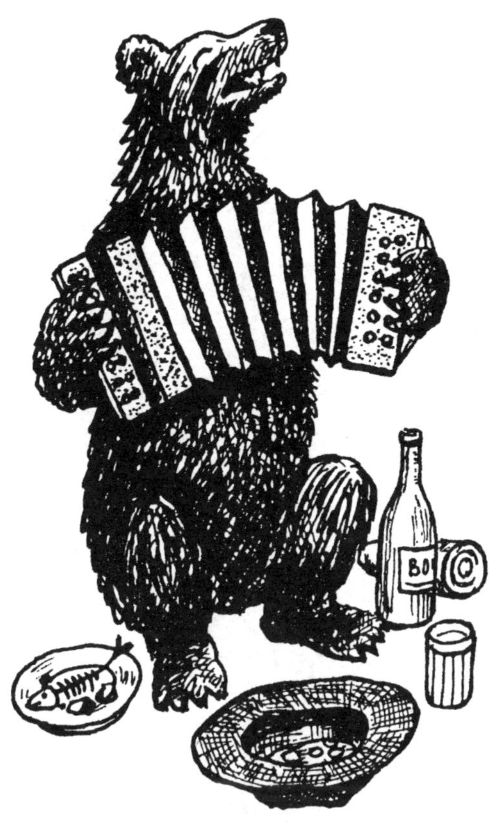

Vologda Transit Prison. 1950s.

A humorous hooligan tattoo, typical in corrective labour camps in the north and the Taiga. The most common name for this tattoo, which is found in numerous different versions, is 'Misha the accordion player'. The wearer was convicted of hooliganism under article 74 of the 1926 Criminal Code of the RSFSR.

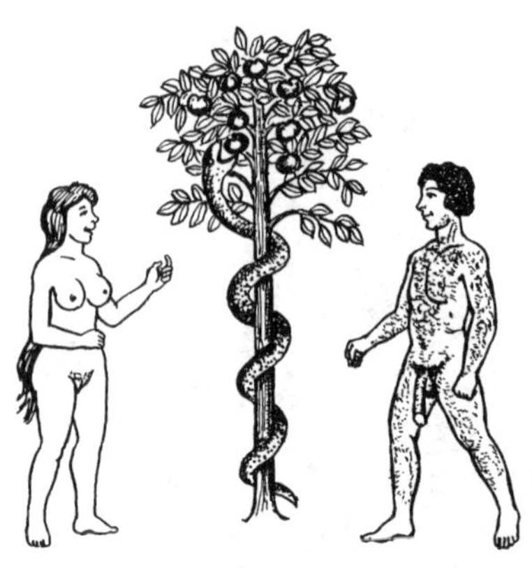

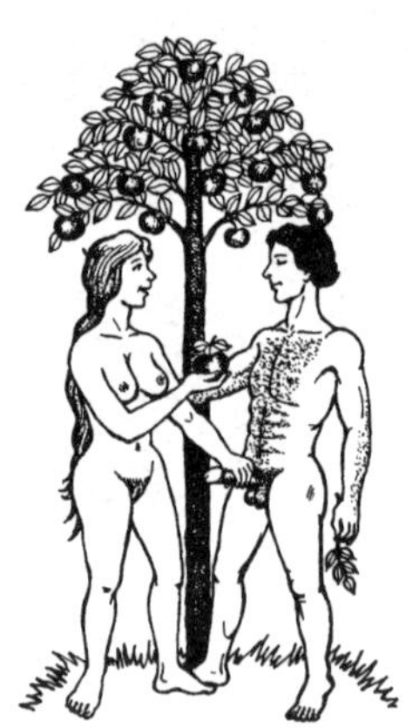

The tattoo of a prisoner nicknamed 'Shaly' (Crazy), convicted under article 74 of the 1926 Criminal Code of the RSFSR. Known as 'Eve pestering Adam' this theme was common in remote camp sites, corrective labour colonies and camps in Siberia in the 1940s and 1950s.

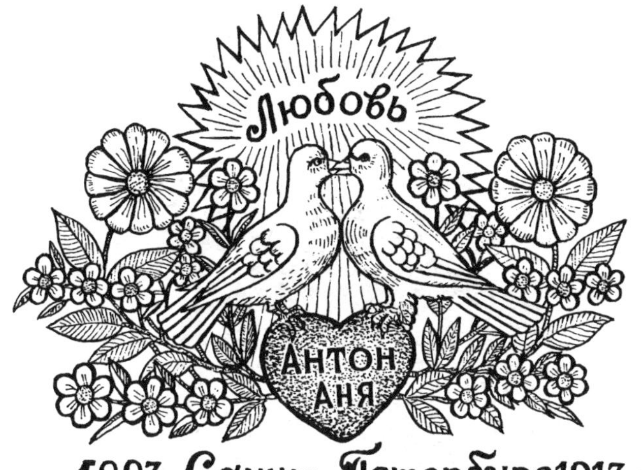

Leningrad Bathhouse No.62, 11 Ilich Lane. 1948-1949.

This tattoo was applied in a house of correction in St. Petersburg. It is from an old thief born in St. Petersburg to a working class family, (his father was employed in the Putilov Factory producing iron and steel). His nickname was 'Happy Anton' (Lucky Anton). The tattoo was applied in 1913 when Anton turned twenty and fell in love with Anya, who was killed in 1919 in Gatchina. He served his first sentence of one year for stealing food, and later served time building the White Sea Canal in both the Urals and Kolyma. He was convicted six times for stealing property.

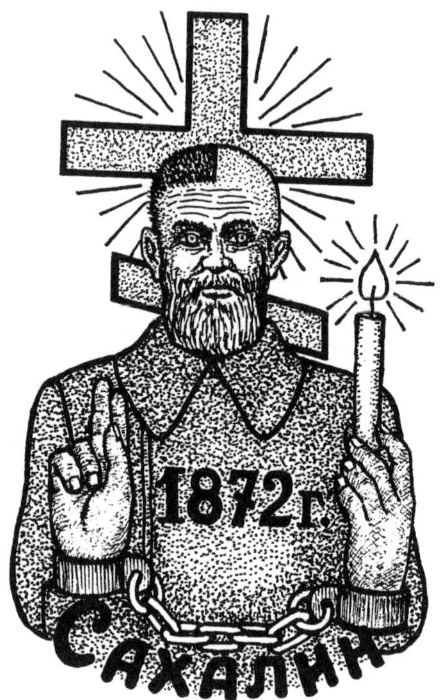

The Kolyma Corrective Labour Camps. 1940s.

'This tattoo shows a convict nicknamed 'Head', with half of his head shaved, holding a candle and set against a cross. It originally belonged to 'Head's' grandfather, who was exiled to Sakhalin with his wife and then released in 1872 under police surveillance. Like his father before him, 'Head' had the tattoo copied on to his body by a convict artist in the Kolyma camps. 'Head' was very proud of his tattoos and regarded them as his inheritance. In Kolyma in the 1940s he was one of only a few remaining old convicts who regarded themselves as hereditary 'legitimate thieves'.

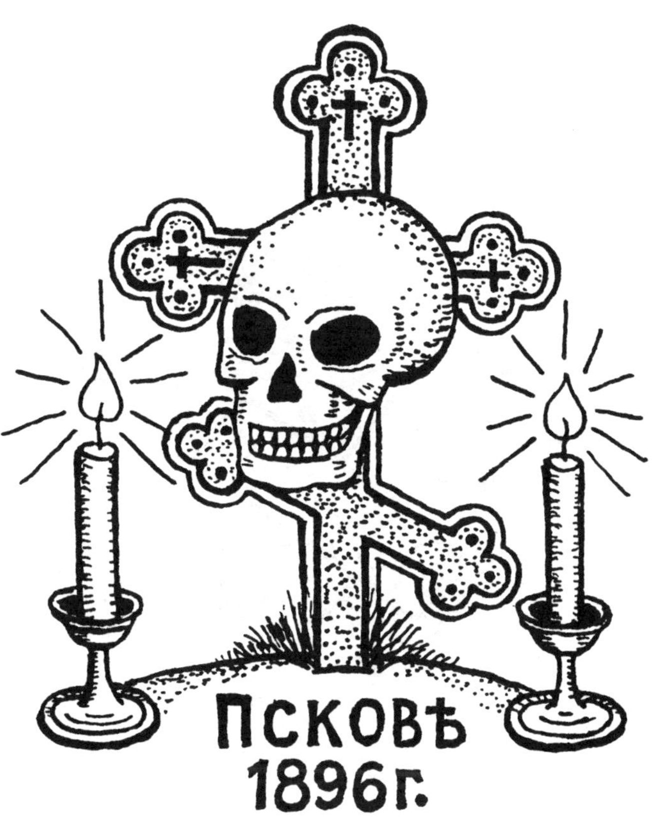

This rare tattoo belonged to an old, repeatedly convicted thief named Shulgin (his thief's nickname was 'Shulga'), whose left hand was missing. He died aged seventy-nine.

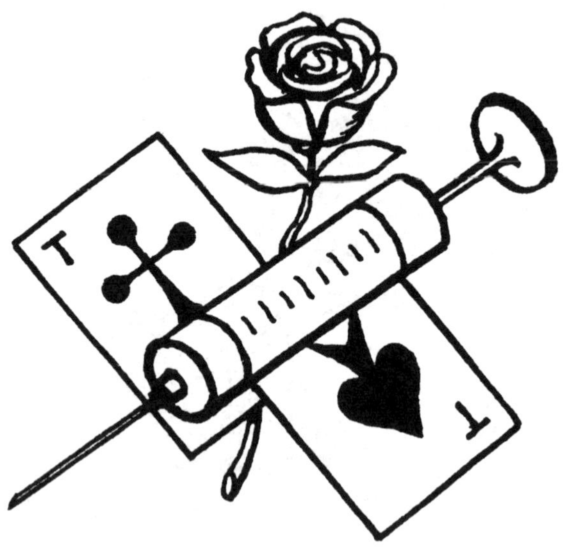

Hip, shoulder, forearm.

A tattoo widespread among young male and female criminals.

Text on the bottles reads **'high'** or **'buzz'**.

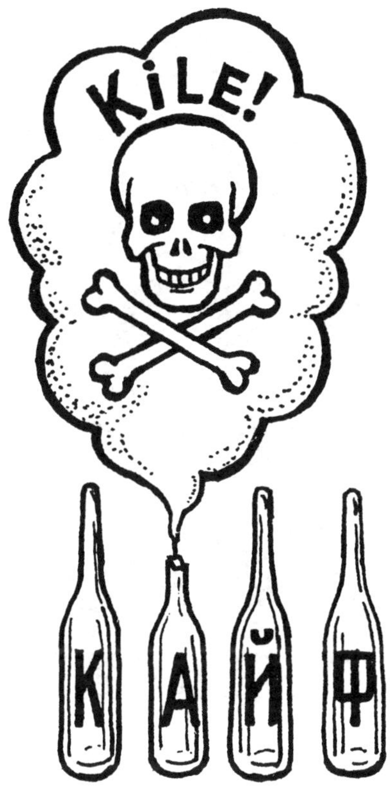

1980s. Hip, stomach, shoulder.

A tattoo found on both male and female youths.

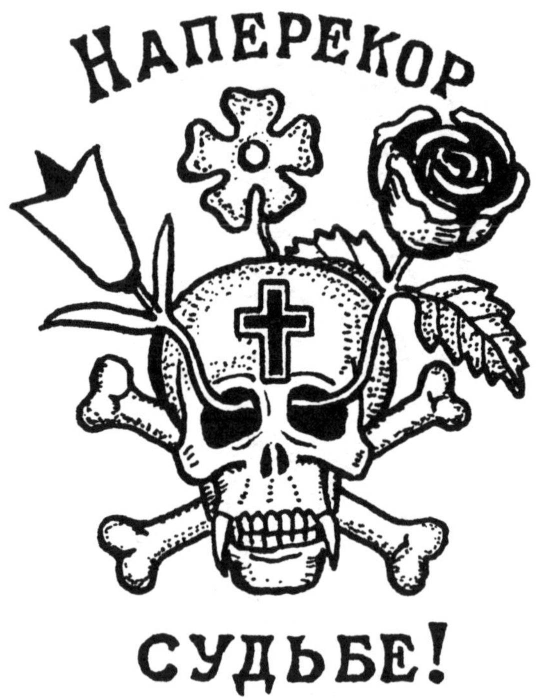

Shoulder, hip.

A young male convict's tattoo.

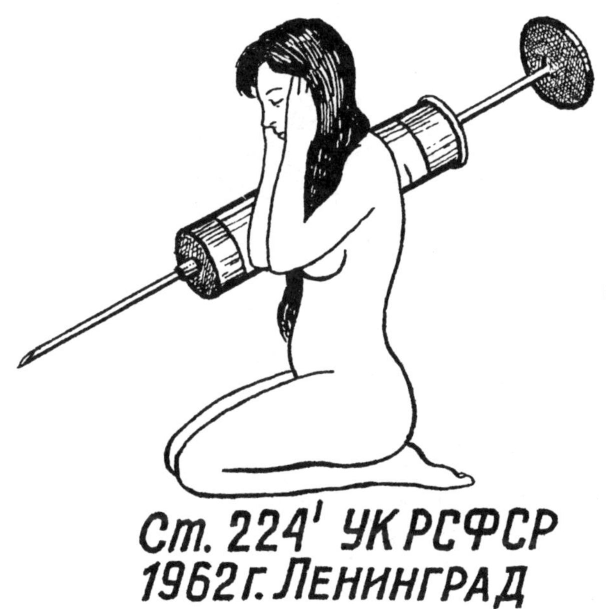

The Lenin District Militia Precinct. 1967. Hip.

A female drug addict's tattoo.

Text on the label reads **'Opium, Vodka, Pontalon'**.

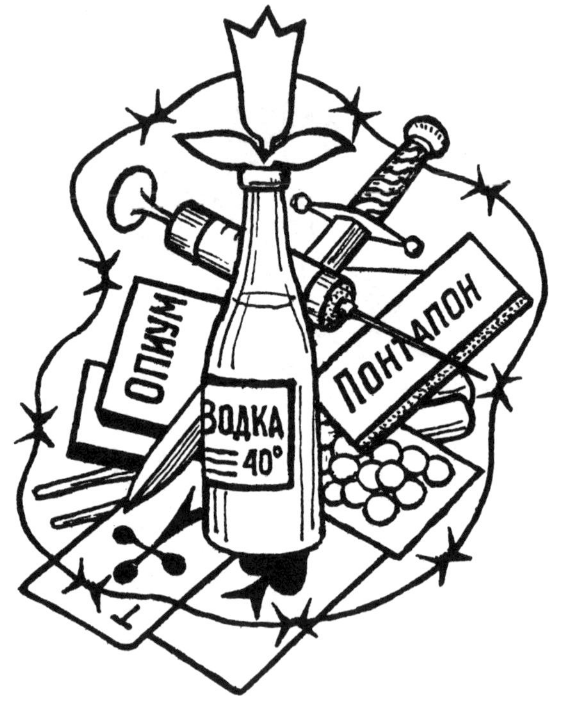

Hip, stomach.

A male youth tattoo conveying the message, 'This is what is destroying us'.

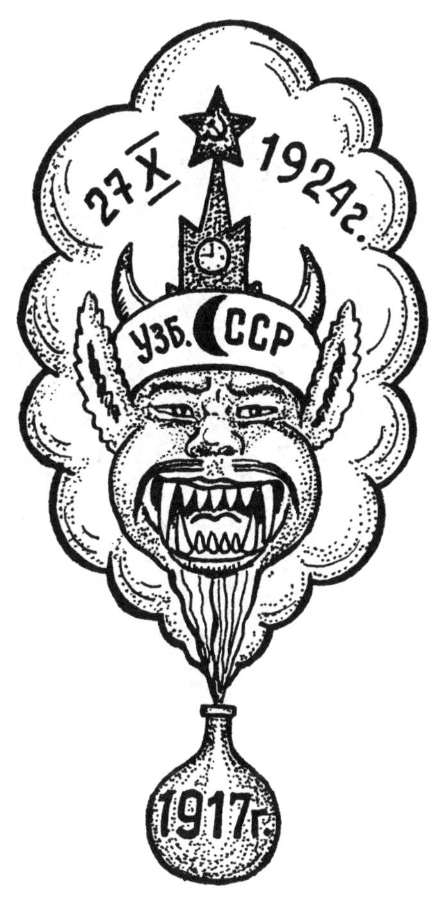

Hip.

A rare male criminal drug-addict's 'grin' tattoo from Central Asia. The date
'27.X.1924' was the day the Uzbek Soviet Socialist Republic was founded.

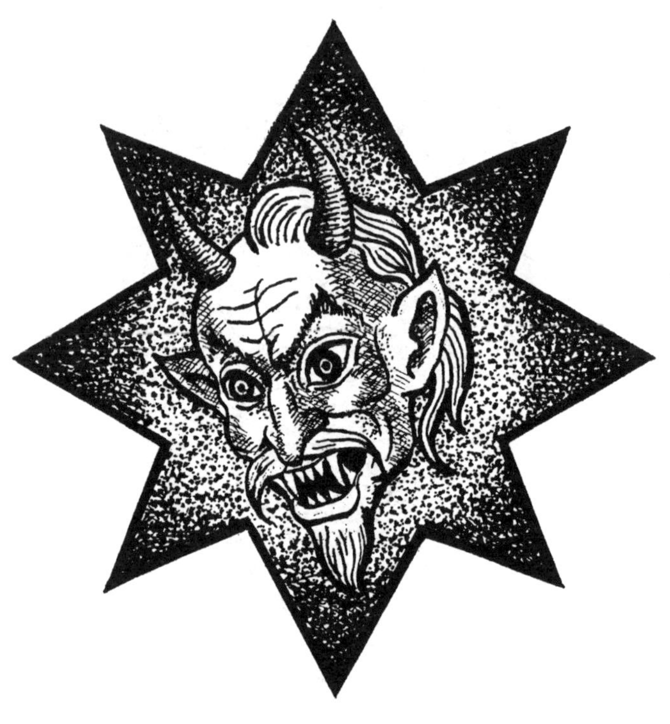

The tattoo of a thief named Orlik, who was convicted twice for burglary and a third time for hooliganism. He claimed indignantly that the 'pigs' specially framed him with the 'cormorant' (the offence of hooliganism), in order to damage his status in the camp zone. According to Orlik, during his previous stretches he spent more than seventy days in solitary confinement, (the credibility of an 'authority' is usually measured by the number of days he has spent in such a cell). The meaning of the tattoo is 'Crush the regime. I have never been happy in this country'.

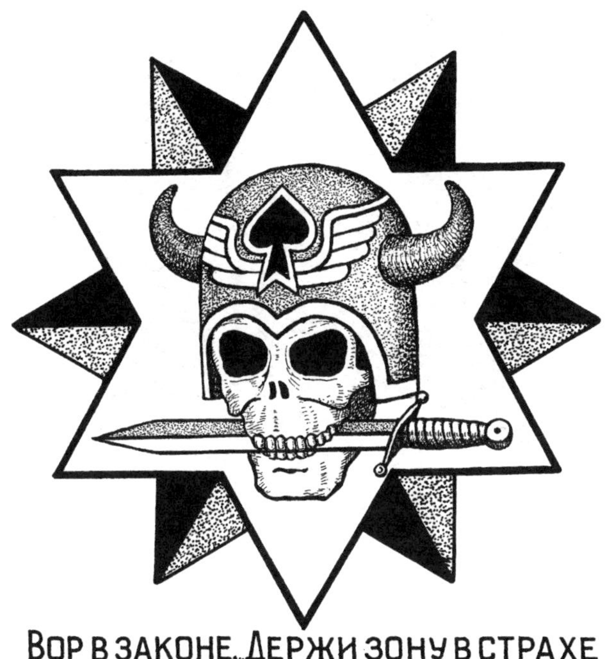

Ushakovka Settlement, Irkutsk. 1967.

A tattoo from an old 'legitimate thief' known as 'Kolya the Chinaman', who spent more than thirty years in the camps of the Kolyma and Angara zones, and who was personally acquainted with Berzin, the head of 'Dalstroi'. His father was a Chinese national, a machine-gunner killed in the Civil War. Kolya the Chinaman and the legitimate thief known as 'Head' gave up crime and lived in the settlement of Ushakovka on what they called 'funds they had served time for'. This was money from convicts which had not been confiscated from them when they had been arrested. It was paid into the accounts of 'Kolya the Chinaman' and 'Head' in gratitude for help they had given them inside the camps.

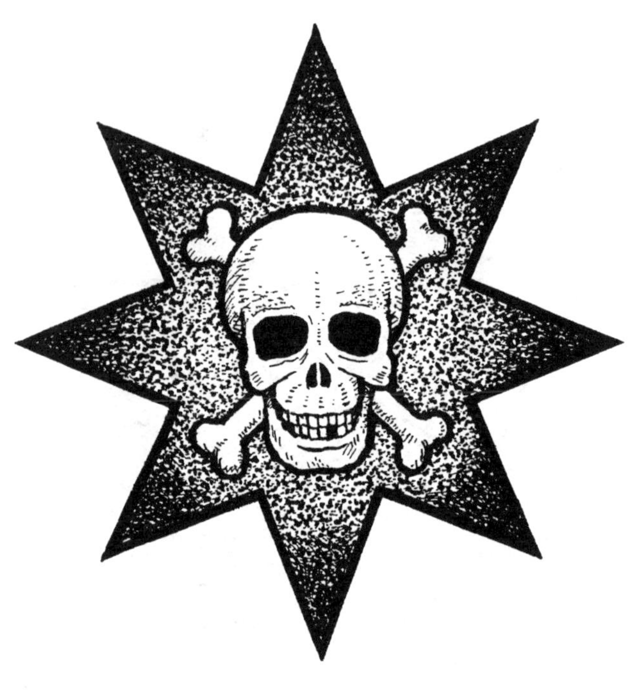

The subclavicular star of a high-status convict in the zone, a 'legitimate thief'. The various meanings of this tattoo include: 'Devoted to the caste of thieves till the end of my life', 'Jail is my home', 'In the zone I'm the boss', and 'Everything for me, nothing from me'. In the 1940s and 1950s subclavicular stars were extremely rare. Only major convict 'authorities' in the camps of Eastern Siberia, the Maritime Territory and Kolyma were allowed to wear them as badges of distinction. After some time these 'badges of distinction' began appearing on other 'legitimate thieves'. This particular star is one of the tattoos of the 'legitimate thief' known as 'Head', a hereditary thief who began his criminal career in 1917 and passed through camps in the Krasnoyarsk zone, the Taishet zone, the Angara zone and Kolyma. While the tattoo was being copied, he confessed that during his time in the camps he had come to realise that the power of the CPSU and the power of 'legitimate thieves' in the GULAG were essentially identical.

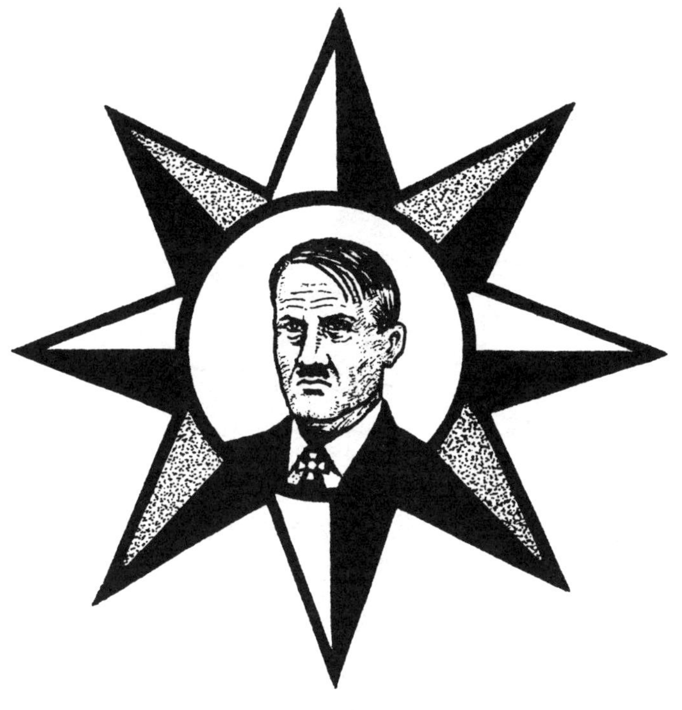

Corrective Labour Camp No.9.

A subclavicular star worn by convicts hostile to the administration in detention camps ('anti-socials'). A Russian national thief's tattoo worn by 'dunces', 'anti-socials' and 'bulls' against the authority of the CPSU and the agencies of law enforcement. Its meaning is: 'Adolf Hitler is a holy martyr', 'Killing communists and Jews is not murder, but cleansing the world of the devil's ambassadors'.

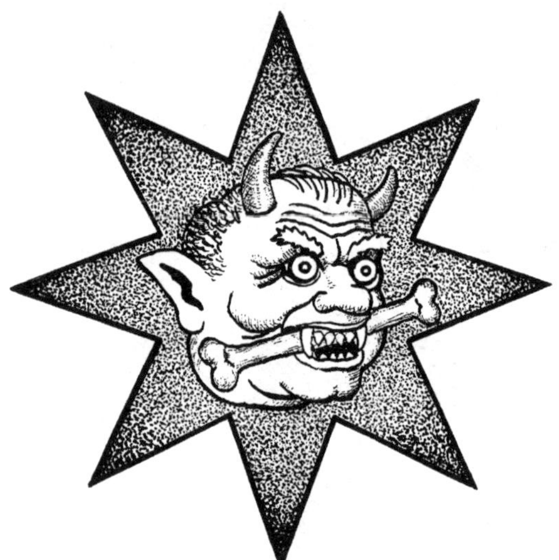

Hospital Morgue, 54 Lermontov Prospect, St. Petersburg.

The 'authority' wearing this tattoo died of an overdose of barbiturates during a settling of accounts dating back to his time in the camps. He was found in the courtyard of 12 Shkapin Street, and identified from his fingerprints as Mitrofanov, a 'legitimate thief' with four convictions. He had served his time in Corrective Labour Colony No.5.

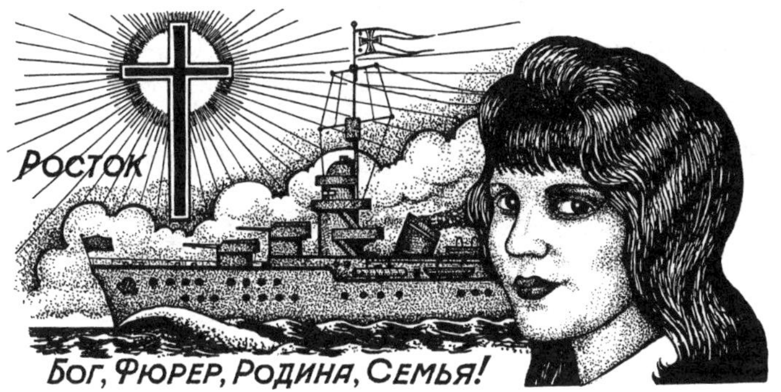

Prisoner of war camp. Sverdlovsk. 1950.

An elaborate tattoo worn by a German prisoner of war had who graduated from a maritime radio college in Rostok and served on cruise ships and minesweepers. He was captured in Eastern Prussia.

German text reads **'A cue from fate!'**.

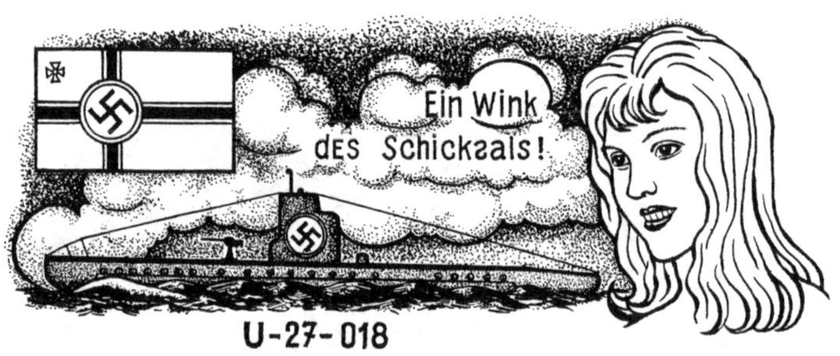

Prisoner of war camp, Leningrad. 1950.

A commemorative tattoo made in Germany. The wearer served as a torpedo operator on a submarine that sank British ships in the North Sea. He was captured while in hospital in Schwerin in 1945.

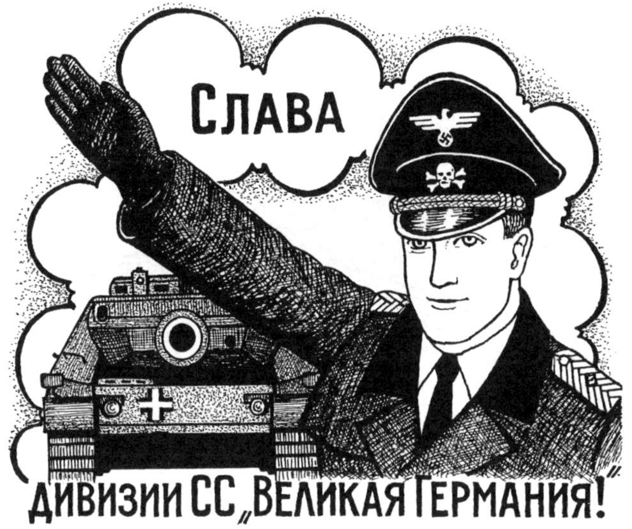

Prisoner of war camp, Nizhny Tagil. 1950.

A German prisoner of war's tattoo worn by a former officer of the 'Great German' SS division. 'Our division perished honourably and heroically in battle when outnumbered five to one by the Russians. That is not total failure. The war, unfortunately, has been lost, but there is no guilt in that. I am sure that Germany will rise from the ruins and ashes'.

German text reads **'Forwards!'**.

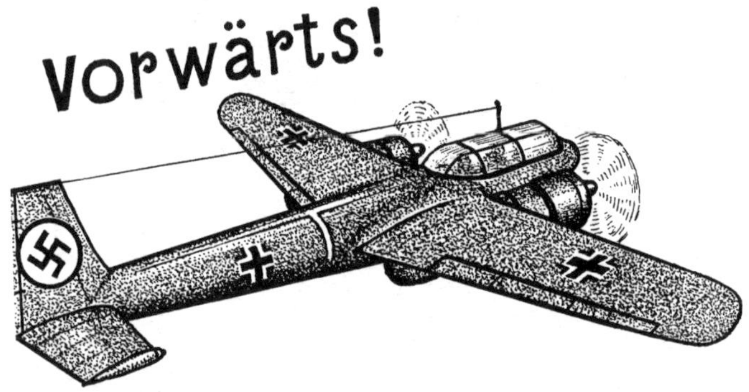

Prisoner of war camp, Nizhny Tagil. 1950. Chest.

This tattoo, worn by a German prisoner of war, was explained as follows: 'I used to fly Junkers 87 and 88 bombers. On command we bombed industrial targets in the enemy's rear; major railway stations, bridges, storage depots and enemy forces. I'm a soldier, I could have been shot for failing to follow orders. It's the same here in Russia and in any army in the world during military conflict. All the miseries inflicted by war are the responsibility of the leaders of the countries at war. I was captured at Kotvus in 1945'.

'Kill the Jews! I'll have the skin stuffed and put in a museum for posterity and send the carcass to make soap' Text on the body reads **'Mimicry, demagogy, greed, insolence are the thirst of power'**.

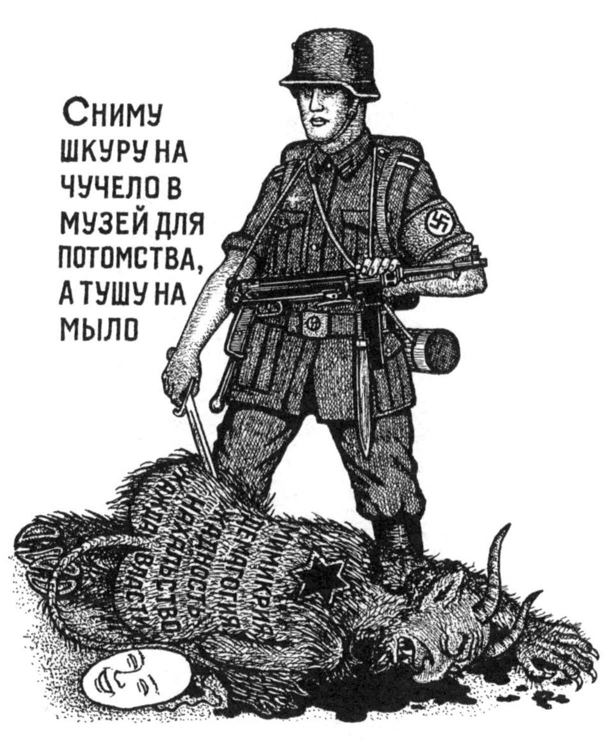

German prisoner of war tattoo.

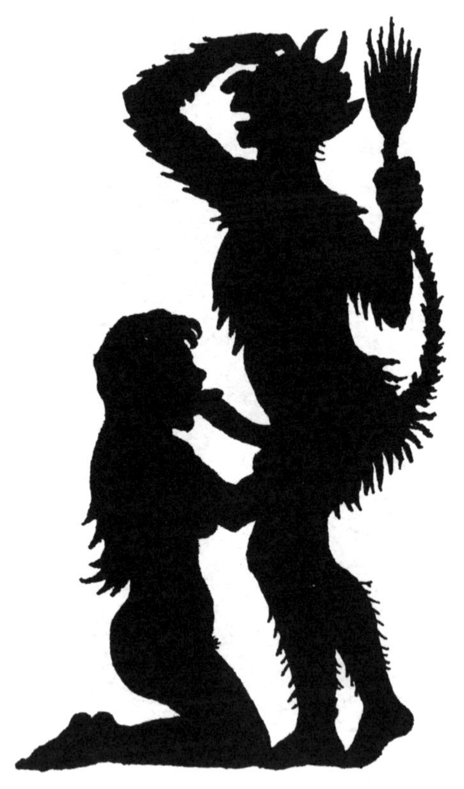

A rare 'silhouette' tattoo worn by both sexes.

Text at the base of the statue reads **'Russia'**. Main text reads **'In Soviet reality it's always as dark as up a nigger's ass'**.

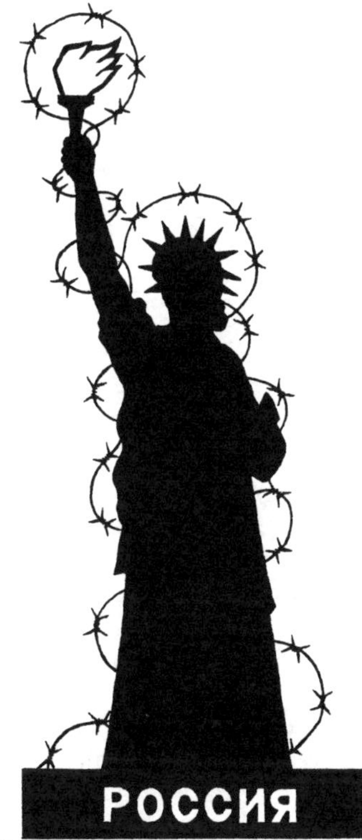

The State Department of Internal Affairs, Special Reception Centre, 10 Bakunin Street, Leningrad. 1963. Hip.

An anti-Soviet convict tattoo.

Test on the hand, from the top:
Five dots: 'Four guard towers and me', 'I've been in prison'.
'MIR' – an acronym that spells the Russian word for peace, but which stands for 'Shooting will reform me'.
Cat's head – a native inhabitant of prison, a thieves' symbol.
Crosses on knucles: 'Trips to the zone' (convictions), 'I've been to prison three times'.
'LARA' – a girlfriend's name.
Forefinger: A 'Leninist' bandit. Leader of a group of expropriators.
Middle finger: 'Convicted for brigandage'.
Third finger: 'Complete orphan. Rely on no one but yourself'.
Little finger: 'Anarchist'.
'PEGA' – nickname.

Text to the right of the hand, from the top:
According to old western heraldry suits of cards had the following meanings:
Clubs – sword.
Spades – spear.
Hearts – shield.
Diamonds – public symbol.
(Thieves, robbers and exploiters prefer clubs and spades).

206

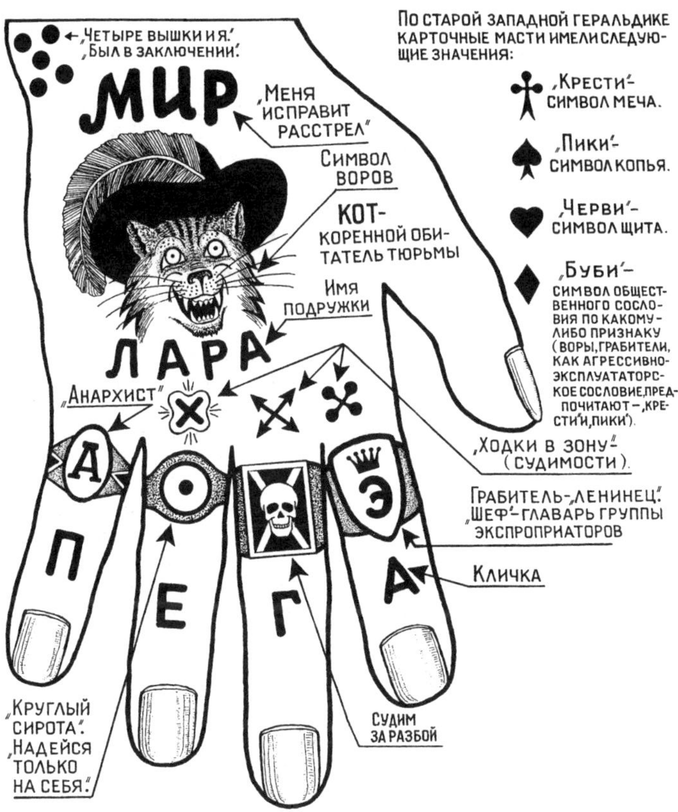
ПО СТАРОЙ ЗАПАДНОЙ ГЕРАЛЬДИКЕ КАРТОЧНЫЕ МАСТИ ИМЕЛИ СЛЕДУЮЩИЕ ЗНАЧЕНИЯ:
„КРЕСТИ"- СИМВОЛ МЕЧА.
„ПИКИ"- СИМВОЛ КОПЬЯ.
„ЧЕРВИ"- СИМВОЛ ЩИТА.
„БУБИ"- СИМВОЛ ОБЩЕСТВЕННОГО СОСЛОВИЯ ПО КАКОМУ-ЛИБО ПРИЗНАКУ (ВОРЫ, ГРАБИТЕЛИ, КАК АГРЕССИВНО-ЭКСПЛУАТАТОРСКОЕ СОСЛОВИЕ, ПРЕДПОЧИТАЮТ - „КРЕСТИ" И „ПИКИ").
„ЧЕТЫРЕ ВЫШКИ И Я." „БЫЛ В ЗАКЛЮЧЕНИИ."
МИР
„МЕНЯ ИСПРАВИТ РАССТРЕЛ"
СИМВОЛ ВОРОВ
КОТ- КОРЕННОЙ ОБИТАТЕЛЬ ТЮРЬМЫ
ИМЯ ПОДРУЖКИ
ЛАРА
„АНАРХИСТ"
„ХОДКИ В ЗОНУ" (СУДИМОСТИ).
ГРАБИТЕЛЬ-„ЛЕНИНЕЦ". „ШЕФ"- ГЛАВАРЬ ГРУППЫ „ЭКСПРОПРИАТОРОВ
КЛИЧКА
А
О
Г
Э
А
П
Е
Г
А
„КРУГЛЫЙ СИРОТА." „НАДЕЙСЯ ТОЛЬКО НА СЕБЯ."
СУДИМ ЗА РАЗБОЙ

i   'I'm a complete orphan' – a youth tattoo that appeared during the 1970s in orphanages for difficult children and juveniles, special labour institutions and educational labour colonies. Known as 'the Round Stone'.

ii   A tattoo belonging to criminals convicted of hooliganism – 'the Cormorant'. In criminals' jargon article 7A of the Criminal Code of the RSFSR of 1960 is known as 'the cormorant article'. In the 'black thieves' zones' hooligans have no status and are subjected to oppressive measures.

iii   'A "Leninist" robber', 'chief expropriator' – the leader of a group of racketeers. A youth tattoo that appeared in the 1990s.

iv   A convicts' symbol – the 'cross of clubs'.

v   The tattoo of a man convicted under article 59-3 of the Criminal Code of the RSFSR of 1926, and article 77 of the Criminal Code of the RSFSR of 1960 for banditry, (subsequently redefined in article 146 of the Criminal Code of the RSFSR for 1960 as 'brigandage'). Known as 'the Stopper', in the thieves' zones of the north and Siberia. 'Stoppers' possess only limited status among the convicts.

vi   A 'Shaggy Thief', a 'Shaggy Face' – a despised convict with no status, who has been convicted for rape and is forcibly subjected to the act of sodomy.

vii   The 'Horn' (head) of a zone in an educational labour colony - the leader of a group of young convicts. An 'anti-social' who is hostile to the existing authorities. A 'horn' is well aware that the laws will not be applied to him in the same way as to adults, and so he shows 'exaggerated bravado', which is then eroded in an adult colony.

viii   Known as 'the Godfather's Suit', 'the Diamond' and 'the Stool Pigeon'. This tattoo is applied forcibly at night in the accommodation zone (under threat of severe beating), to inmates exposed as informers (or of having connections with the operations unit of the remote camp site, corrective labour colony or camp).

ix   'Within Bounds', 'A Place Man' – a convict who is not subject to oppression, who occupies a middle-rank position in the prison camp hierarchy, observing the laws. A member of a convicts' 'suit' or group. A 'place man' can serve criminal bosses or 'authorities' by working as a 'table honcho' or a 'bed honcho', and he can be a member of a 'family of thieves' – a group that defends its own interests against aggression from other groups and the 'suit' of cormorants, (hooligans). This is the largest group of prisoners. Convicts from a 'family of thieves' eat together, and in the living accommodation zone they have their own 'dosses' on beds or bunks beside each other. They share food parcels, drink 'chifir' (extremely strong tea) together, and buy goods in the zone shop.

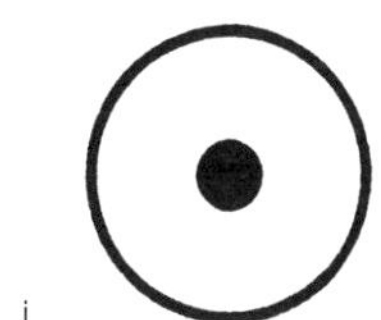

i

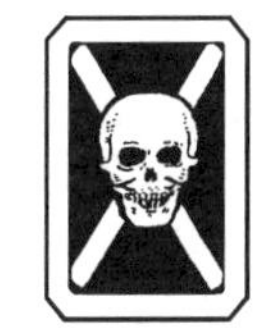

ii

iii

iv

v

vi

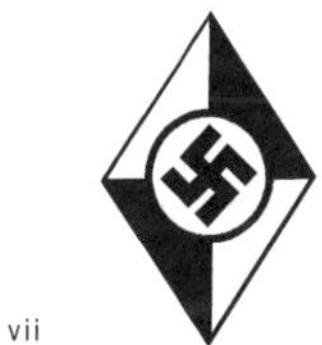

vii

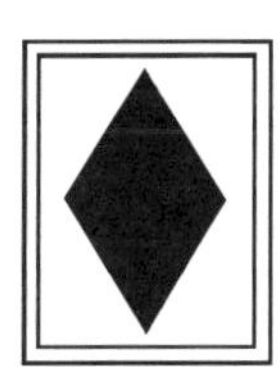

viii

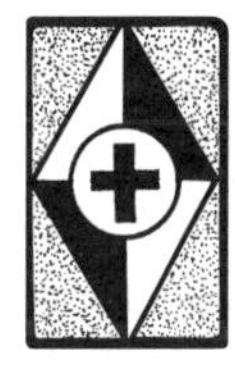

ix

x   'I was born a thief'. Usually applied to the thumb as a 'talisman'.

xi   'A racketeer and proletarian expropriator', 'A collector of the Abyssinian tax' from protected owners of trading kiosks, offices, etc.

xii   A scarab beetle – the symbol of success as a thief and material prosperity. An old pre-revolutionary tattoo. A distinctive 'talisman'.

xiii   'A racketeer of Caucasian nationality', in particular a Chechen. A rare tattoo.

xiv   'Always remember (I always remember) the zone (educational or corrective labour colony)', 'Thrown overboard from life'.

xv   'I am fatherless', 'I became a thief because of poverty and a broken home'.

xvi   'Before I was imprisoned I served in a military construction unit'. '130' is the number of the construction unit, stationed in Leningrad at Novaya Derevnya.

xvii   'Convicted for robbery'. As a second shadow power in places of detention, 'traditional' convicts, including 'legitimate' thieves, despised violent robbers or 'brigands', preferring 'clean' thefts with no violence to the victim – since outside prison they themselves were not guaranteed against attack by a brigand.

xviii   'Convicted for brigandage'. In the GULAG and corrective labour camps a thief who had committed grievous bodily harm or murder forfeited his status and was called a 'flatiron', or even a despised 'cormorant' – a hooligan. They are rarely accepted into 'criminals' camp families'.

xix   'I was raised in an orphanage', 'An Orphan' (with living parents who are good for nothing). Juveniles usually have this tattoo applied by juvenile criminals in educational labour colonies in order to enhance their status among their peers.

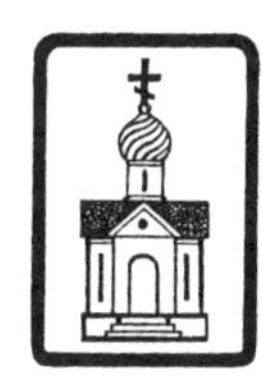

x

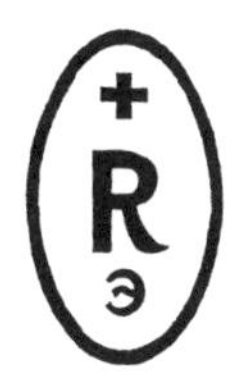

xi

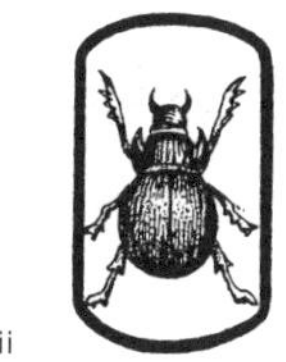

xii

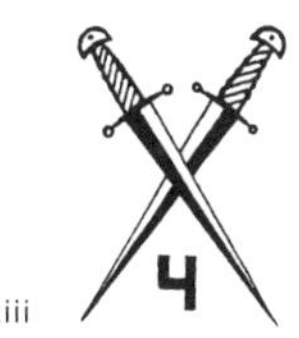

xiii

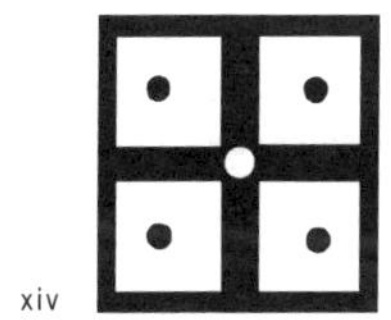

xiv

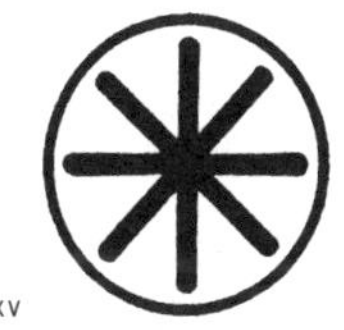

xv

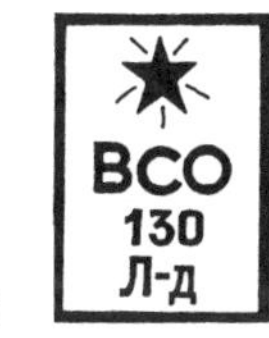

xvi

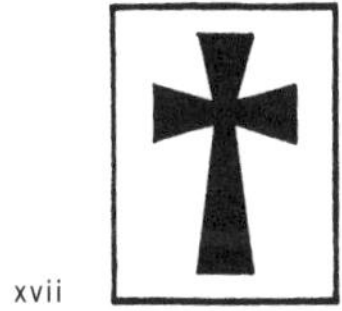

xvii

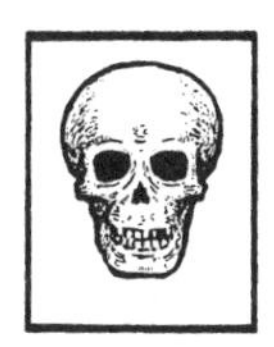

xviii

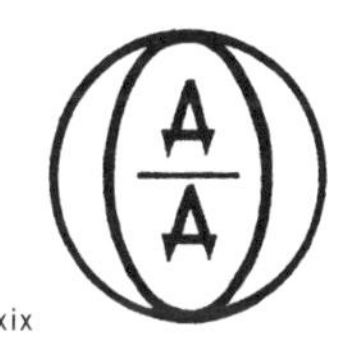

xix

xx Tattoo of a cat's head – a thieves' symbol. 'KOT' – an acronym that spells the Russian word for 'cat', but which stands for 'a native inhabitant of jail'.

xxi 'I spent two years in a disciplinary battalion for military crime'.

xxii 'Convicted for murder', 'Convicted for inflicting grievous bodily harm', 'Butcher'.

xxiii A touring thief who travels round various towns, commiting thefts. 'Trotter', 'Here today, there tomorrow'.

xxiv The tattoo of a criminal boss or 'authority' – the 'Crown' of a 'legitimate thief'. In the GULAG and corrective labour camps they had almost unlimited power over prisoners.

xxv A symbol meaning 'I am a thief'. According to prison and camp law, prisoners convicted for crimes that do not involve property have no right to wear this tattoo in places of detention.

xxvi A 'Polish thief' – a pickpocket who commits his crimes alone. The expression appeared in 1840 following the partition of Poland. The number '9' is the length of the sentence in years, '3' is the number of convictions.

xxvii 'I've been through the "Crosses"', – meaning in solitary confinement (solitary confinement cell No.1).

xxviii A 'sixer' – the lowest position in the camp hierarchy of convicts. This person acts as a servant to the thieves' 'authorities'. A 'sixer' irons clothes; cleans shoes; acts as a messenger; writes letters and notes; brings food from the canteen; prepares 'chifir' (extremely strong tea); washes bed-sheets, socks and foot-wrappings; acts as a bodyguard; reports on the mood among the convicts; exposes informers; maintains order in the accommodation and production sections of the zone; collects the 'Abyssinian tax' from convicts under 'protection'; guards the food locker; washes the 'authority' in the bathhouse; procures passive homosexuals and men who give fellatio; opens up and makes the bed; and, on the orders of the 'authority', collaborates with the operations unit of the remote camp site, corrective labour colony or camp. An 'authority' in a camp can have ten or more of these 'sixers'.

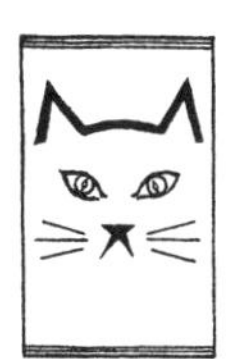

xx

xxi

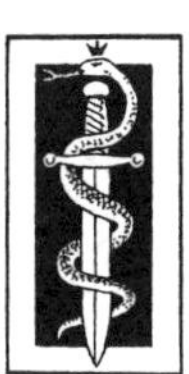

xxii

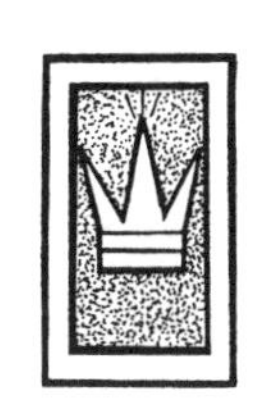

xxiii

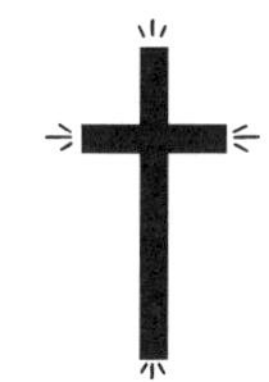

xxiv

xxv

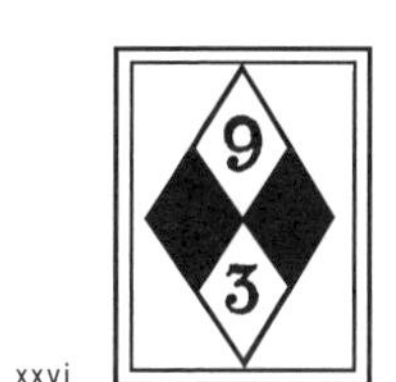

xxvi

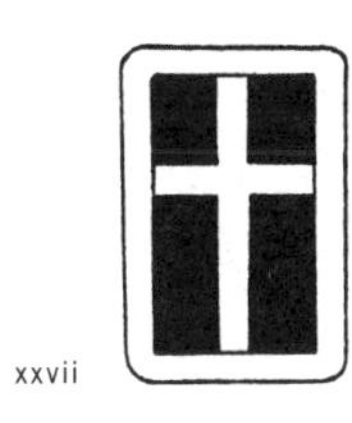

xxvii

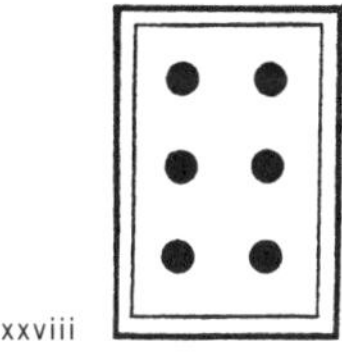

xxviii

xxix A tattoo symbolising 'I will revenge my desecrated love'. Rarely encountered among convicts.

xxx 'A lover of women', 'A lover of group sex'. Convicts call men with this tattoo 'cunt-struck' and 'sex maniacs'.

xxxi 'A shaggy thief', 'A shaggy safe-breaker', 'A cunt-struck lover', 'One cigar, ten years hard labour', 'Drowned in the twat' – the tattoo of a man convicted for raping children, adolescents or women. In places of detention rapists are often forcibly subjected to acts of buggery, sometimes by groups - they are 'lowered', degraded to the 'bottom' of the camp and they become 'untouchables'.

xxxii 'Garbage' – a slovenly, dirty, stupid, mentally and physically degraded passive homosexual, from whom nothing should be taken, not even a match, so that you do not 'filthy yourself', 'get scummy' or 'get polluted'. A 'garbage' is regarded as unclean, you cannot even sit next to him. In the canteen and the club, this bottom level of the camp have their own seats. Their crockery and spoons are marked with drilled holes and washed separately. When they are released or transferred their dosses (beds) are burnt to purge them. 'Garbages' (or 'slimes') carry out the dirtiest cleaning jobs. In the accommodation section they have their own hut or corner.

xxxiii 'Waffle eater' – the tattoo of a man who gives fellatio and swallows sperm. This is usually done by homosexuals and prisoners who are entertainers or actors. Men who give fellatio are also known as 'strokers'. A passive homosexual who engages in prostitution is known as an 'old tart'.

xxxiv 'I stayed in till the bell' – a prisoner who served his sentence in full, without any amnesty or reduction of the length of sentence. After serving two thirds of their time an inmate might get a conditional early release, but only if they had exhibited exemplary behaviour, or worked well and over-fulfilled the plan. Forcibly applied 'garbage' and rapist tattoos were concealed by being overdrawn with this tattoo.

xxxv 'Love and cherish freedom' – a widespread tattoo among young convicts.

xxix 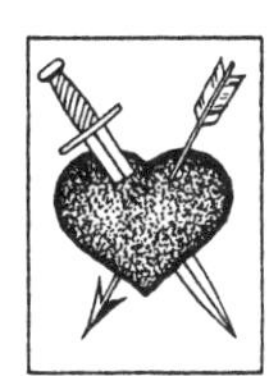

xxx 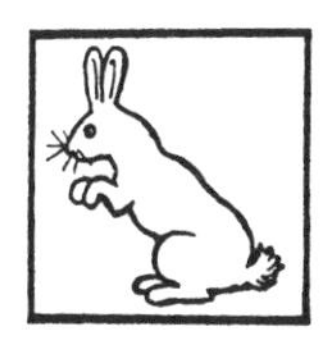

xxxi 

xxxii 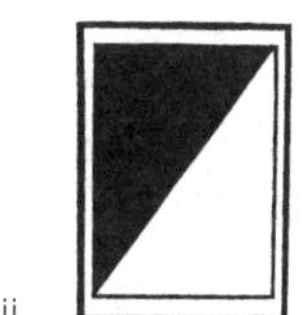

xxxiii 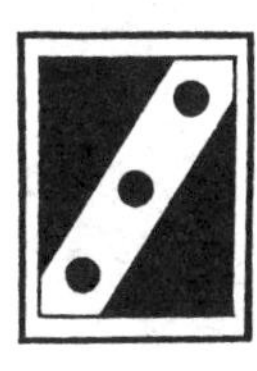

xxxiv 

xxxv 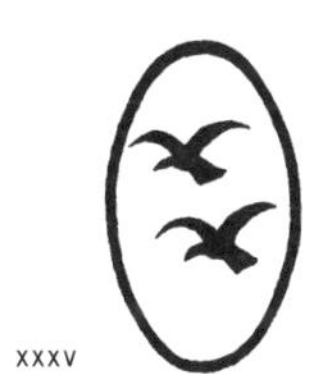

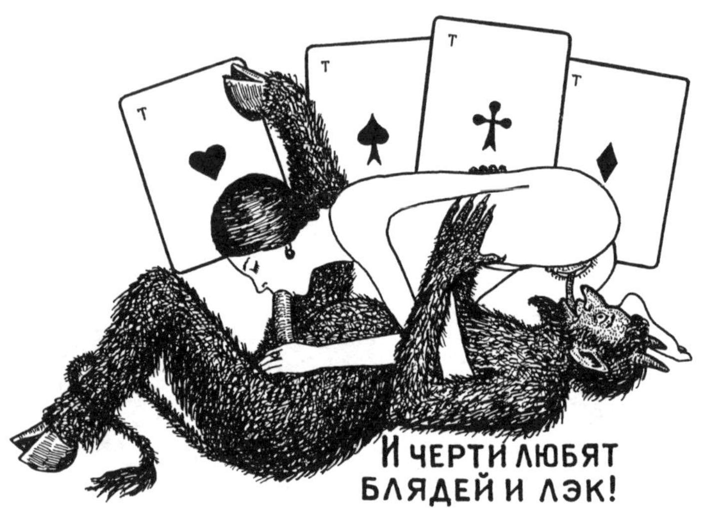

1994. Back.

A tattoo drawn on a man who had lost at cards in Corrective Labour Colony No.9. According to the rules of the game, the loser has to comply with the winner's wishes. He is also forced to pay the artist for making the tattoo.

'Section 20/5, Corrective Labour Colony No.5. Oppressed by a cunt-lackey. Art[icle] 120 of the Criminal Code of the RSFSR'.

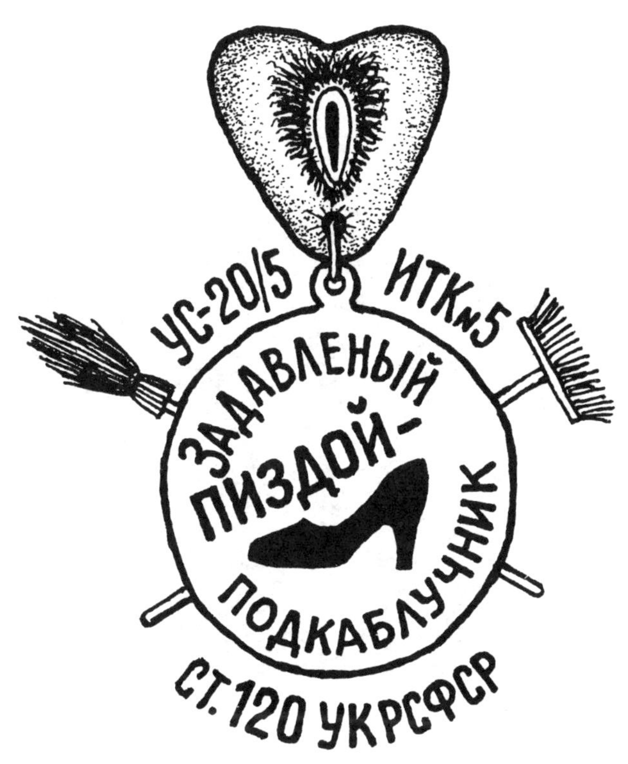

A tattoo forcibly applied to a 'degraded' convict, also known as a 'lackey's medal'. According to other convicts, the wearer of this tattoo got married after his mother's death, and moved his wife and her daughter from a previous marriage, into his flat. His strong-willed wife subjected him to many humiliations, including making him wash her own and her daughter's underwear. Eventually, to get rid of her husband, his wife got him drunk on his birthday and planted her fourteen year old daughter in his bed. In his sleep he mistook the daughter for his wife and embraced her. The militia detail that was summoned, along with the wife's friends present at the birthday party, subsequently reported 'an attempted rape'.

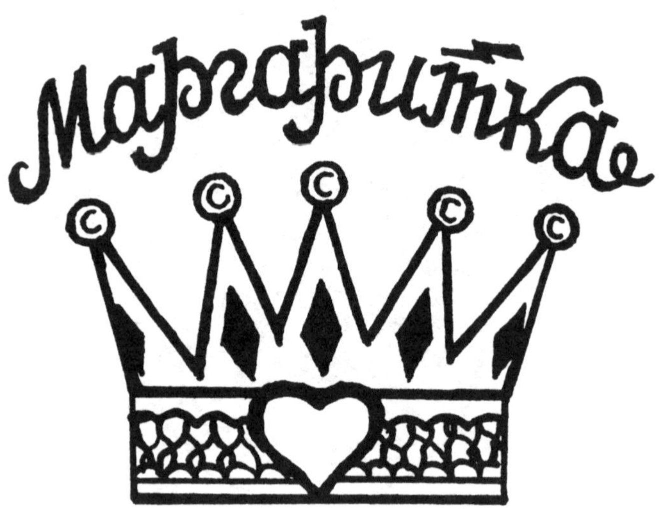

Back.

This is the tattoo of a 'passive' homosexual that has been forcibly applied in prison. In criminal jargon a passive homosexual is also called a 'daisy', 'Mashka' (a woman's name), 'cockerel', 'coxcomb', 'queer', 'cocksucker', 'gay' or 'piglet'.

The acronym and text reads **'Educational Labour Colony, Tyumen'**.

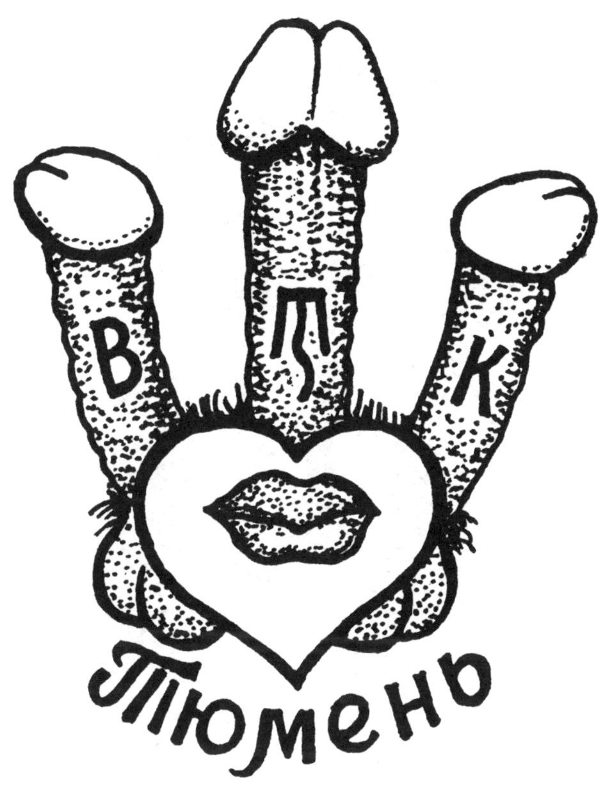

A 'passive' homosexual's tattoo.

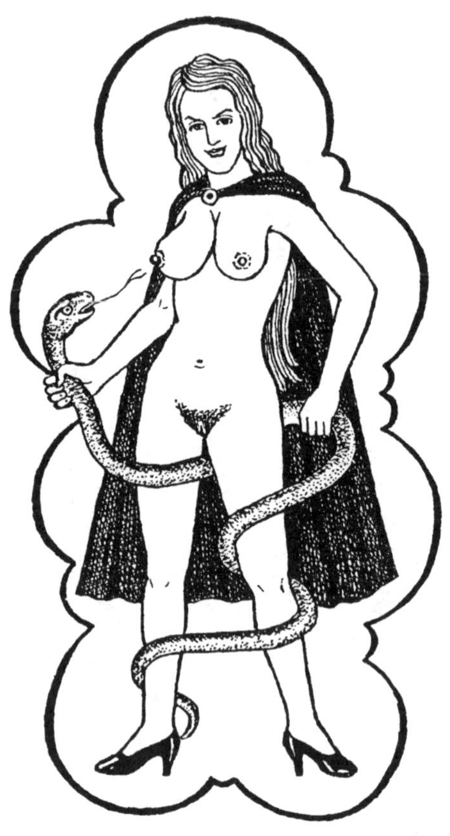

A tattoo worn by a 'congenitally' homosexual actor who was killed by his friend, an active homosexual, in a fit of jealousy. The murderer was arrested at 9 Ilich Lane by district militia officer Ganush, and the operations group of the Fourth Militia Precinct of the Frunze District of Leningrad.

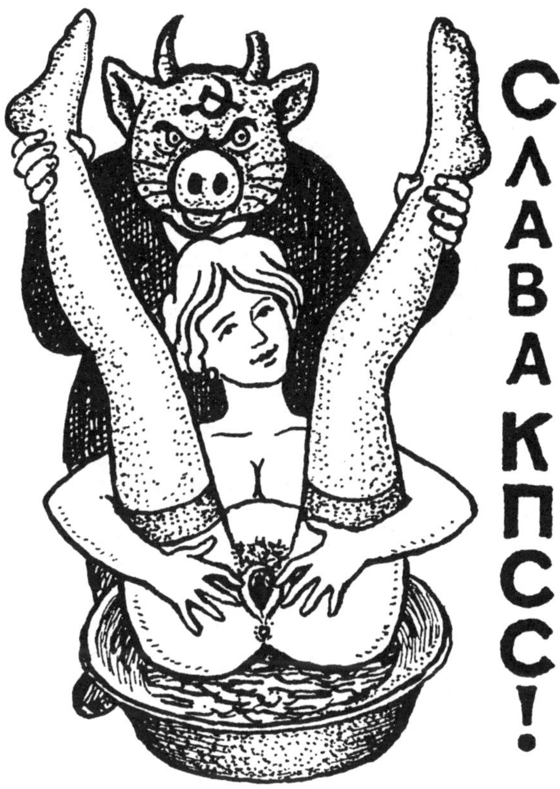

A tattoo drawn on a prisoner who lost at cards in the strict regime Corrective Labour Colony No.9 in the 1980s. This distinctive 'grin', directed at the authorities, always raised a laugh with other convicts.

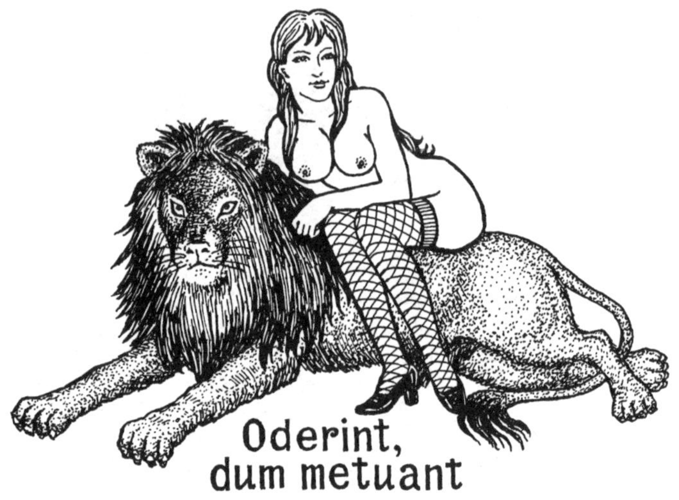

Oderint,
dum metuant

'Death to whores!'

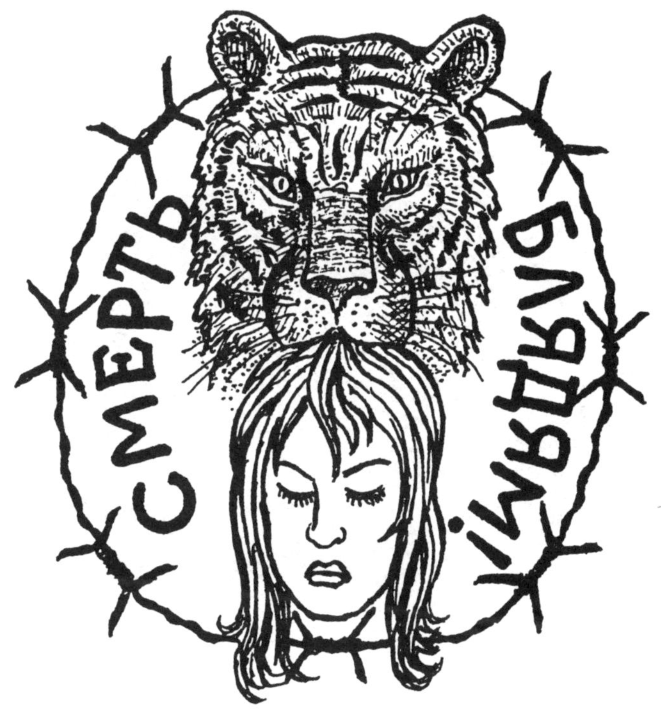

Khabarovsk Corrective Labour Colony. 1956. Shoulder.

A male hooligan's tattoo. The wearer was convicted of murdering his mistress under article 136 of the Criminal Code of the RSFSR.

'**N**ow, bitch, tell me how you were unfaithful to your husband!'

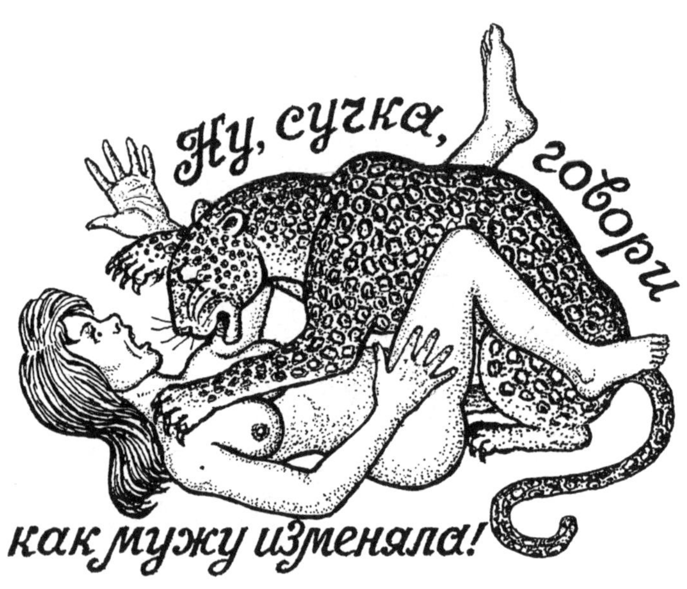

Ministry of the Interior Inter-Regional Hospital, Leningrad. 1944.

A male hooligan's tattoo worn by a man convicted for hooliganism under article 206 of the Criminal Code of the RSFSR.

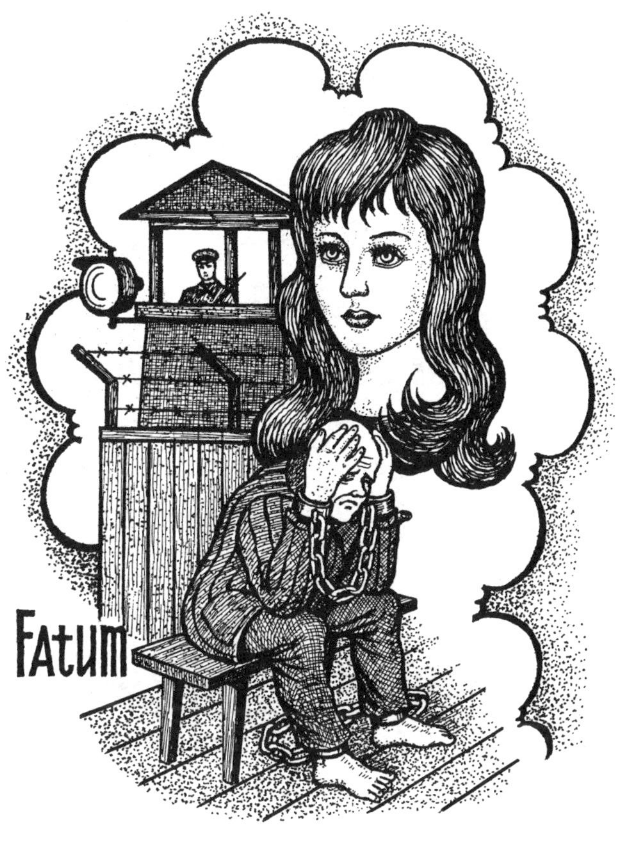

Leningrad. 1960s. Stomach.

A tattoo based on a photograph.

Latin text reads **'No sooner said than done'**.

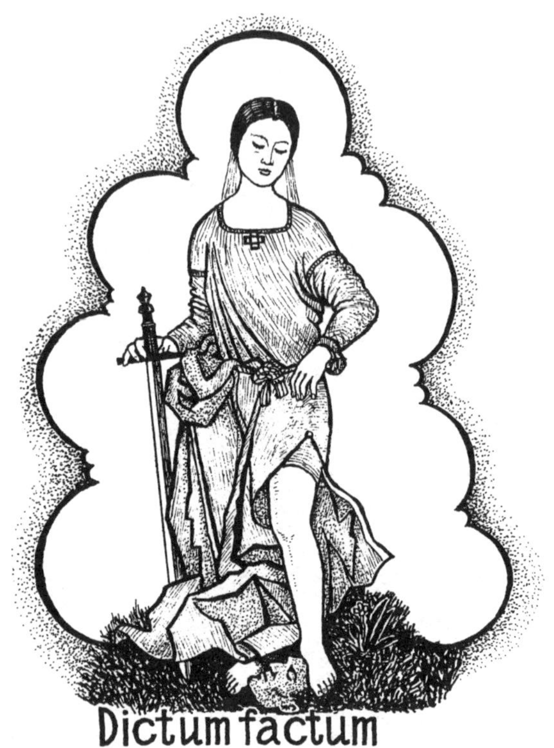

Vladivostok Prison. 1950s. Chest.

A rare tattoo from a sailor sentenced to two years imprisonment for failing to pay alimony under article 152 of the 1926 Criminal Code of the RSFSR. The depiction of 'The beheading of John the Baptist' represents himself and his wife, who took him to court and had him imprisoned. He said that after he had served his time he would no longer be able to go on foreign voyages, and from now on his fate would be to 'hang about inshore', in other words to work on unchartered coastal vessels.

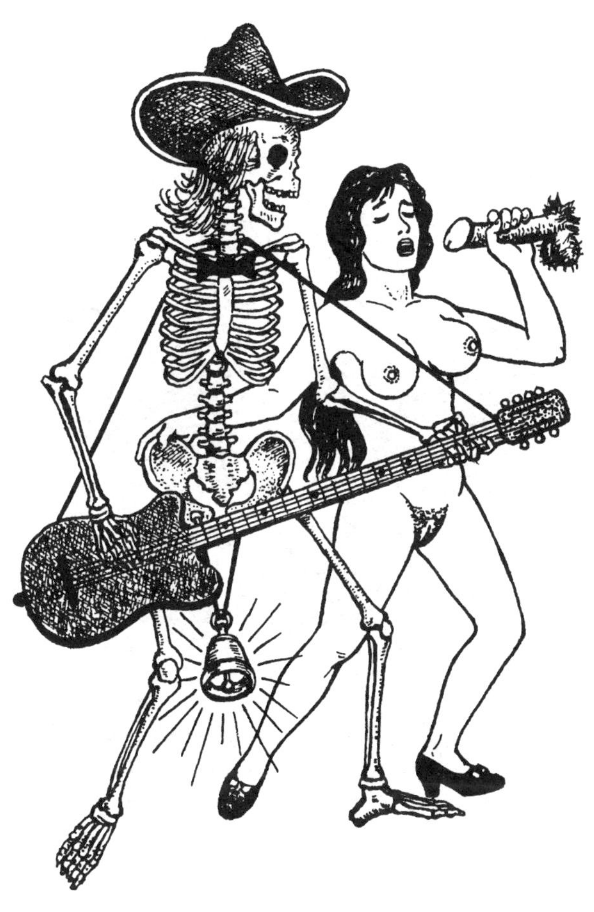

Corrective Labour Colony No.9. 1986.

A humorous youth tattoo which is known by convicts as 'Duet with sleighbells'.
Sometimes accompanied by a text, usually vulgar rhymes.

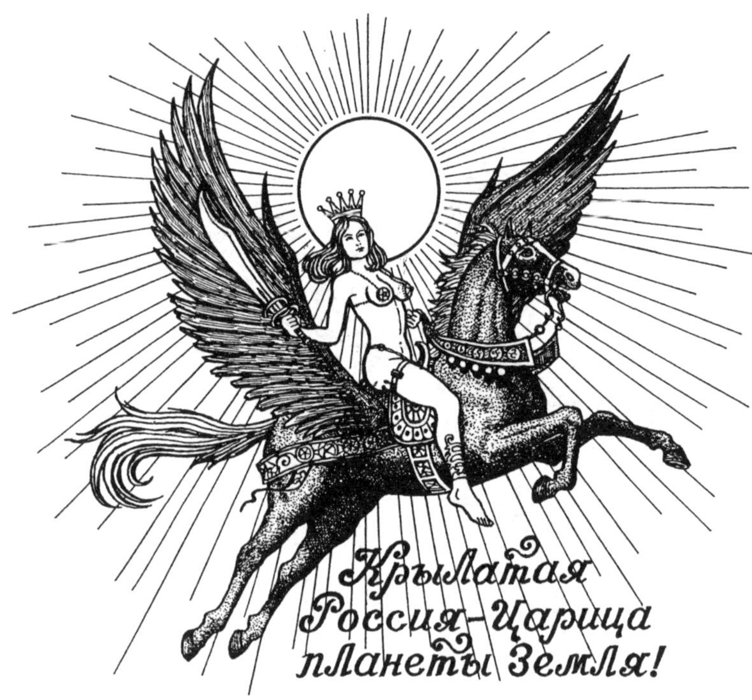

Isolation Cell Block, 7 Arsenal Enbankment, St. Petersburg.

A finely drawn tattoo made in a Moscow tattoo salon in 1994.

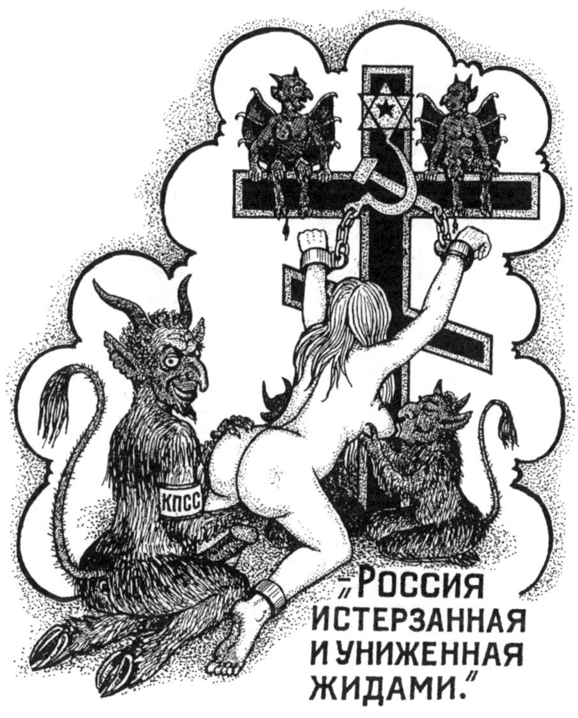

Special Vagrant Reception Centre, 10 Bakunin Street. Leningrad. 1972. Stomach.

An anti-Semitic tattoo. The wearer, who had three convictions for theft and robbery, was arrested in a brothel at 44 Ligovsky Prospect, where he was living with a prostitute.

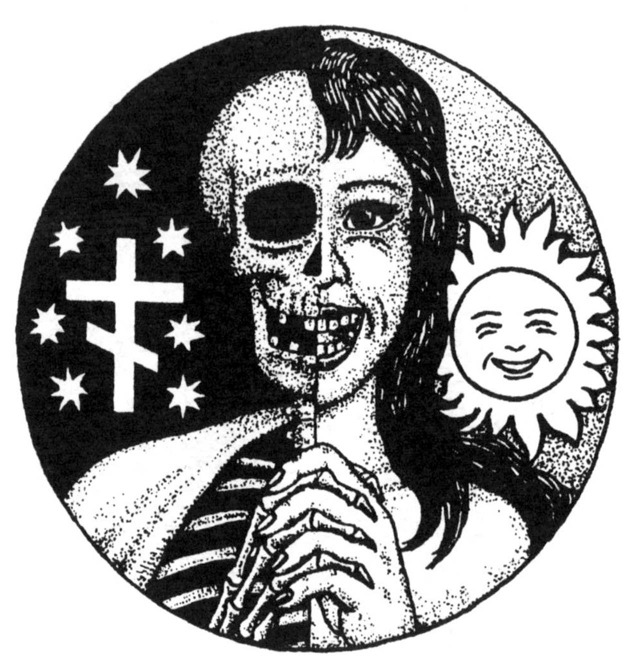

Camp Site, Krasnoyarsk Camp Zone. 1960s. Stomach.

A rare tattoo worn by a criminal 'authority' known as the 'Docent', (an under educated man).

'Karly Marly and the lighthouse of communism'. Text on the penis reads **'Communism'** and bears the Soviet seal of manufacturing quality. The book is Karl Marx's **'Capital'**.

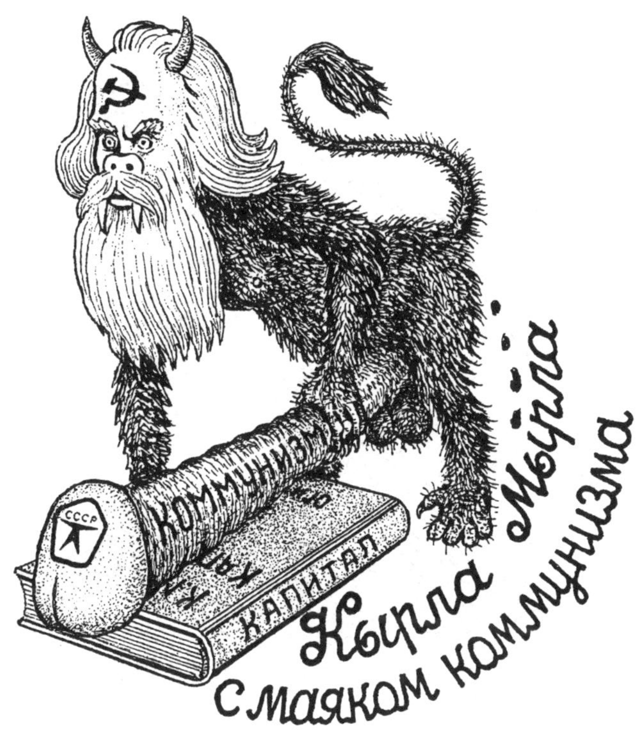

Kashchenko Hospital. 1970s. Stomach.

An anti-communist tattoo. The wearer, known as 'Shaft', had been convicted for hooliganism.

Text on the sickle reads **'Forward into communism!'** The text under the drawing reads **'The chief gang boss of the CPSU'.** The book is Karl Marx's **'Capital'.**

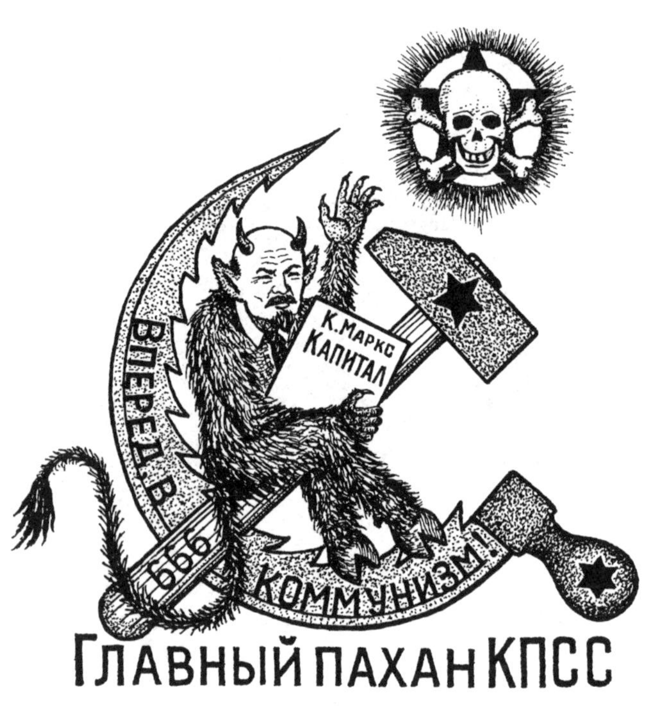

Hip.

A finely drawn anti-Soviet tattoo from a military construction worker previously convicted of theft.

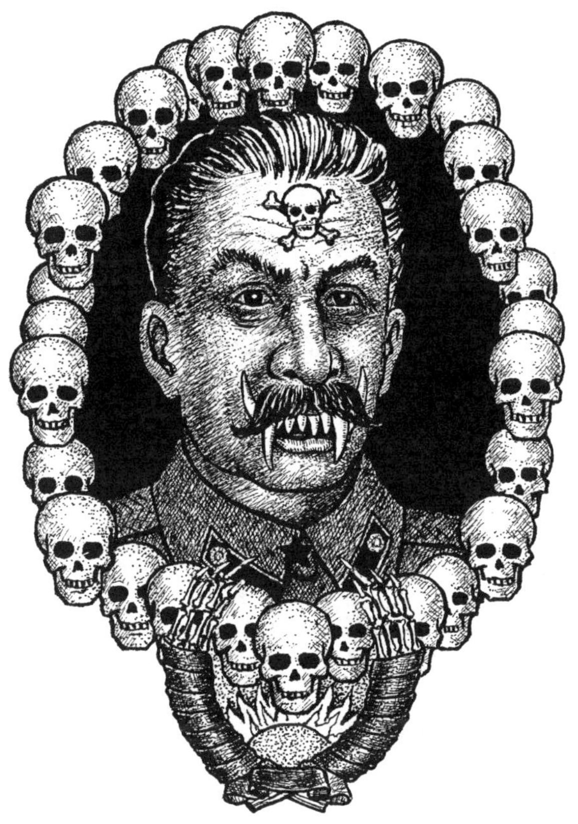

A tattoo from a criminal 'authority' from the town of Tambov, who spent more than forty-two years in various places of detention. It is known as 'The Great Cannibal – the organiser of the Great Terror' or 'We were born to make Kafka reality'.

'Who else can I help!'

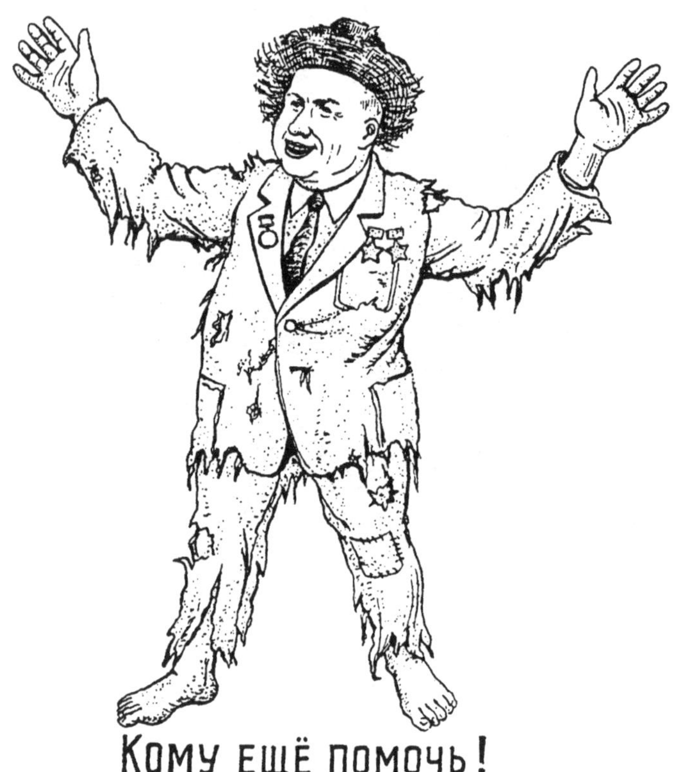

1963. Hip.

'A certain actress for a laugh sucked the General Secretary's cock off.
Look how brilliant he is, look how sexy he is!'

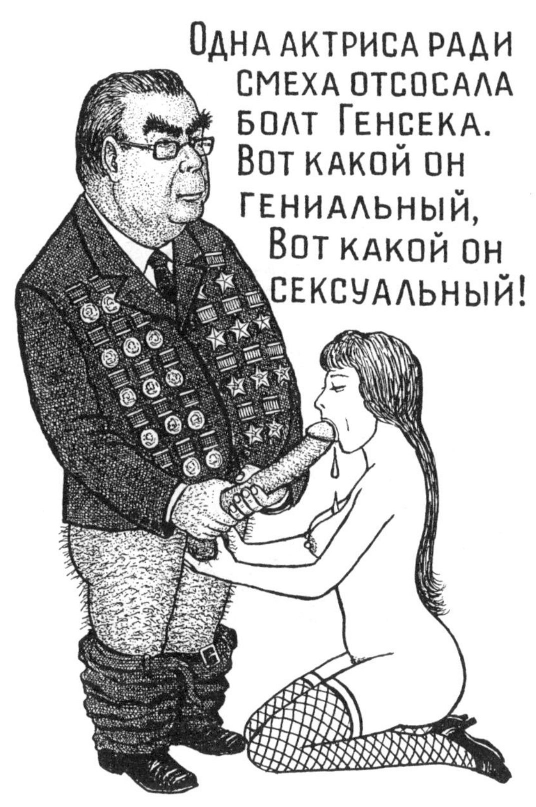

Corrective Labour Colony No.4.1972. Back.

A derisive tattoo applied to a loser at cards who failed to pay his debt.

'Everything for us and nothing from us...' Text on the pig reads 'The CPSU is the mind, honour and conscience of our era'. Text on the trough reads 'Privileges'.

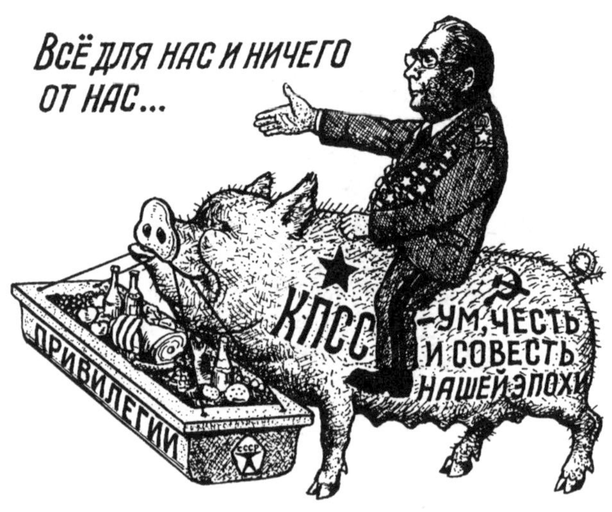

1970s.

A rare caricature tattoo, drawn on the left side of a former convict by the artist Vladimir Fedorov in a studio at 202 Ligovsky Prospect, Leningrad.

'Boris, you're right! I have always grasped and still grasp my glass with firm and steady hands! I'm not a runt like Mishka Gorbachev, who only drinks ryazhenka' (a yoghurt-like product). Text on Gorbachev's forehead is **'Enemy of drunkenness!'**.

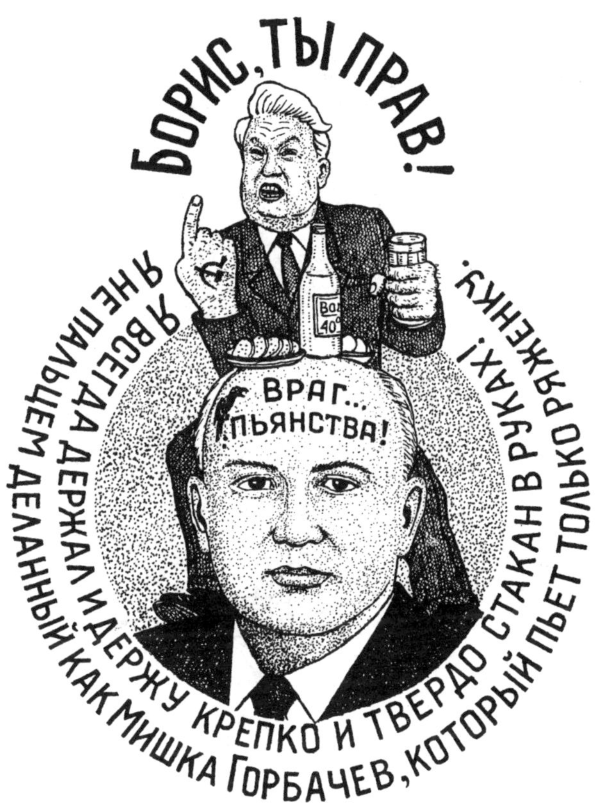

A humorous youth tattoo worn by a man twice convicted for hooliganism.

From the top the text reads **'Giant of Soviet thought, C₂H₅OH** [the molecular formula for alcohol]. **Down the hatch, Cheering Kremlin Heart Drops, For victory over Chechnya!!!!!'**.

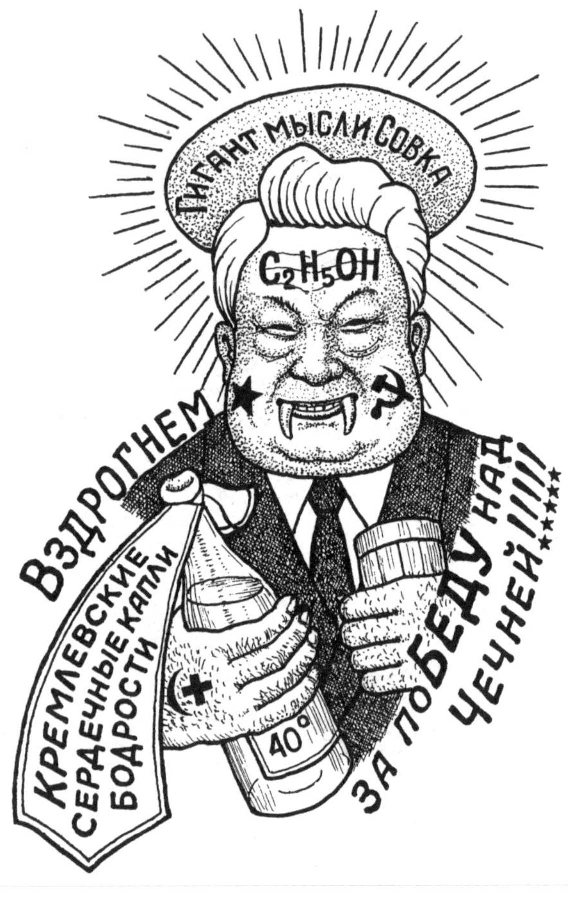

A caricature known as 'Japanese eyes'. The wearer fought in the Chechen war of 1994–1996.

**'I'm going to feel her extra-Marxist cunt and tits, I'm not afraid of anything,
I'm going to marry Furtseva'.** Furtseva, (Soviet Minister of Culture) has the
Soviet seal of manufacturing quality on her body.

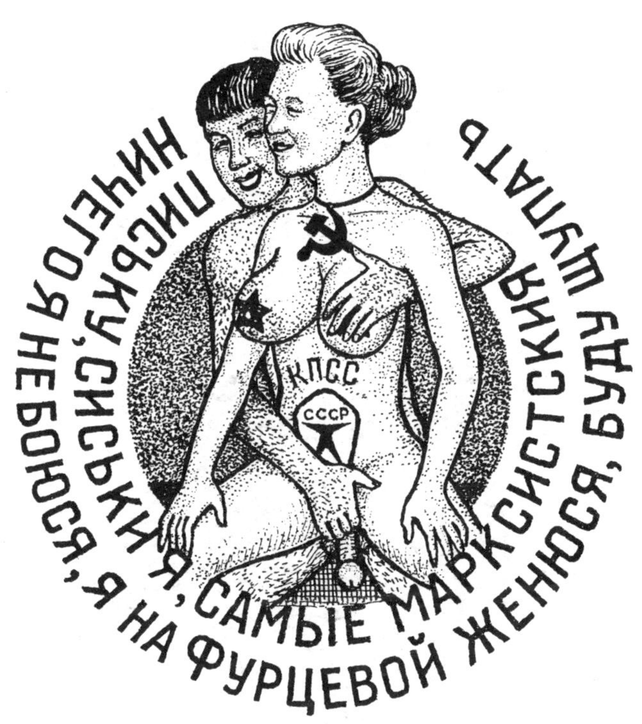

An artistic caricature tattoo, an 'anti-Party grin'.

The text reads 'Everyone knows our Soviet crest, a hammer on the left, a sickle on the right, and you can reap and you can beat, but all the same you'll get fuck all!' The text in the barbed wire reads 'Forwards into communism!'. The text on the crest reads 'GULAG, MVD, USSR'.

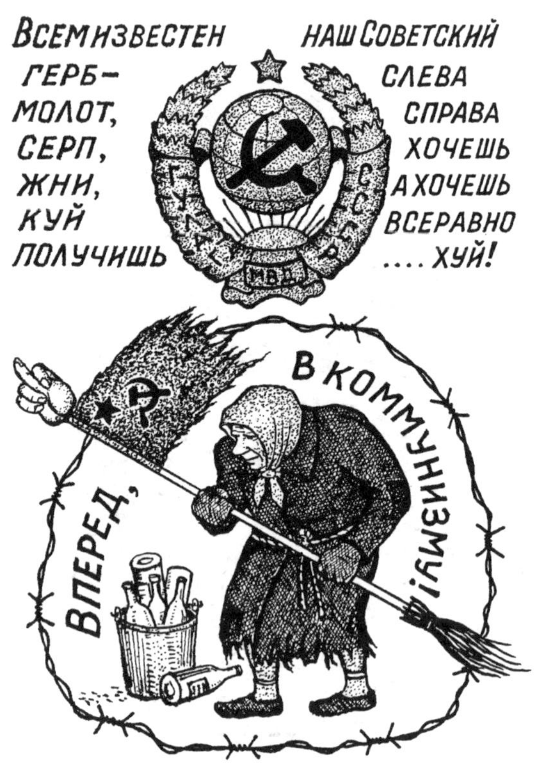

1997

This tattoo, from a man convicted of speculation under article 154 of the Criminal Code of the RSFSR, is known as 'The October 1917 granny'. The wearer had completed his second term of imprisonment – for engaging in private business activities.

'**CPSU – Forward to communism! The GULAG** plan at any price!' The text on the scythe reads '**The bright future**'.

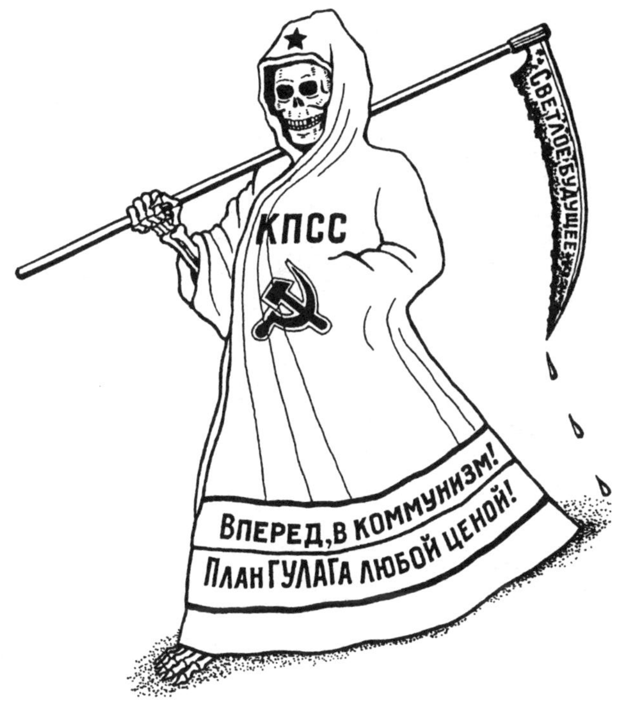

Morgue, 47 Zagorodny Lane, Leningrad. 1960.

A male convict's tattoo belonging to a recidivist known as 'The Professor'.

'You little Soviet shit, you are still kow-towing, arse-licking and flogging away for the **CPSU** and being paid zero point fuck-all and do you want to be a cripple? Think about it!'

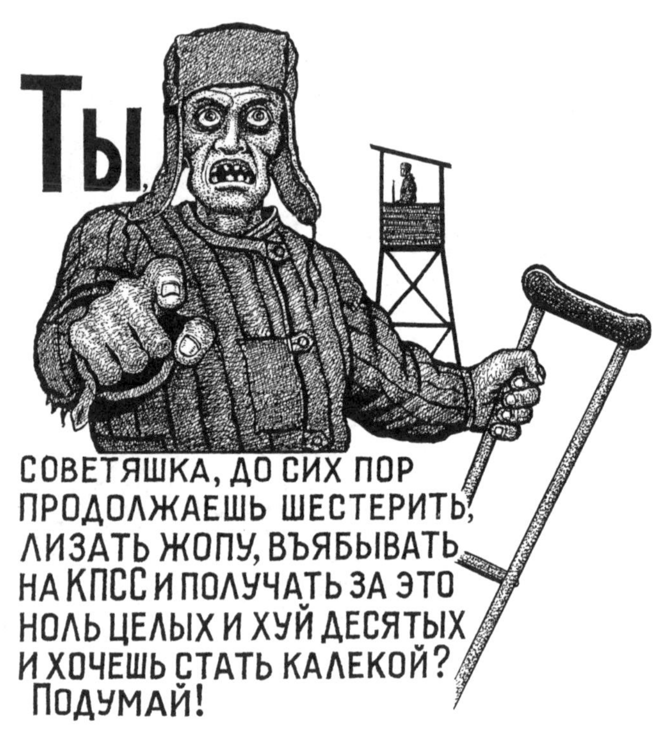

A tattoo widespread in the camp zone in the 1950s and 1960s. An imitation of a well-known Civil War poster.

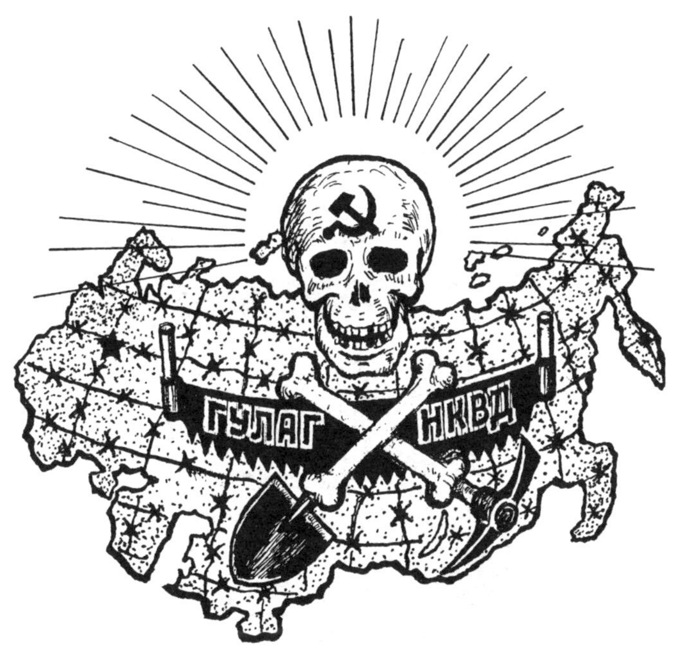

Coal Mining Camp Site, Bukachacha, Chita Region, Transbaikal, Eastern Siberia. 1950s. Back.

A tattoo known to convicts who have spent time in the camps as 'The experimental zone of Satan and the Devil', 'The zone of Marxist-Leninist communism', 'Stalin's socialist camp of communism', 'The CPSU zoo' and 'The universal cemetery'.

'Into the north-eastern camp zone for a seventh trip > there is no way back!'. The text on the devil's chest reads 'MVD'.

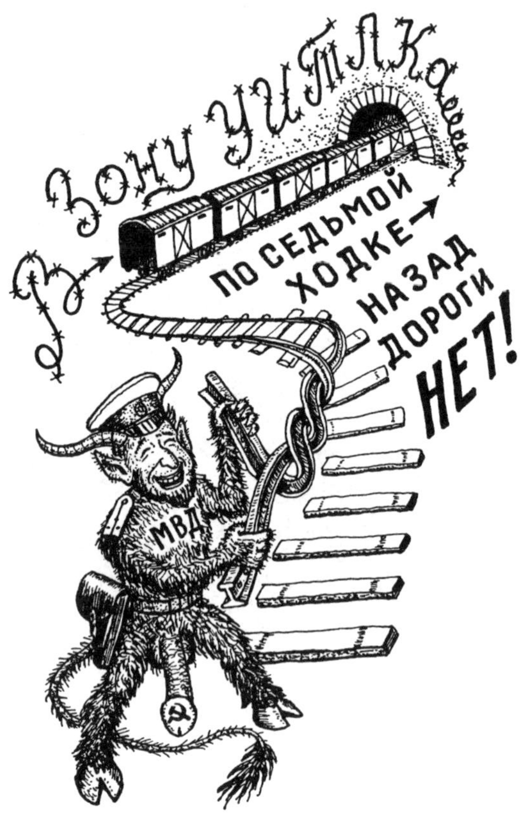

Krasnoyarsk Camp Zone. 1956. Back.

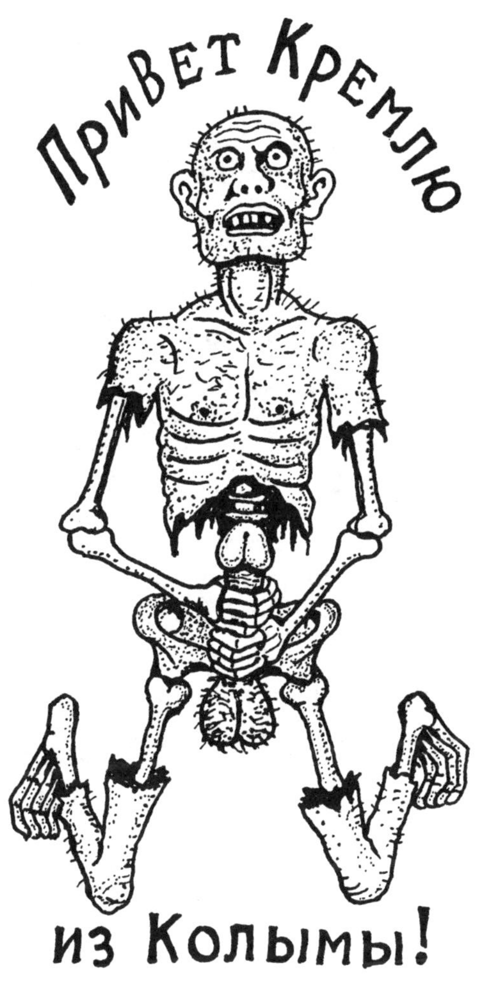

Special Reception Centre for Persons Arrested for Petty Hooliganism.

An anti-social thieves' tattoo.

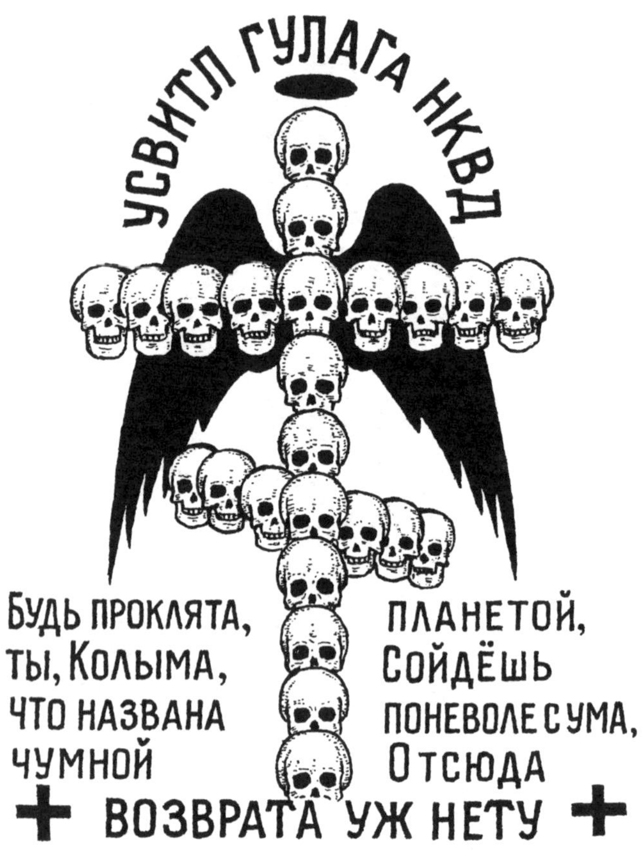

A tattoo that is known as 'The Kolyma cross of the Angel of Death'. Before
the Second World War the wearer was twice convicted under article 162 of
the 1926 Criminal Code of the RSFSR.

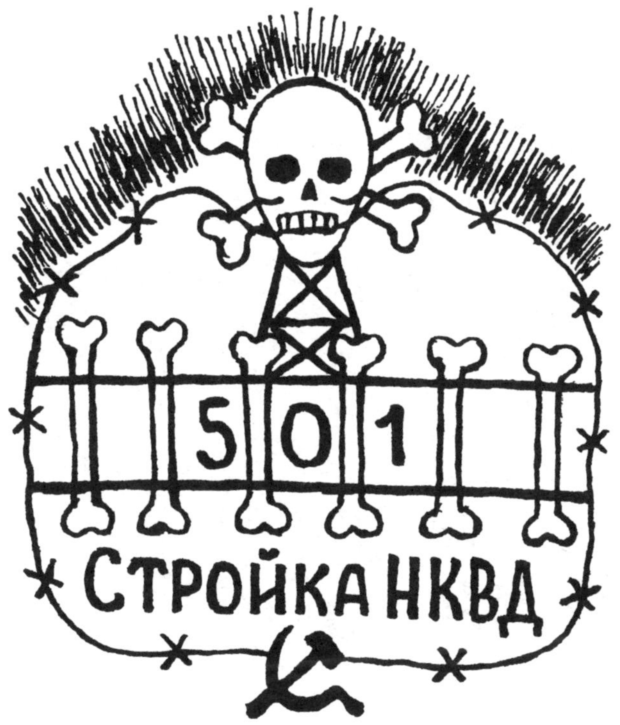

Ministry of the Interior Inter-Regional Hospital. 1951.

This convict served his sentence on 'Construction site 501', building the 'Road of Death' – the railway line running 1,300 kilometres from Labytnangi to the port of Igarka on the Yenisei. Convicts died in their hundreds of thousands during its construction, 'collapsing' into the bogs and the tundra.

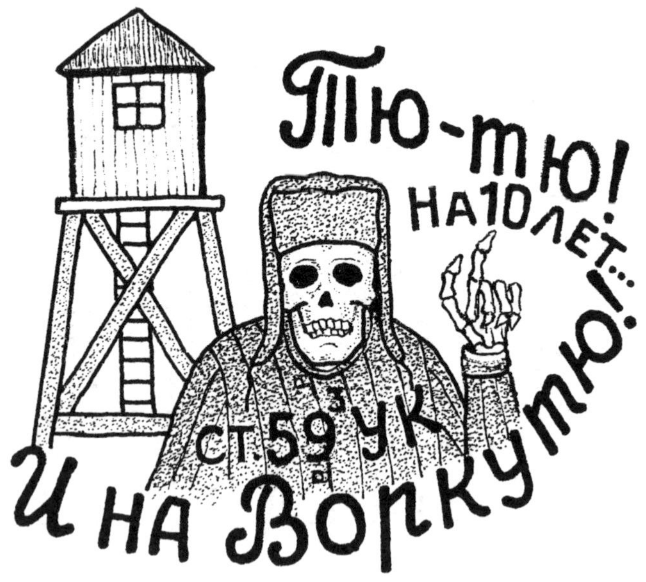

Leningrad in 1972. Stomach.

A tattoo worn by a prisoner convicted under article 59-3 of the 1926 Criminal Code of the RSFSR for being a member of a gang of robbers. He was sentenced to ten years imprisonment.

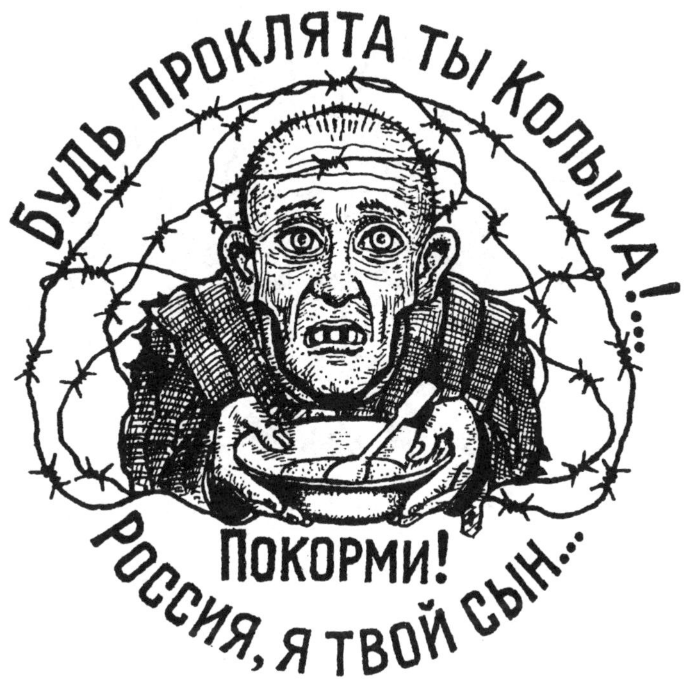

Irkutsk. 1967. Located below the breastbone over the stomach.

A tattoo from a criminal 'authority' nicknamed 'Luba', (from his surname Lubov).

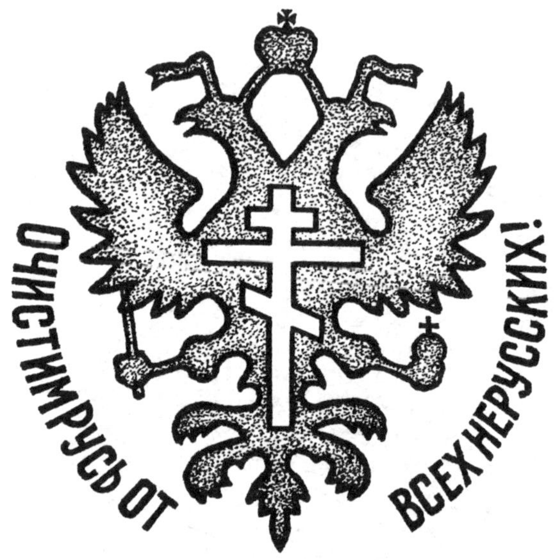

Leningrad, 1972. Stomach.

This convict explained the reason for his tattoo: 'When I was free I worked as a turner. It was a bit cold in our workshop and I used to wear a black sleeveless jacket. There was this Russian wanker in the shop, working as a labourer, he saw me and he yelled, 'Hey you, Tatar, help me get this electric motor off the trolley!' So I helped him: for calling me 'a Tatar', (a Russian), I smashed him on the snout and broke his nose. I've got a third-class boxing certificate. I graduated from a technical college in Kazan, and I got so I couldn't stand those vicious bastards – Tatars and Yids. When he took Kazan, Ivan the Terrible slaughtered the lot of them, from the little snakes at the breast to the old. If it was up to me, I'd send them all off to that Allah of theirs – the Yids too. We should purge all the Russian lands: the Urals, Siberia, Russia'.

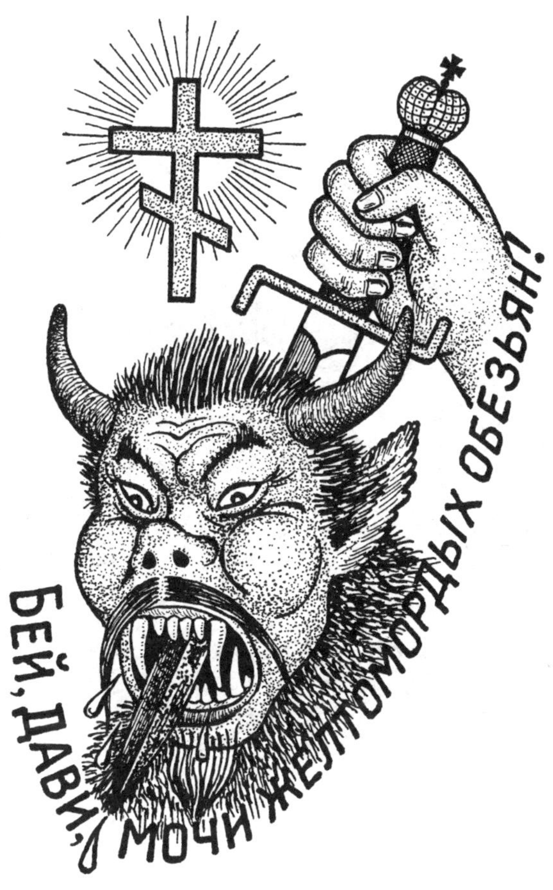

'Beat, crush, kill the yellow-faced monkeys!'

Vladivostok City Jail. 1949. Chest.

A tattoo worn by a 'legitimate' thief with multiple convictions for theft, known as 'Sotnik' (Centurion), 'Kalin' and 'Ryaboi' (Pock-marked).

The numbers on the crest refer to letters from the alphabet that spell out the words **'Kill the Yid'**.

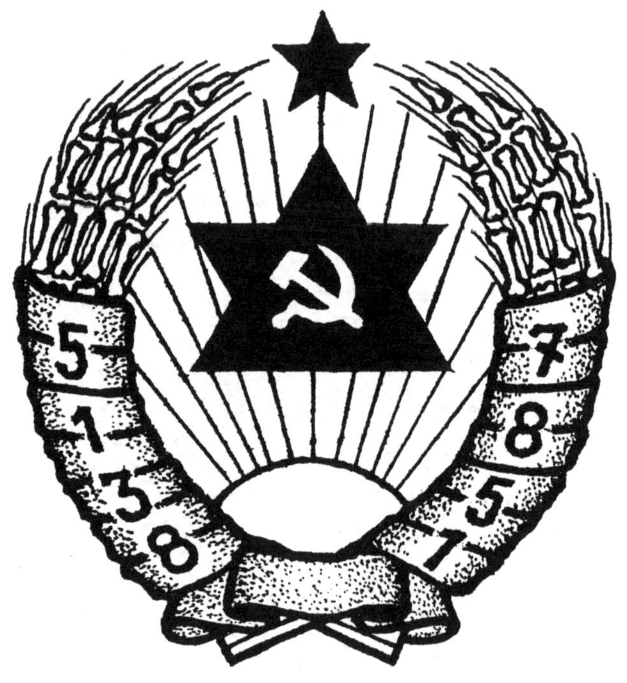

1960s-1970s.

A Russian nationalist anti-Soviet tattoo.

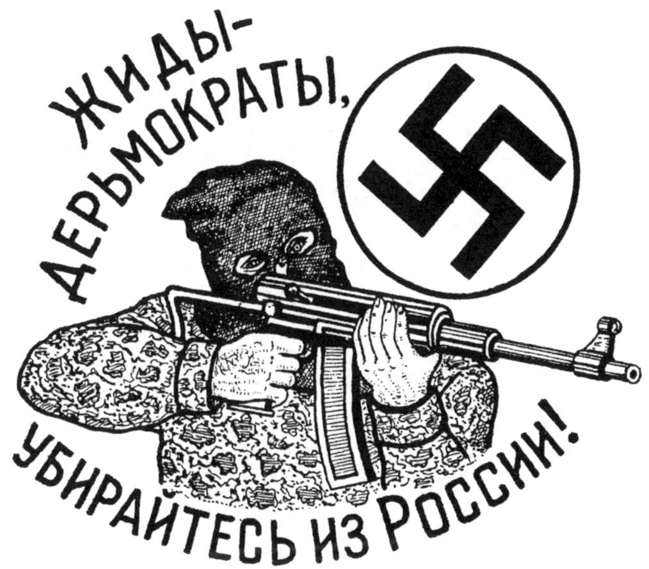

1991. Hip.

A male youth fascist tattoo.

Letters stand for **'The Jews have turned the Russians into their guinea-pigs'**.

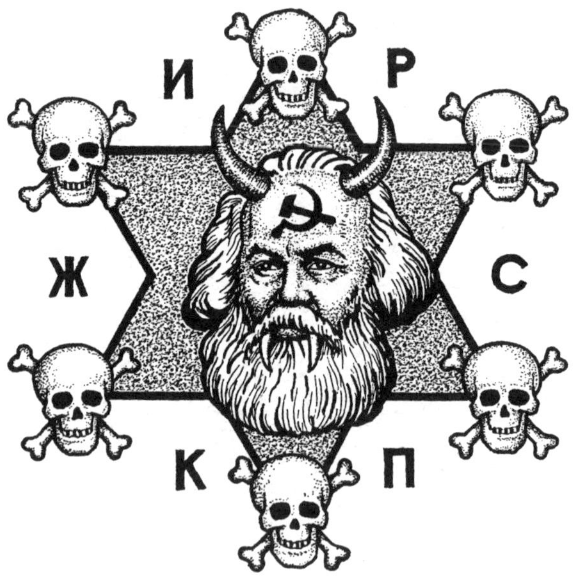

Konyashin Hospital No.21, Leningrad. 1985. Left shoulder-blade.

A rare tattoo.

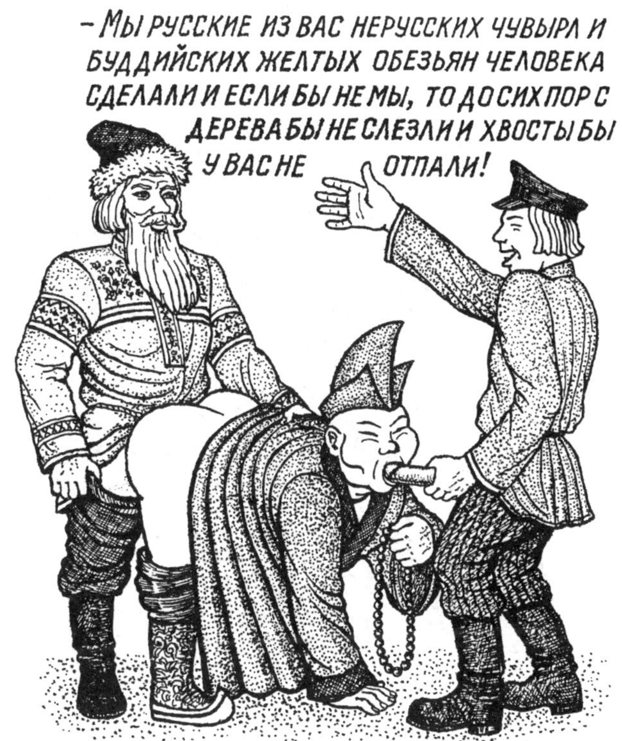

Ulan-Ude Jail, Buryato Monglian Autonomous Soviet Socialist Republic. 1952.

A pornographic tattoo from Borovsk, belonging to a member of a Russian Old Believer family from the Bichursky province of the Buryato Monglian Autonomous Soviet Socialist Republic, a 'legitimate' thief and 'authority' with several convictions. Made by a Russian artist in the town of Kyakhtav.

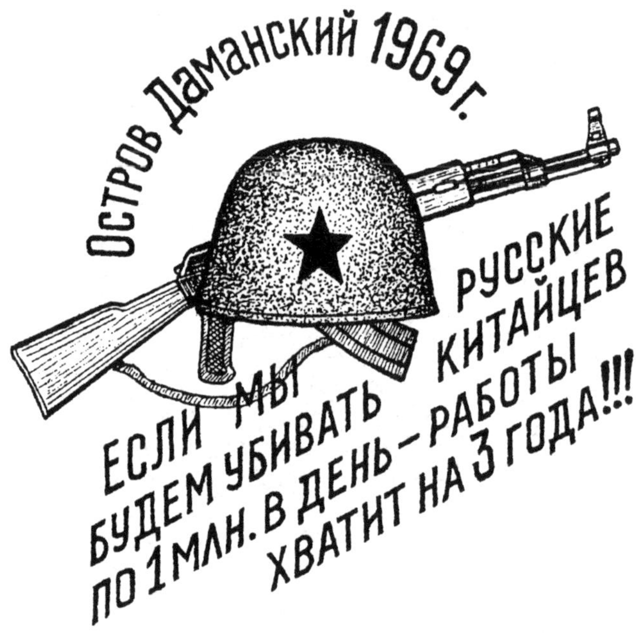

Peter and Paul Fortress, Leningrad. 1970. Hip.

A Russian chauvinist tattoo from a convict who fought in the battles with the
Chinese on Daman island.

The acronyms on the lower skulls stand for **'The State Committee of the Interior (NKVD)'** and **'The State Camp Administration (GULAG)'**. The letters around the Star of David are **'CPSU'**.

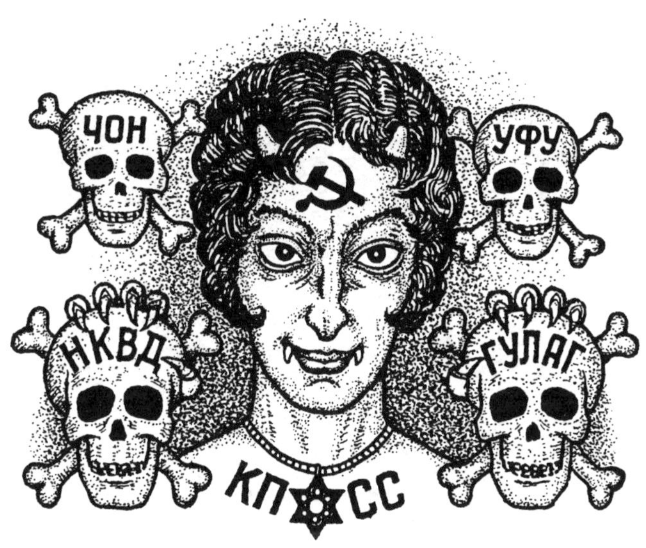

An anti-communist, anti-Jewish tattoo worn by an inveterate transgressor of the prison regime in Corrective Labour Colony No.9, with two convictions for theft.

The German text reads **'The height of the power of USSR-Russia was in 1945, and then a rapid decline set in'**.

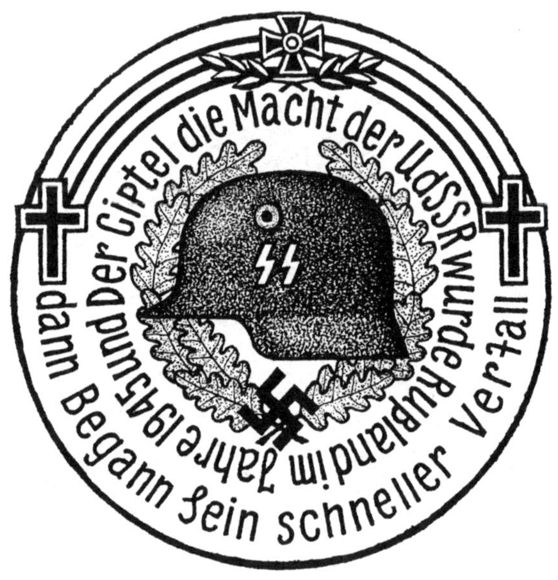

Minister of the Interior Inter-Regional Hospital. 1963.

A German SS forces helmet, crosses, a swastika and oak leaves. The wearer of the tattoo, an Estonian, was convicted under the Supreme Soviet Presidium decree of 4th June 1947 for group theft from a military depot in 1949, and sentenced to twenty years imprisonment. The convict's mother was a White Russian émigré and his grandfather fought in the forces of General Yudenich. His Estonian father was killed fighting in the 20th Estonian SS Division in 1943. When the tattoo was copied the prisoner was suffering from an acute form of tuberculosis.

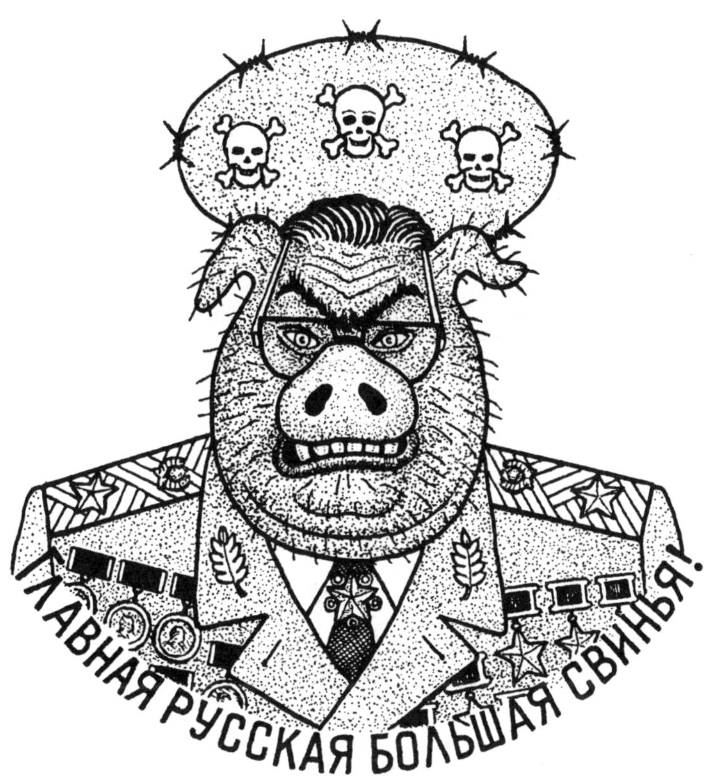

Special Reception Centre for Temporary Detainees, State Department of Internal Affairs, 6 Kalyaev Street, Leningrad. 1981.

A 'grin' directed against the authorities, drawn on the left buttock, (the right buttock had an image of the order of Lenin), of a prisoner convicted for speculating in foreign goods acquired from merchant seamen.

'The aggressive, eternally hungry, drunk Russian swine asks the West to help…'

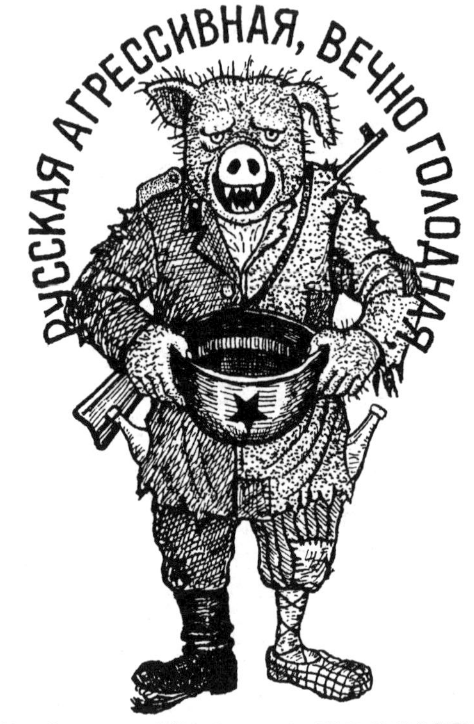

Zelenogorsk. 1997.

The parents of the owner of this tattoo were exiled to the Komi Autonomous Soviet Socialist Republic in 1945, only surviving by a miracle. His mother's two brothers were shot in Daugavpils prison for working in a military equipment repair shop while Latvia was occupied by the Germans.

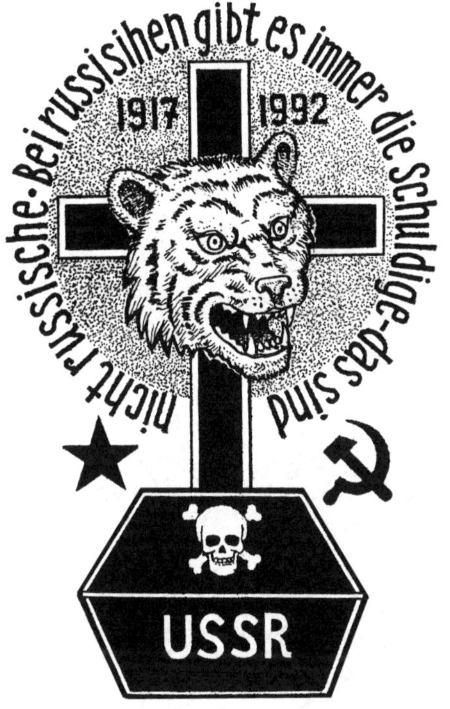

Swimming pool, 19 Konstantinovsky Prospect, Leningrad. 1994.

In 1949, when the owner of this tattoo was two years old, he and his parents
were exiled to the town of Usolie-Sibirsk in Eastern Siberia under the
supervision of the NKVD commandant's office. In 1957 the family returned
to Latvia. He was convicted for the first time in 1966 for refusing to serve in
the Soviet Army, and then a second time for attempting to escape to Switzerland.
He served his ten year sentence in camps in the Komi Autonomous Soviet
Socialist Republic and was only released in 1993, following the collapse of
the Soviet Union.

The Lithuanian text reads **'Long live the freedom of the Lithuanian people! Kill communists and Jews – the deadly enemies of Lithuania!'**.

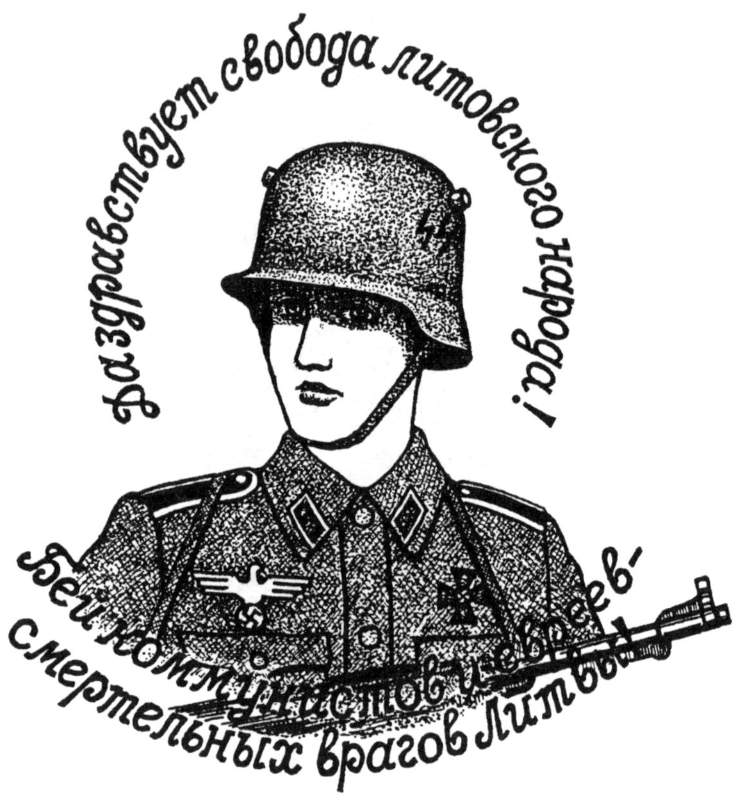

Isolation Cell Block. 1966.

The owner of the tattoo explained: 'After the occupation of Lithuania in 1940 the NKVD, the Lithuanian communists and the Jews began hunting people down. I managed to hide, but my parents and thousands of other people were exiled to Siberia'.

The Lithuanian text reads **'For Lithuania without communists, Russians and Jews! Vilnius'**.

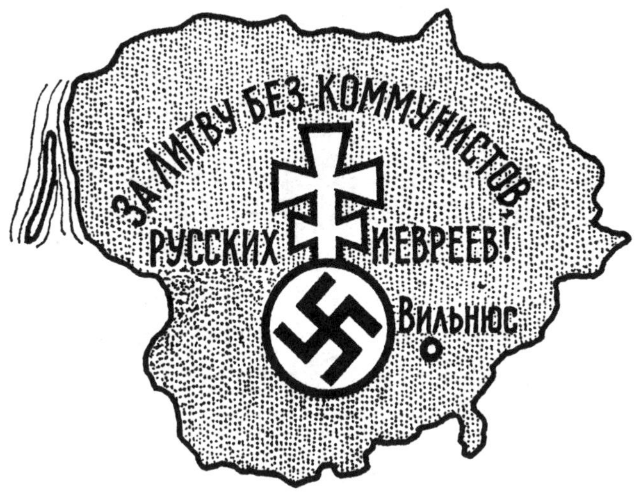

Ozyora Camp Zone, Eastern Siberia. 1950s.

This convict explained the meaning of his tattoo as follows: 'The Russians, deceived by the Jews, began to believe in absurd communism and in 1940 they decided to export it to Lithuania. The first thing they did was to start liquidating their 'class enemies', and sent away hundreds of thousands of citizens of the Baltic countries, which made absolutely everybody hate them. When the German forces arrived in 1941 many Lithuanians, including myself, volunteered to serve with them'.

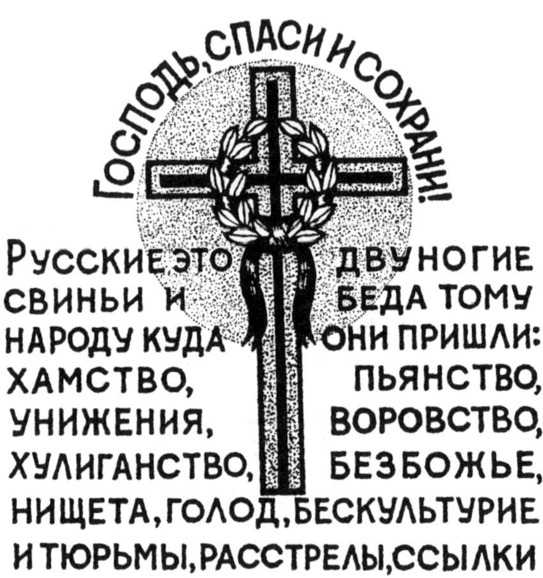

St. Petersburg. 1994.

An anti-Russian tattoo. Janis, the owner of this tattoo, recounts how in 1946, when he was seven, he and his parents were exiled from near Kaunas to the Krasnoyarsk Territory. His two elder sisters, aged sixteen and seventeen, were sold to criminals by the NKVD, somewhere in the Urals. They were dragged out of the exiles' carriage by their hair and tossed into the criminals' carriage. Janis never saw them again. He saw his father shot dead in front of him as he attempted to defend his family with a spade. Janis was left with his mother and two younger sisters, aged nine and twelve. Together with the other Lithuanians they were taken off the train at Yenisei Station, where his mother and sisters died of bowel infections. He was then taken in by another family.

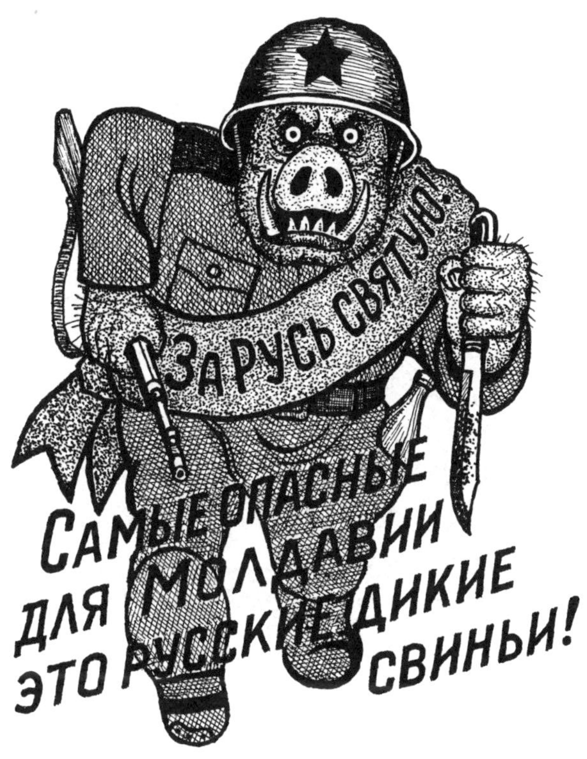

Leningrad. 1984. Hip.

An anti-Russian tattoo belonging to a man convicted of resisting representatives of a volunteer security patrol under article 191, and for hooliganism under article 206 of the Criminal Code of the RSFSR. The owner of the tattoo explained that when he was detained for being drunk, they demanded that he pay a bribe 'since he was Moldavian'. When he refused the volunteer patrolmen attempted to search him, but he 'gave them a good smacking'. For this he was sentenced to five years imprisonment, which he served in the Komi Autonomous Soviet Socialist Republic. He was released in 1979.

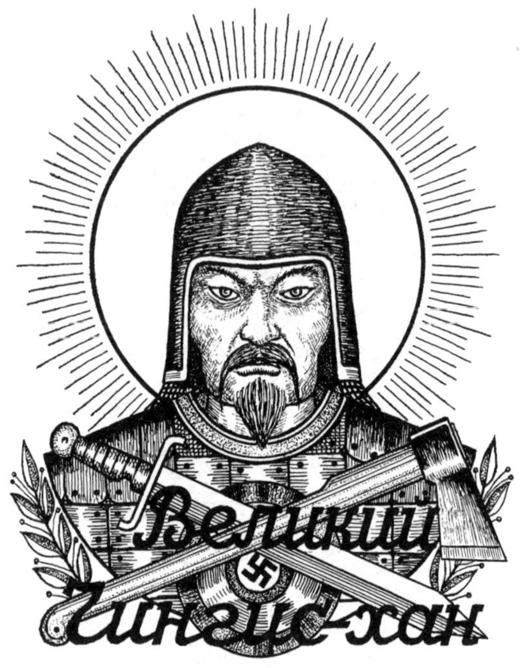

Bathhouse, Smolnaya Street, Ulan-Ude. 1975. Chest.

This tattoo was made in the 'Djidastroi' Corrective Labour Colony in the Buryato-Mongolian Autonomous Soviet Socialist Republic. It belonged to a convict named Dorzhap, and was drawn by the artist V. Makushkin, with whom he was sentenced in the late 1950s under article 74 of the 1926 Criminal Code of the RSFSR for hooliganism, specifically for fighting with six Russian Old Believers in Ulan-Ude. According to Dorzhap, the Old Believers called them 'yellow-faced monkeys who have only just lost your tails', and 'slanty eyes'. Since they were skilled in eastern martial arts, Dorzhap and Makushkin easily dealt with the name-callers, who were from the Bichursk region of the Buryato-Mongolian Autonomous Soviet Socialist Republic. They were sentenced to five years imprisonment, working in a mine at the 'Djidastroi' Corrective Labour Colony.

'Kill the Russian swine! Allah be praised! The Russians are a people of self-eaters, sacrificially, mindlessly, annihilating themselves and others and living nature'

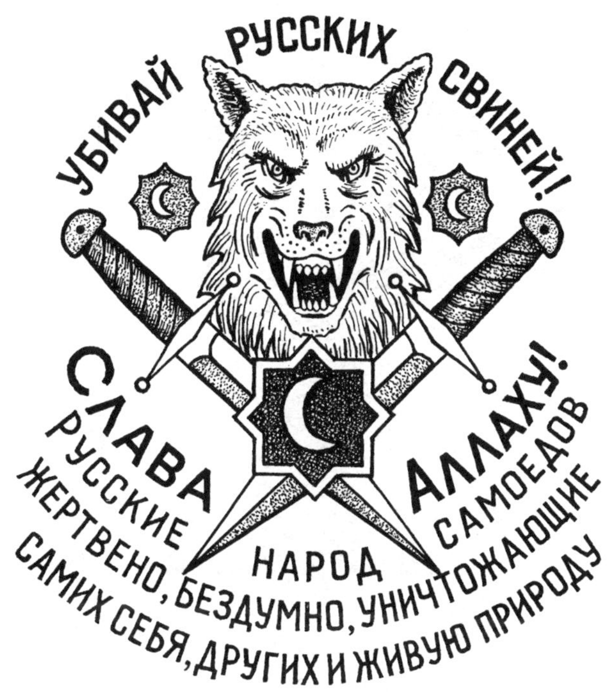

Isolation Cell Block No.1. 1980.

The tattoo was made in the town of Ordjonikidze (Vladikavkaz), in the 1970s. The upper text was originally in Arabic and the lower text was in Karachaevo-Balkarian. It was worn by a Karachaevan who was exiled to Kazakhstan with his parents in 1944. He was convicted under article 102 of the Criminal Code of the RSFSR, for murder and causing grievous bodily harm to two Russians who abused and struck him at the Moscow Station in Leningrad.

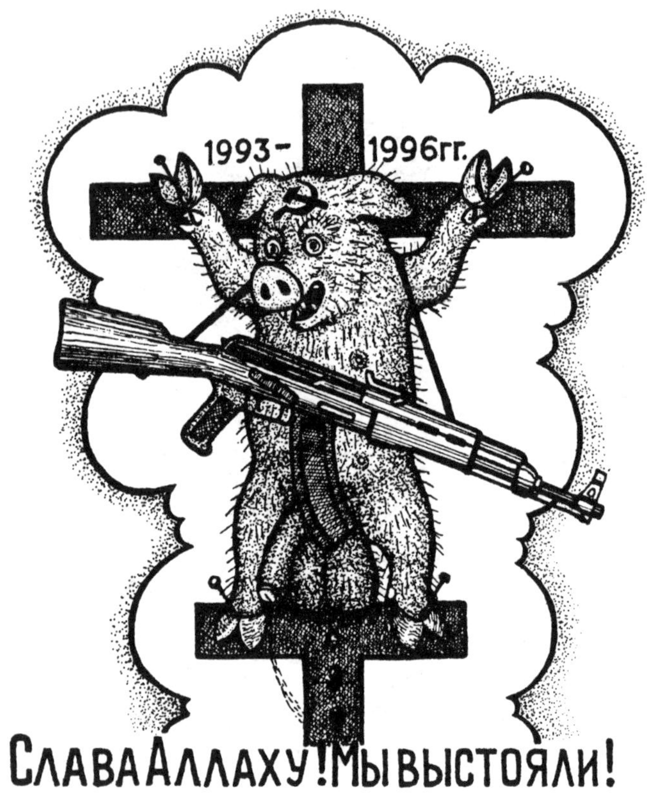

The Watchman's flat, St. Petersburg Mosque. 1997.

According to the owner of this tattoo, a Chechen called Musa who was personally acquainted with Djokhar Dudaev and his relatives, 'the general was betrayed by Chechen infidels, devils and swine, who showed the federal forces where he was'. Musa himself took an active part in the war against the Russians from 1993 to 1996, first in Grozny and later in the Argun and Gudermes regions. He had the tattoo made in Makhachkala in 1997.

The acronym at the top of the tattoo stands for **'We will make the Russian and German anti-semites into frightened sheep'.** The lower text in Latin reads **'Crush the arrogance of the rebellious'.**

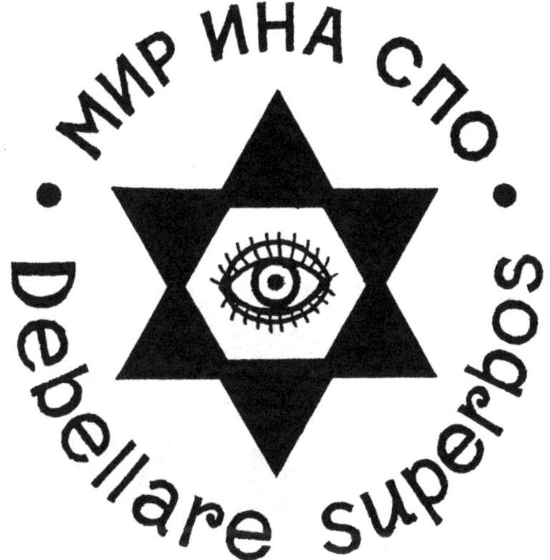

1950s-1960s.

A Jewish nationalist tattoo, dipicting the Star of Zion and the all-seeing eye.

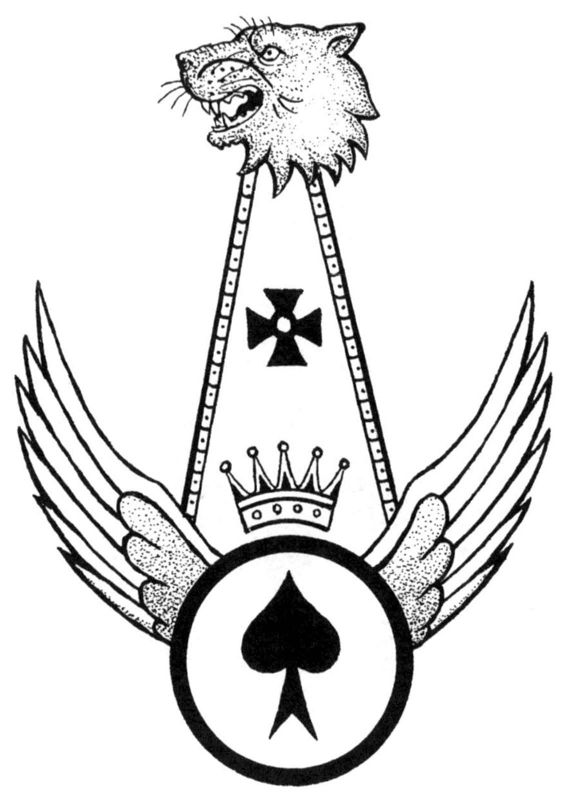

A shoulder tattoo worn by a 'winged' convict, a major camp 'authority'. It's meaning is: 'God grants to each his own', 'How am I worse than the communist shitocratic thieves?', 'May God forgive me my sins'.

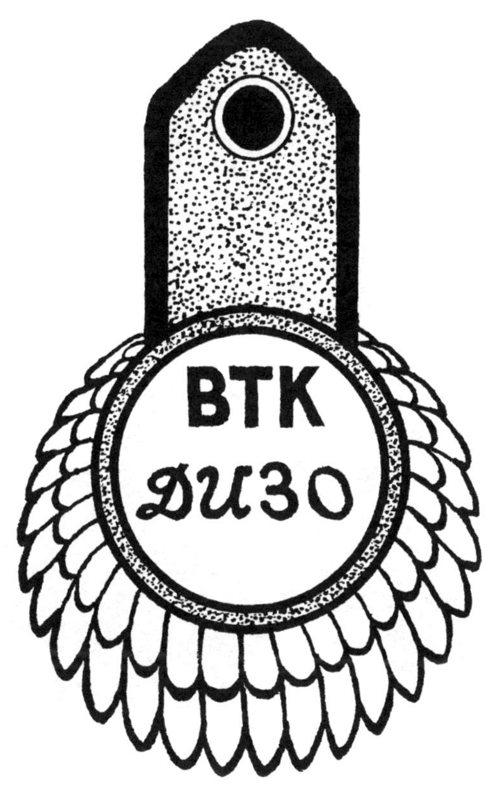

A shoulder tattoo from a young convict in an educational labour colony, where he spent at least fifty days in solitary confinement.

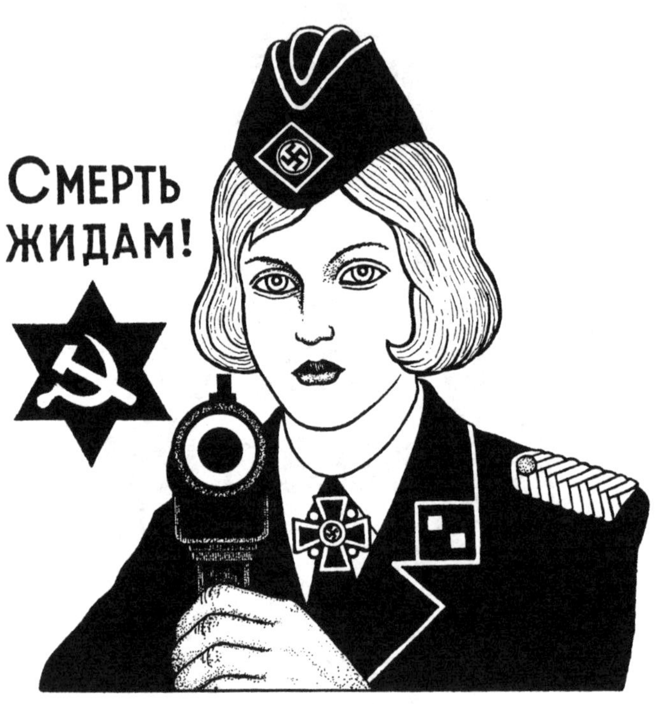

Isolation Cell Block No.1. 1969. Stomach.

A fascist anti-Semitic tattoo belonging to a convicted car thief who steals cars from 'grasping Jews working in the trade' and resells them in Ukraine and the Caucasus.

The lower text reads **'9 grams for every communist!'**. (The weight of a bullet.)
Text on the wings reads **'Angel of Death'**.

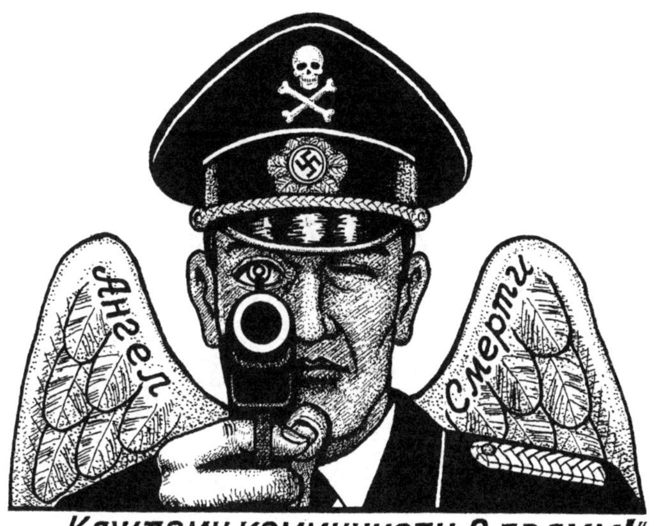

1970s-1980s.

An widespread anti-communist youth tattoo known as the 'Angel of Death'.

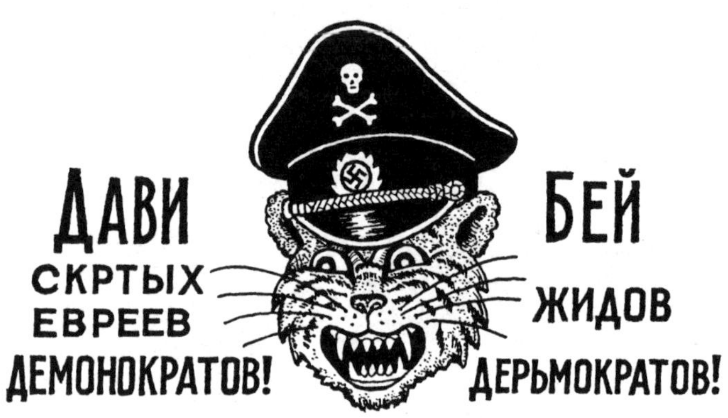

Corrective Labour Colony No.6. 1994.

A Russian anti-Jewish tattoo made in the Kolpino Educational Labour Colony.

'Communism is an invention of the Jews. Yids are parasites for the whole globe'

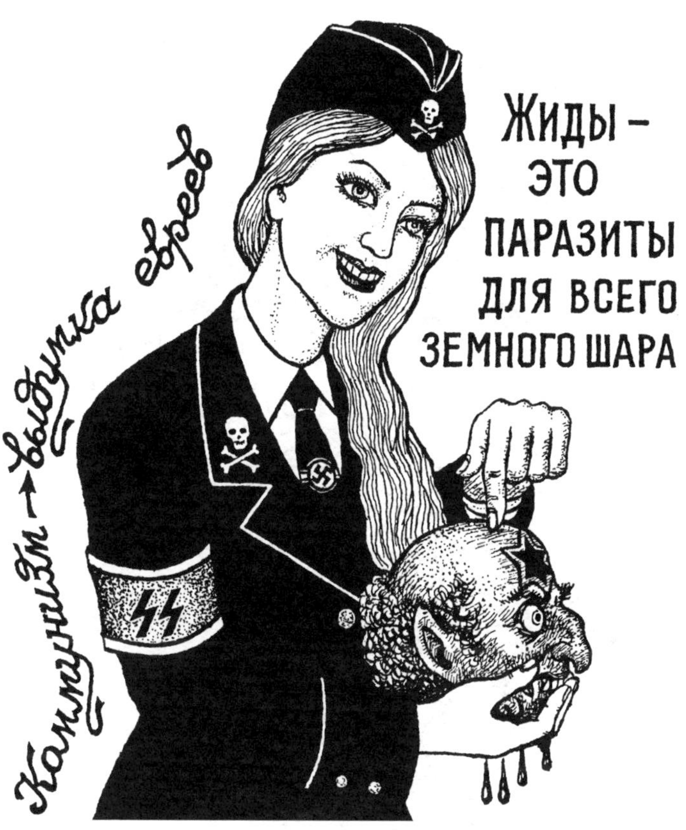

Bathhouse, Ulan-Ude. 1975. Stomach.

A fascist anti-Semitic tattoo belonging to a criminal boss or 'authority' imprisoned for theft.

'**Take him by the ear and out into the sunshine!**'. The letters on the cuff read '**NKVD**'.

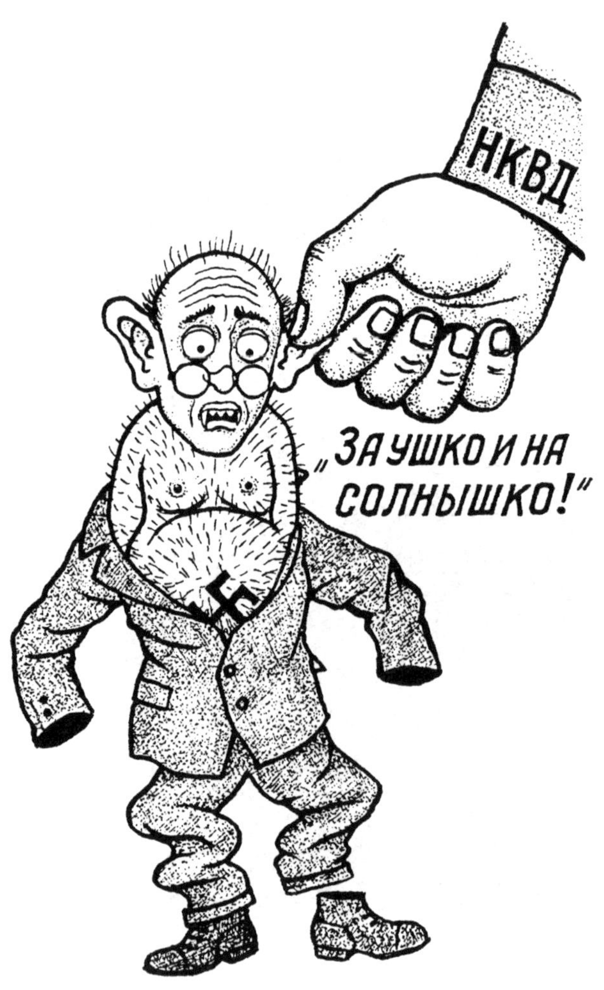

4 Liteiny Prospect, Leningrad. 1963.

A tattoo belonging to Sergei Peremyshlin, an employee of the management office in the Leningrad Administration. He later tried to have the tattoo surgically removed.

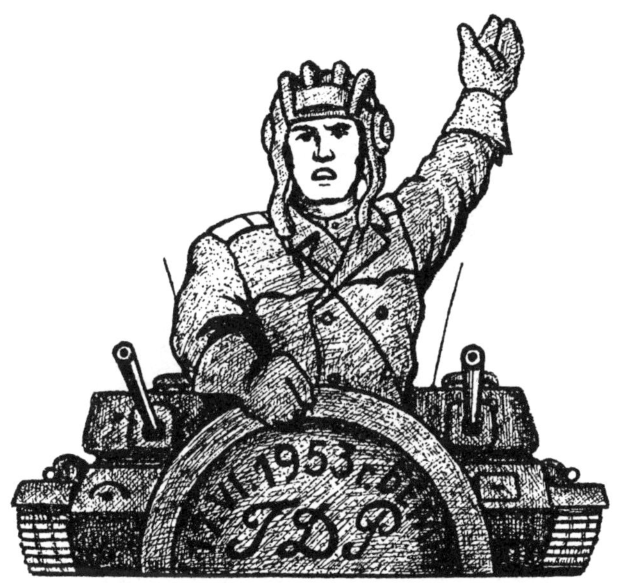

Konyashin Hospital, Leningrad. 1985.

A tattoo worn by a former soldier who was involved in the events in Berlin in June 1953.

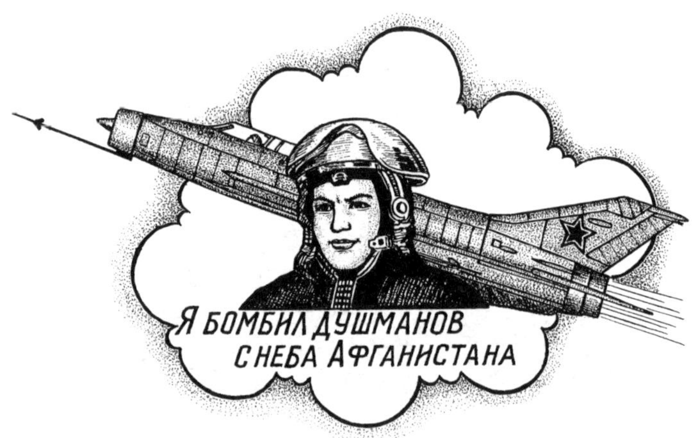

Swimming pool, 70 Glory Prospect, St. Petersburg. 1996. Left side of the chest.

A commemorative tattoo from a former military pilot who fought in the war in Afghanistan.

'Kill the Asians – the enemies of the **USSR** and lackeys of the **USA**. 1980-1982. Kabul-Kalat-Kandahar'

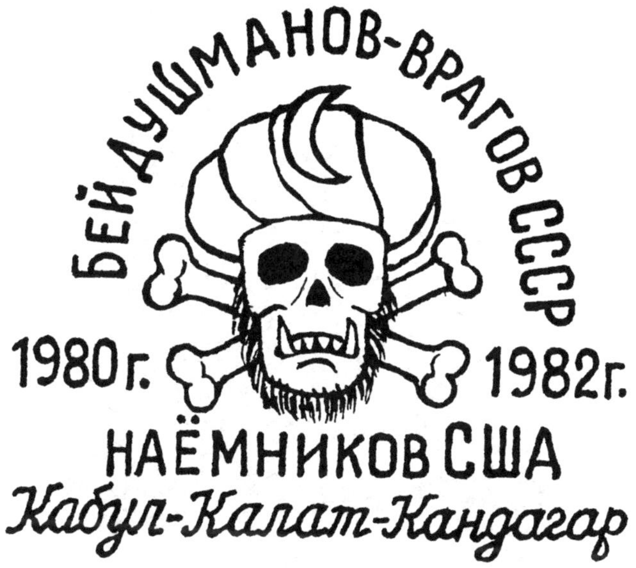

Carburettor Factory, Leningrad. 1986. Shoulder.

A tattoo belonging to a man who fought in the war in Afghanistan.

Text on the flag reads **'The Dawn of Communism Collective Farm'**. Lower text reads **'First Tractor Driver of the Collective Farm'**.

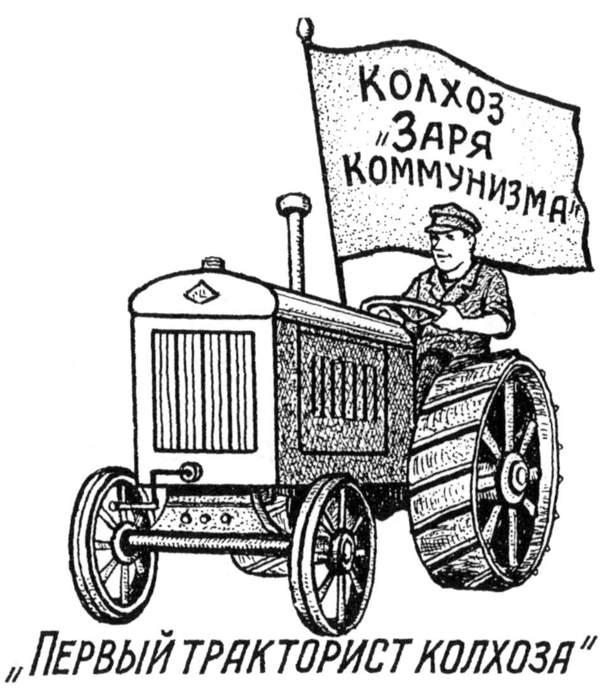

1943

A tattoo worn by Pavel Rubtsov, the driver of a tractor used for pulling a tank with a 45mm canon. He served in the motorised construction unit of the 61st tank division stationed in the town of Bayantumen (Choibolsan) in the Mongolian People's Republic.

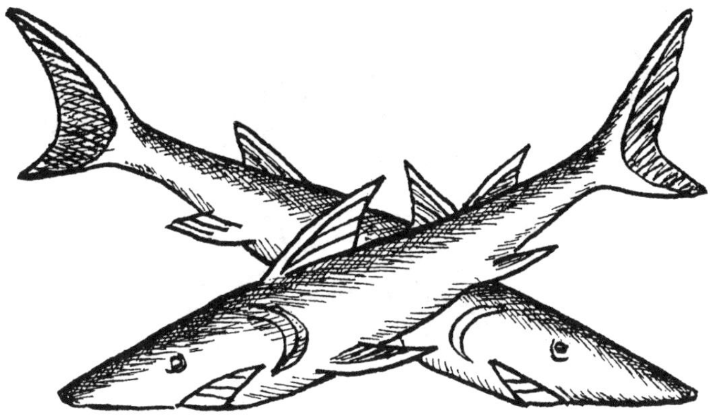

Khabarovsk Corrective Labour Camp. 1954.

A horoscope tattoo worn by a convict imprisoned under articles 146 and 74 of the Criminal Code of the RSFSR for hooliganism and causing grievous bodily harm in the port of Nakhodka, where he had previously worked as a stoker in the fishing fleet.

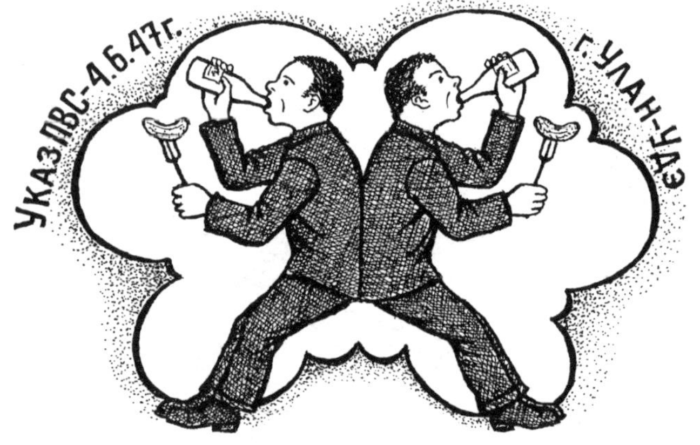

Strict Regime Corrective Labour Colony, Bulato-Mongolian Autonomous Soviet Socialist Republic, Ulan-Ude. 1952.

A 'Gemini' horoscope tattoo worn by a man convicted of theft under the Supreme Soviet Presidium decree of 4th June 1947. He was sentenced to fifteen years imprisonment.

'We are twins and our spirit is young!'

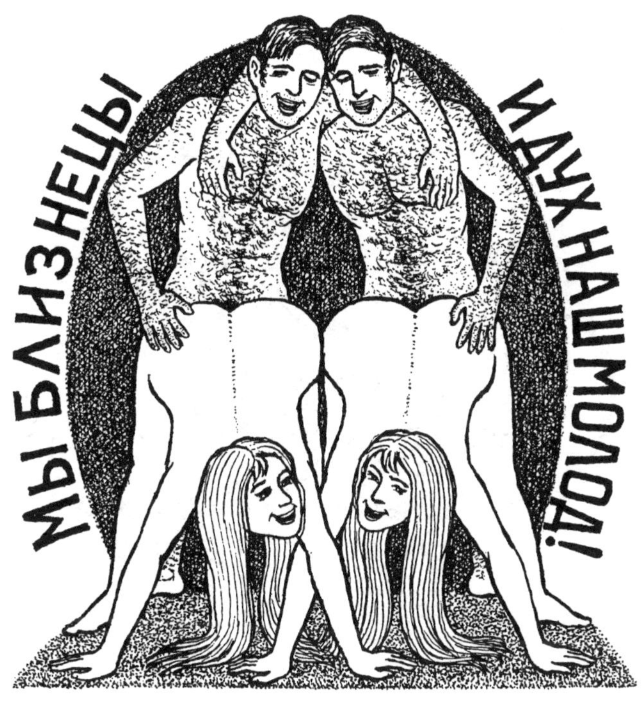

A hooligan horoscope tattoo belonging to a prisoner with two convictions for theft. It was made in a corrective labour colony in the Komi Autonomous Soviet Socialist Republic during his first sentence.

The acronym on the animal stands for **'Internal Order Section'**, in the cloud **'18.VIII.1963'** (date of birth). Text below reads **'Rostov-on-Don'**.

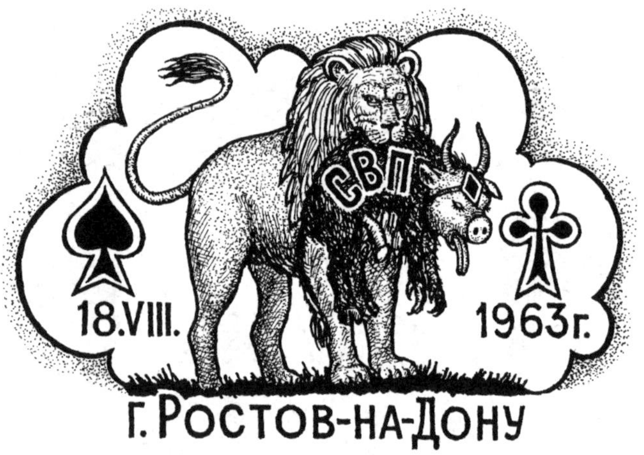

Isolation Cell Block No.1. 1980.

A tattoo from an 'anti-social' convict who was an 'authority' in the zone.

'Fate plays with man, but man never plays with fate!' Text on the scales reads **'The will of the chemical zone. FATE'**.

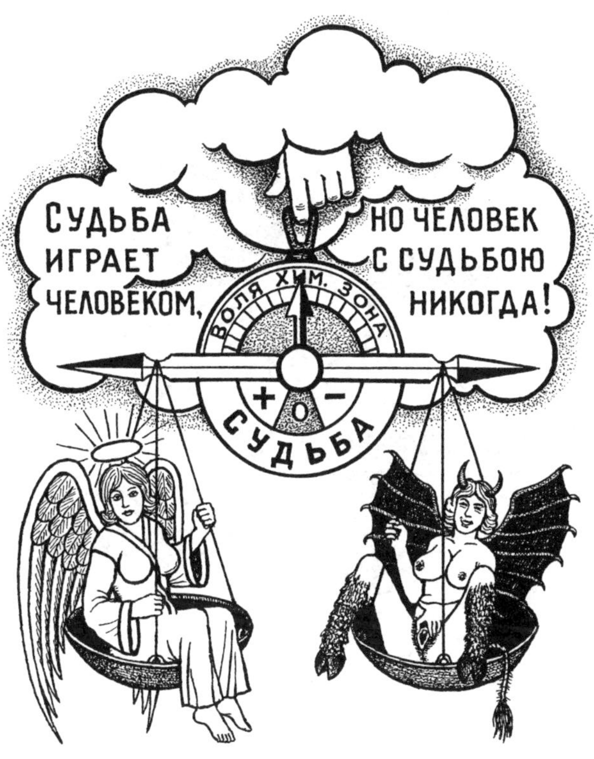

Corrective Labour Camp No.9. 1976.

A tattoo from a convict from the cast of 'anti-socials' with four convictions, two under article 144 of the Criminal Code of the RSFSR and two under article 89. The tattoo was made during his second 'zone trip' to a corrective labour colony in the Chelyabinsk Region.

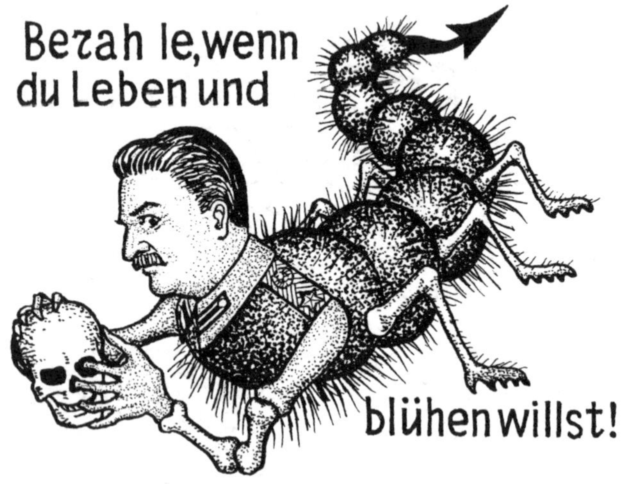

Isolation Cell Block No.2. 1989. Hip.

The 'talisman' tattoo of a racketeer convicted of extortion under article 148 of the Criminal Code of the RSFSR and sentenced to three years imprisonment.

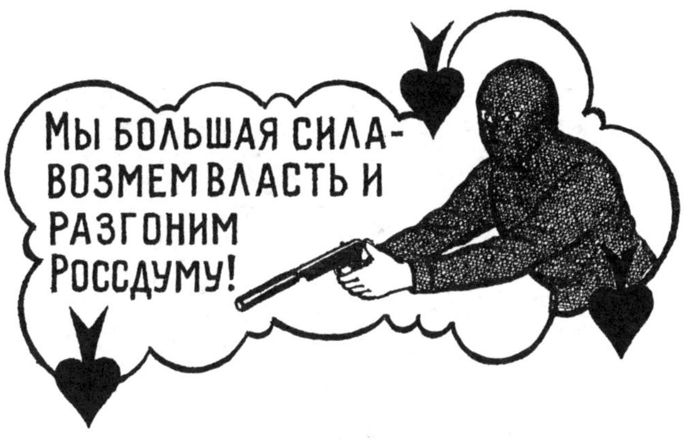

Swimming Pool, 70 Slavy Prospect, St. Petersburg. 1997. Hip.

A youth tattoo worn by a racketeer from a St. Petersburg mafia group. The inverted 'spade' symbol signifies ruthlessness and death.

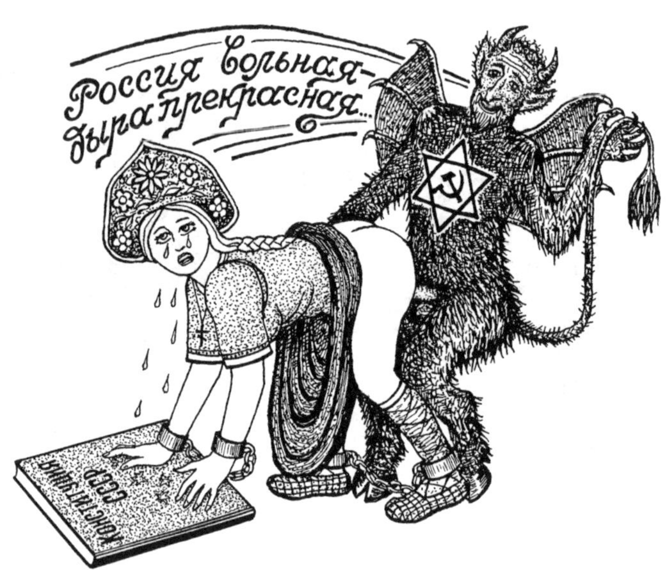

Ministry of the Interior Inter-Regional Hospital. 1975.

Made in the Vyatka camp zone in 1972 this is an anti-Soviet, anti-Semitic pornographic tattoo, worn by A. Ivlev, an inveterate transgressor of prison routine with four convictions for theft and hooliganism.

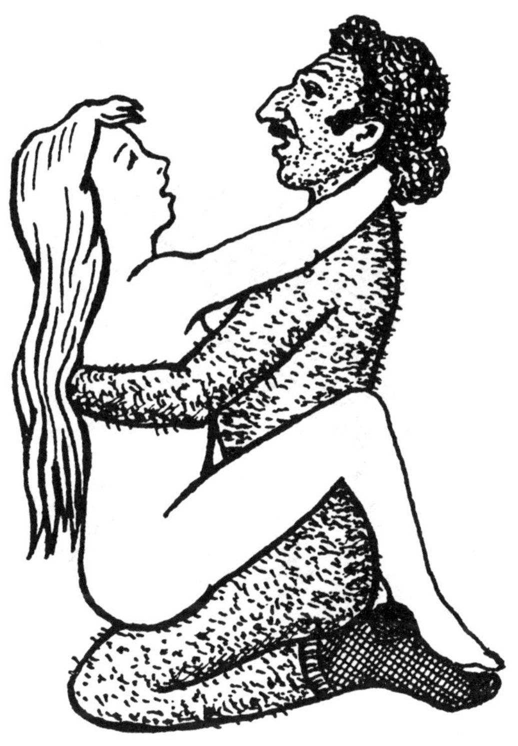

Hip, shin.

This tattoo is called 'Love for ten roubles'.

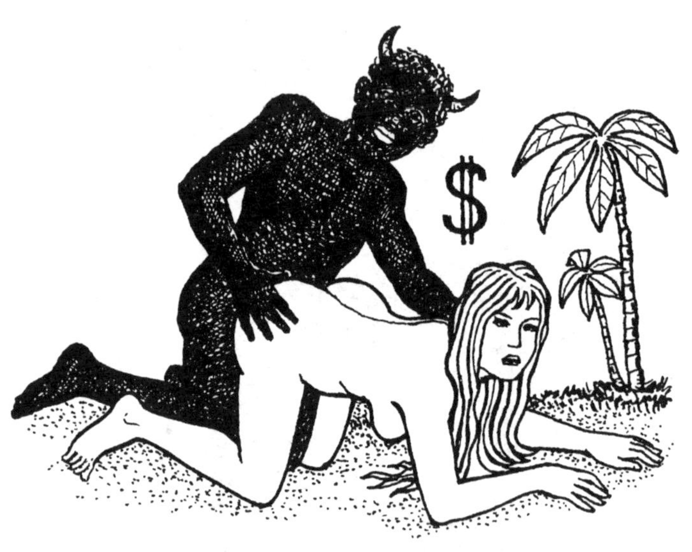

Hip.

This tattoo is called 'The hot black shaft' or 'The greedy whore'.

Drawings. Female Tattoos

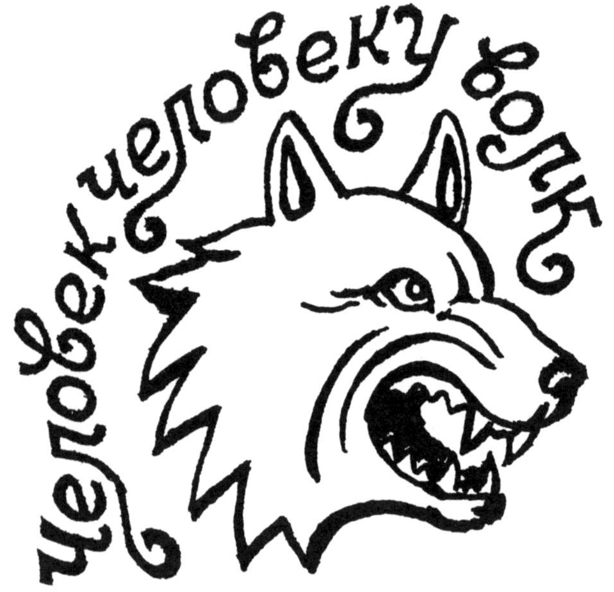

Hip.

This tattoo signifies: 'I am angry with my fate, my life is a failure'.

The acronym stands for **'If you're unfaithful, I'll cut your balls off'**.

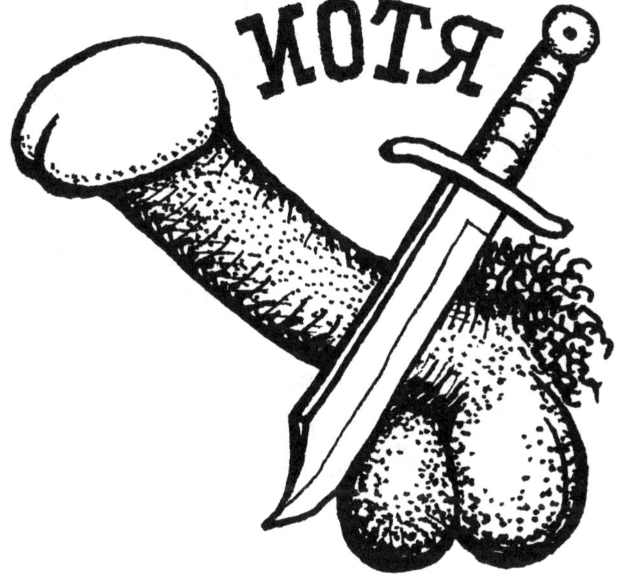

Hip.
___

A hooligan tattoo.

'There you are! Take a bite on that!'

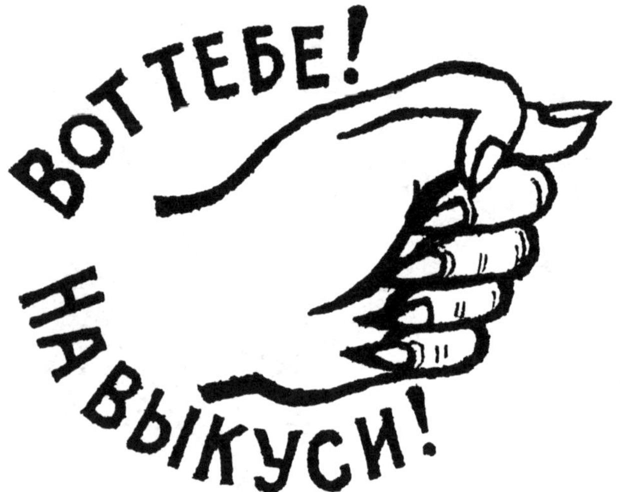

Shoulder, forearm.

A humorous tattoo.

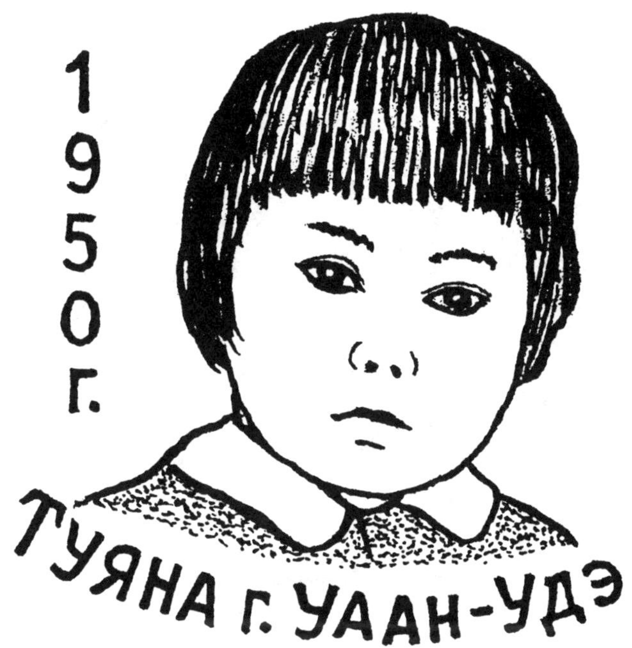

Ministry of the Interior Inter-Regional Hospital. 1975.

A tattoo from a women's corrective labour colony in Ulan-Ude. The wearer was sentenced to eight years for embezzlement under the Supreme Soviet Presidium decree of 4th June 1947. Tuyana was the convict's daughter, born in 1950, who remained with the woman's mother and husband.

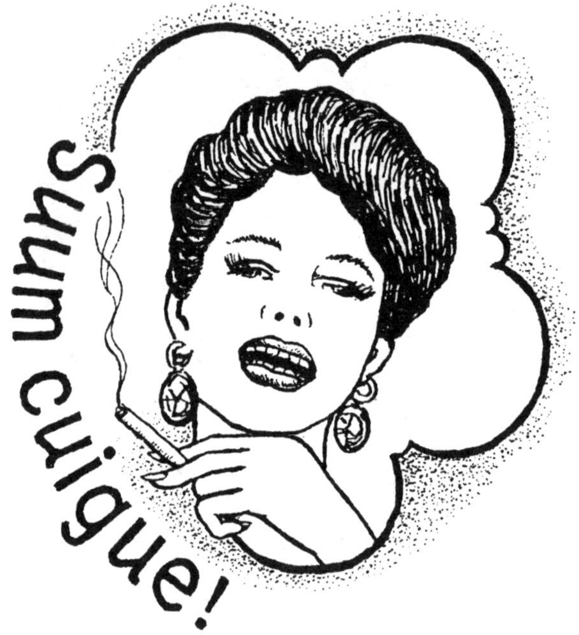

Corrective Labour Colony, Angara Camp Zone. 1953. Stomach.

A tattoo from a woman with two convictions for hooliganism under article 206 of the Criminal Code of the RSFSR. According to the wearer of this tattoo, all her hooliganism consisted of was being in an 'emotional state' in the communal kitchen, and pouring a saucepan containing cabbage soup over her neighbour's head. She claimed the neighbour had been abusing her, calling her a whore and a slut simply out of envy – 'no one ever came to her place'. The tattoo was made by the wearer's friend, a fireman, following the first sentence.

'Super sex. Fellatio'

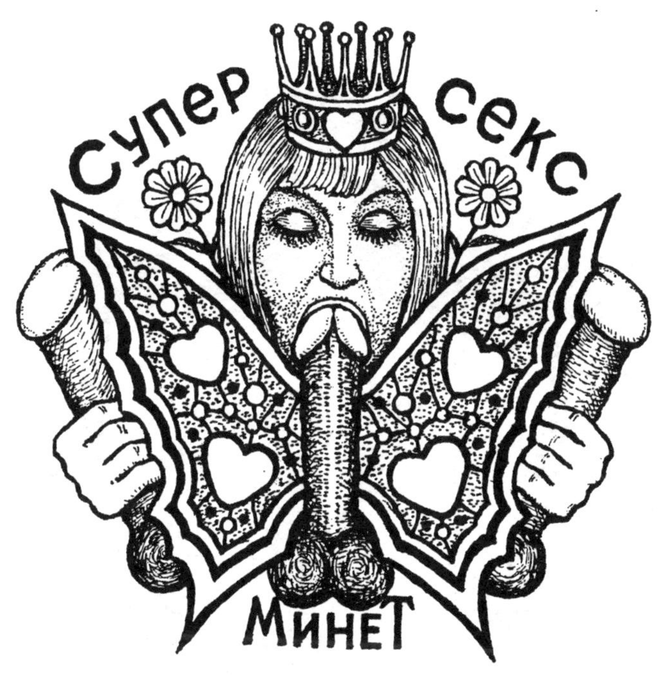

Morgue, 47 Zagorodny Prospect. 1964. Pubis.

A tattoo from a prostitute killed in a brothel at 126 Ligovsky Prospect.

'Stay with me a while, darling, I want you so badly...'

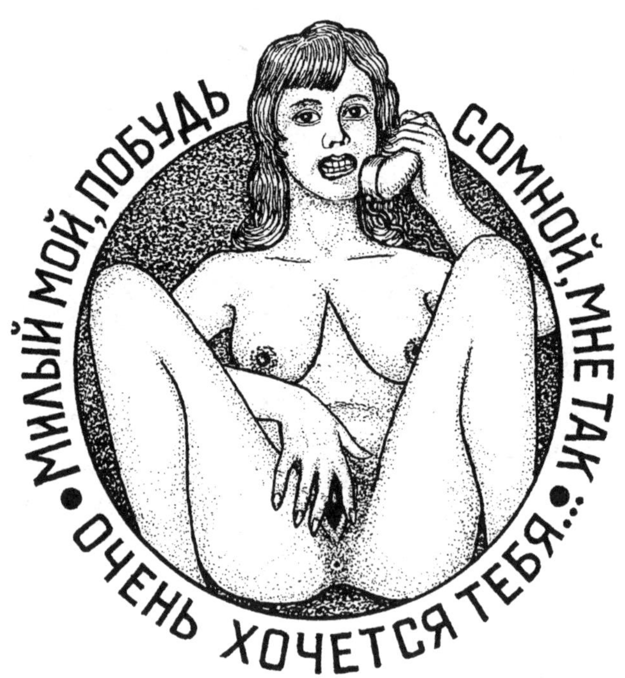

K. Devize Workshop, 202 Ligovsky Prospect, Leningrad. 1979. Left shoulder-blade.

This tattoo belonged to Marina, a twenty-two year old waitress who worked in the restaurant of the Moskovskaya hotel. It was made in an art studio attached to the 'Pictorial Design Combine'. She had two convictions for hooliganism under article 206 of the Criminal Code of the RSFSR.

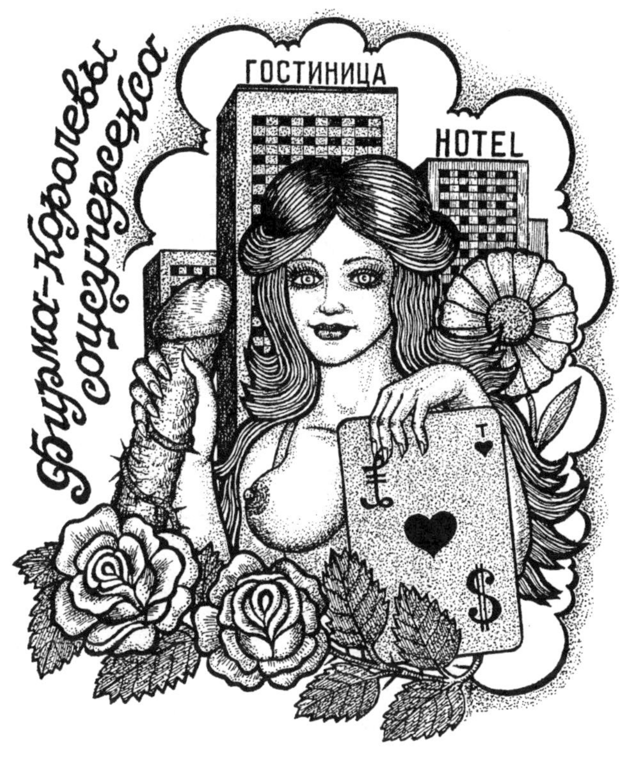

Hip.

A prostitute's tattoo.

An acronym which stands for **'I'm dying for a hot fuck!'**.

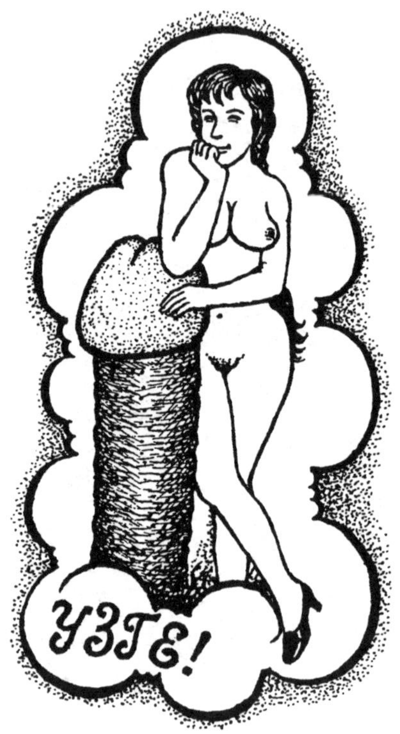

1960s-1970s.

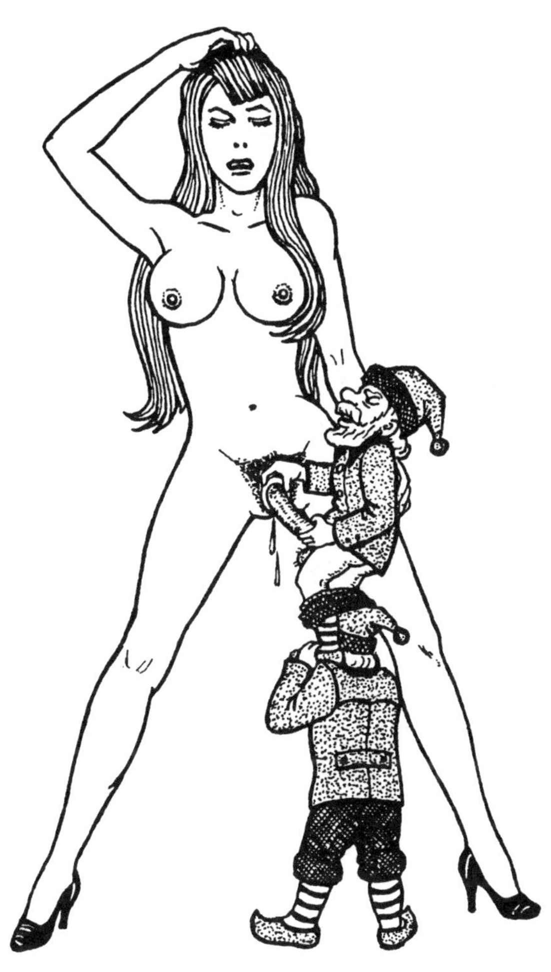

A youth tattoo from a former hard-currency prostitute and morphine addict.

Widespread criminal finger-ring tattoos. Female.

From the top:
Five dots – 'Four watch-towers and a convict'. 'I've been in the zone' (very frequently found on convicted criminals).
'OMUT' – an acronym that spells the Russian word for 'whirlpool', but which stands for 'It's hard to get away from me'.
Devil's head – a 'grin' meaning 'I hold a grudge against the authorities'.
Crosses on knuckles: 'Trips to the zone'. 'I've been to prison twice'.
Forefinger: An 'anti-social' – an inveterate transgressor of prison regime.
Middle finger: A thieves' cross.
Third finger: 'I've been through "The Crosses"'.
Little finger: 'In the Circle of Thieves'.
'PUMA' – nickname.

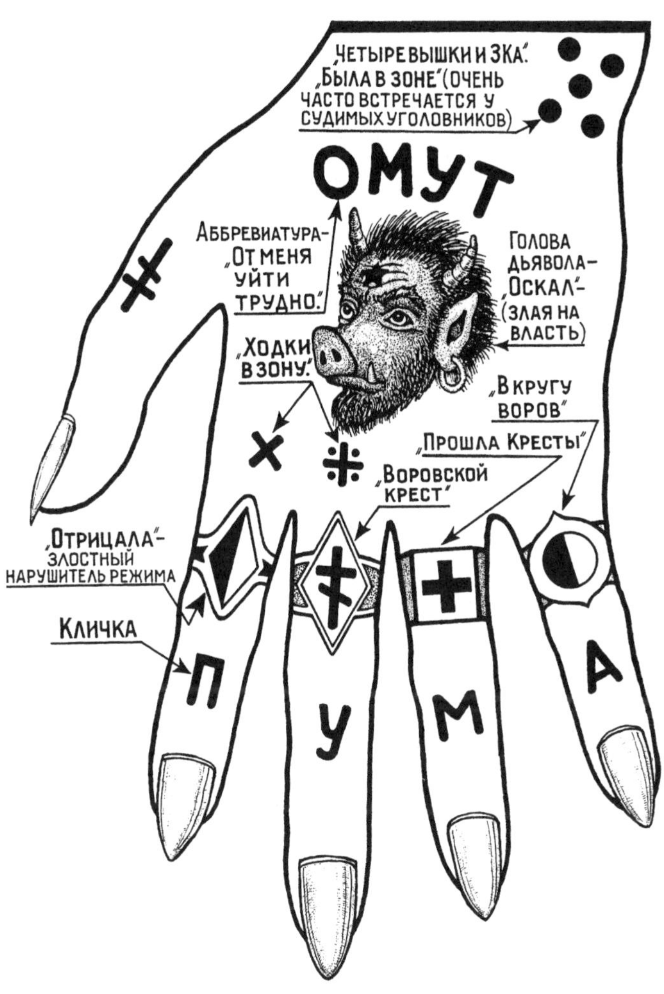

„ЧЕТЫРЕ ВЫШКИ И ЗКА".
„БЫЛА В ЗОНЕ"(ОЧЕНЬ
ЧАСТО ВСТРЕЧАЕТСЯ У
СУДИМЫХ УГОЛОВНИКОВ)
ОМУТ
АББРЕВИАТУРА-
„ОТ МЕНЯ
УЙТИ
ТРУДНО."
ГОЛОВА
ДЬЯВОЛА-
„ОСКАЛ"-
(ЗЛАЯ НА
ВЛАСТЬ)
„ХОДКИ
В ЗОНУ."
„В КРУГУ
ВОРОВ"
„ПРОШЛА КРЕСТЫ"
„ВОРОВСКОЙ
КРЕСТ"
„ОТРИЦАЛА"-
ЗЛОСТНЫЙ
НАРУШИТЕЛЬ РЕЖИМА
КЛИЧКА
П
У
М
А

i   'I was convicted for hooliganism'.

ii   'Shine for the thieves, not the public prosecutor'.

iii   'I was convicted for theft'.

iv   'I served a juvenile's sentence in an educational labour colony'.

v   'In the circle of male and female thieves'.

vi   'I was the only underage detainee in my circle of friends'.

vii   'I won't give my hand to the cops'.

viii   'I've been through "The Crosses"' – Leningrad prison No.1.

ix   'Authoritative female thief'.

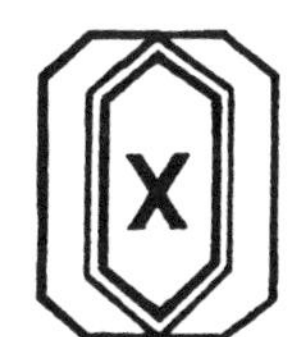

i

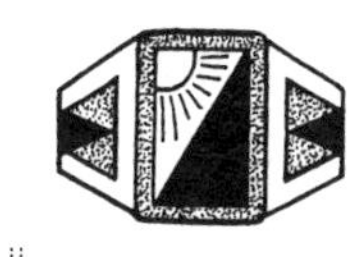

ii

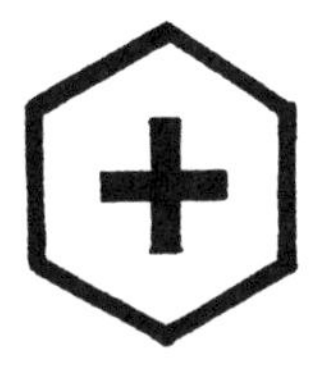

iii

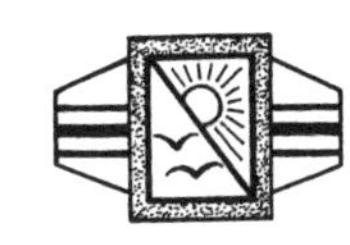

iv

v

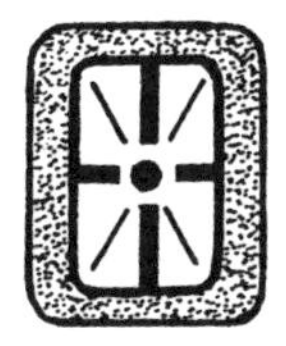

vi

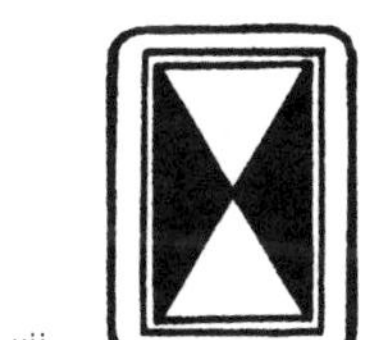

vii

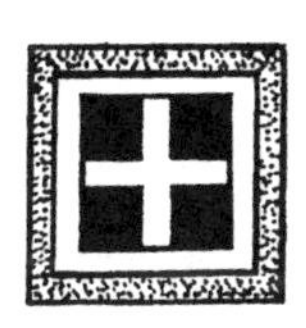

viii

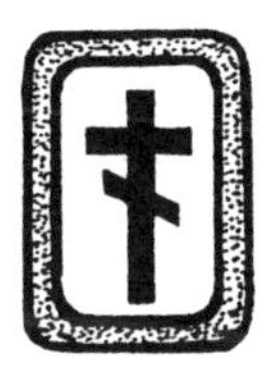

ix

x   An 'anarchist anti-social' – an inveterate transgressor of prison regime who refuses to work.

xi   A female 'legitimate thief' – a woman with high status in the criminal world.

xii   'Bulldyke' – an active lesbian criminal boss or 'authority'.

xiii   An 'anti-social' – an inveterate transgressor of prison regime who refuses to work.

xiv   'They don't convict them (juveniles)'.

xv   'Drug addict' – the letter 'F' stands for 'free'.

xvi   'I was convicted for stealing property'.

xvii   'I spent two years in a special school for difficult children'.

xviii   A 'girl thief' – a young criminal with connections with male and female thieves.

x

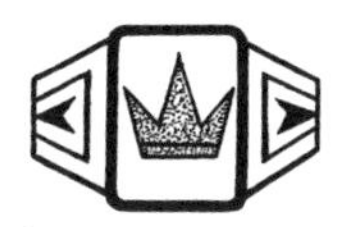

xi

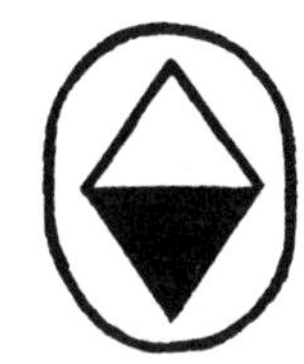

xii

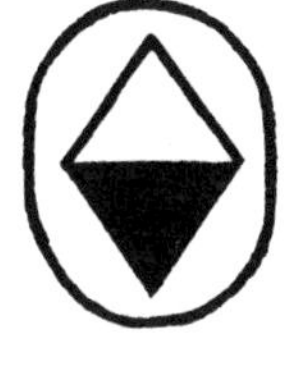

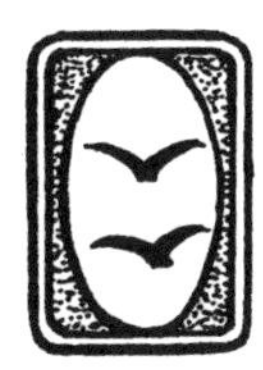

xiii

xiv

xv

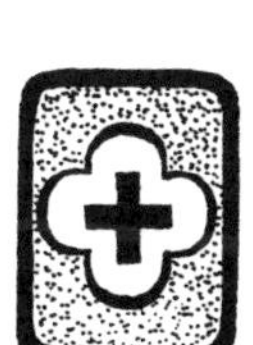

xvi

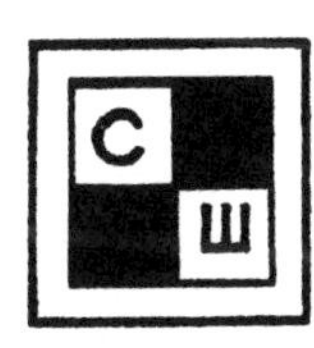

xvii

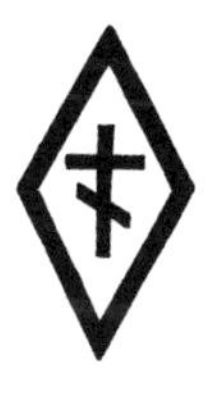

xviii

xix   An 'authority', repeatedly convicted for theft and robbery.

xx   'I served my sentence in a corrective labour colony' (the lines indicate the number of years).

xxi   'I served my sentence in an educational labour colony'.

xxii   'Greetings to thieves, male and female' – indicates membership of the criminal community.

xxiii   'I began stealing out of poverty and hunger in this Soviet life'.

xxiv   A 'girl thief' – an underage thief with connections in the criminal world, infected with criminal romanticism.

xxv   'First conviction'.

xxvi   A 'bitch and a piglet', a 'sloppy cunt' – someone who doesn't keep her promises, is mentally and physically degraded, slovenly, takes no care of her appearance or bodily cleanliness. This tattoo is applied forcibly.

xxvii   A 'shagger', 'slut', 'crab louse' – women convicted for killing their own children. This tattoo is applied forcibly.

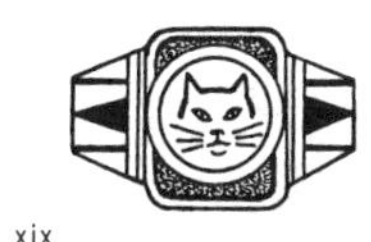

xix

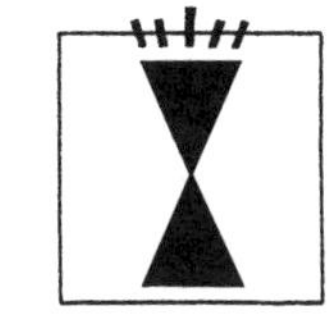

xx

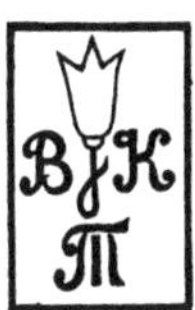

xxi

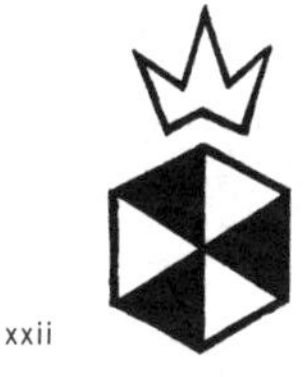

xxii

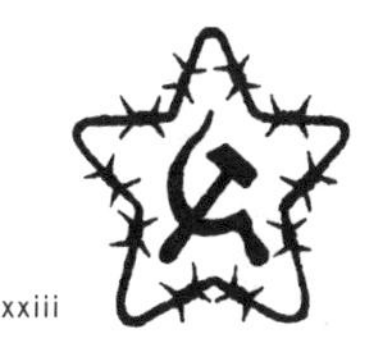

xxiii

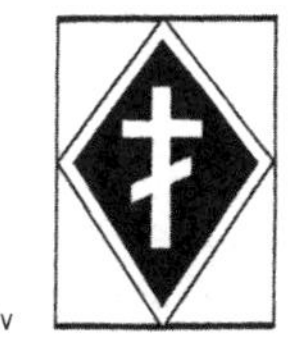

xxiv

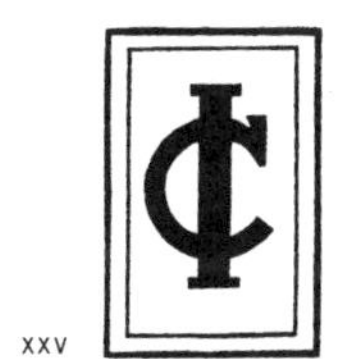

xxv

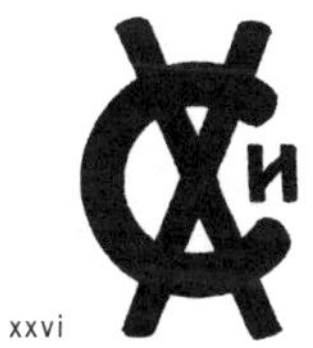

xxvi

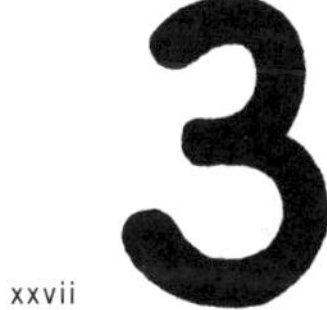

xxvii

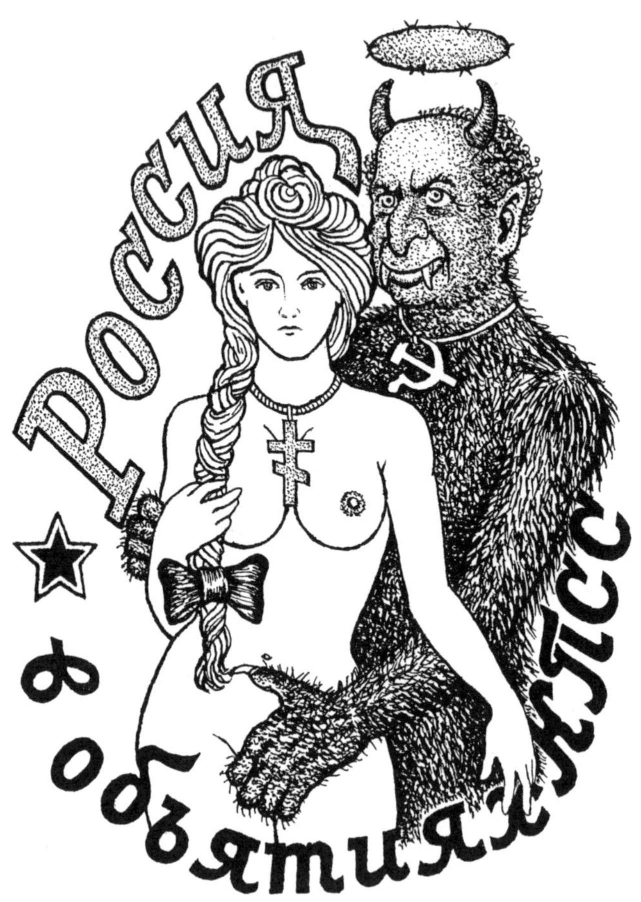

Vagrants' Reception Centre, 10 Bakunin Street. 1977.

A rare anti-communist 'grin' made in a corrective labour colony in the Komi Autonomous Soviet Socialist Republic.

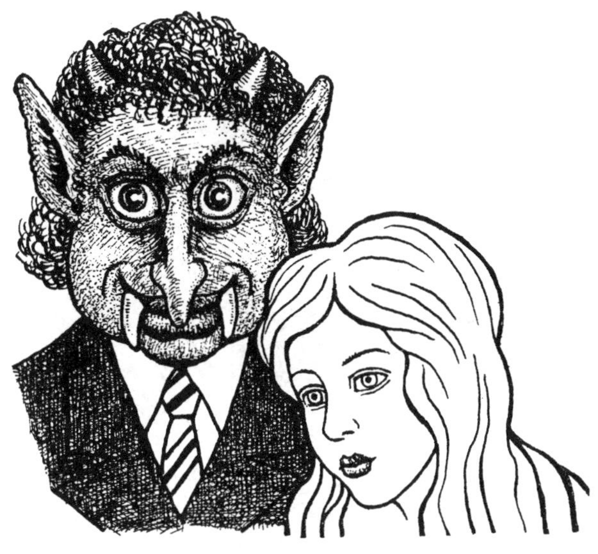

Corrective Labour Colony, Angara Camp Zone. 1953. Stomach.

An anti-Semitic tattoo worn by a woman convicted under the Supreme Soviet Presidium decree of 4th June 1947, for stealing food from a depot. The owner of this tattoo said that for a long time she cohabited with a Jew who was the head of the food depot where she worked. When she had a child by him, the Jew stopped seeing her and took up with a different lover - a young Russian girl. Soon afterwards this girl gave the single mother a shopping bag containing grain and sugar and a note for the security guards written by the director of the depot. But she was detained at the checkpoint, the militia were called and the note was destroyed in front of her by the head of security. That was how the director got rid of her, when all she had asked of him was help for her child. After she was 'put away' her half-Jewish child was cared for by her mother and brother.

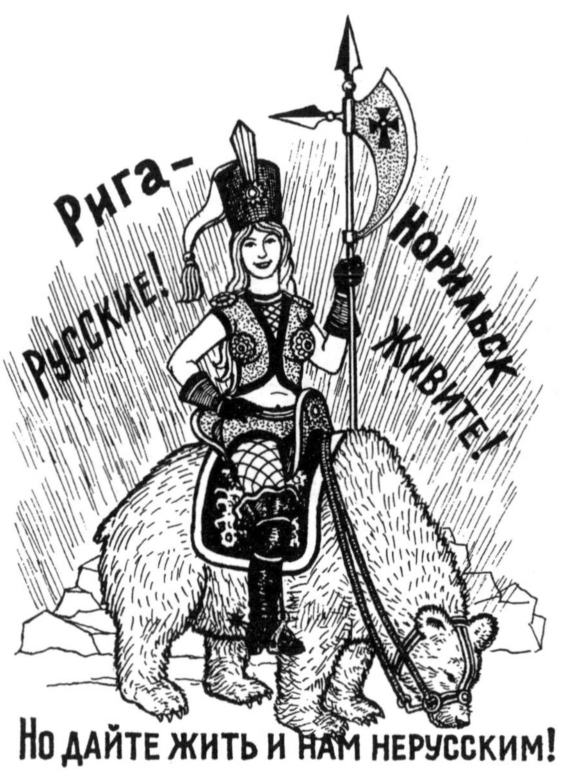

Isolation Cell Block No.2. 1949.

A Latvian tattoo, typical of individuals who have spent time in northern camps. This tattoo belonged to Else Shaltis, who at the age of twenty-three was sent to the GULAG together with her family. It was made by a friend in the Norilsk camp zone. Her parents, younger sister, and brother all died in the camps. After her release in 1957 she lived in Riga.

The text (translated from Polish) reads '**A Russian woman convict is a red Soviet swine who doesn't like work and thinks she is a higher race, she's malicious and envious, abandons her own children, loves getting drunk, thieving, acting like a hooligan and humiliating everyone**'.

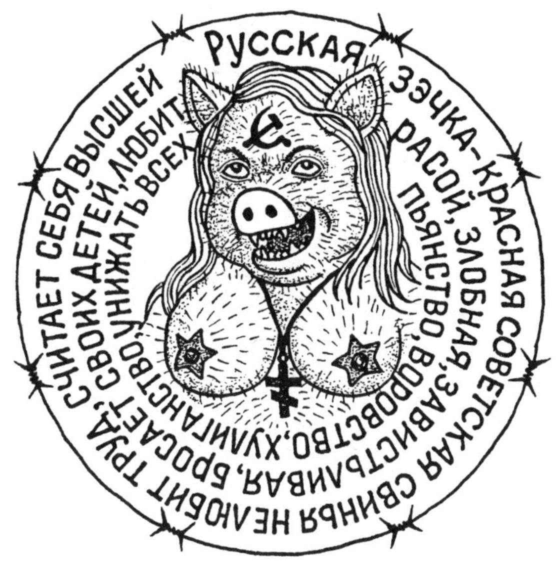

A Polish 'grin' worn by a Polish woman called Bronja who was exiled from Belostok in 1940 and sent to a criminal's camp. She was orphaned when young and from the age of nine was raised in a Jewish family that owned two shops, where she worked as a sales assistant after finishing grammar school. At the age of twenty Bronja was exiled under armed escort with her adopted parents because they were listed by the NKVD as 'an alien bourgeois element'. At Sverdlovsk the NKVD armed escort separated all the young Polish women from their parents and older relatives, and Bronja and the others were taken to the Taishet Camp Zone. There she organised a group of Polish and Baltic girls to resist against the Russian women criminals who were supported by the administration of the remote camp site. Bronja was a beautiful girl with a good figure who looked a bit like Sophia Loren.

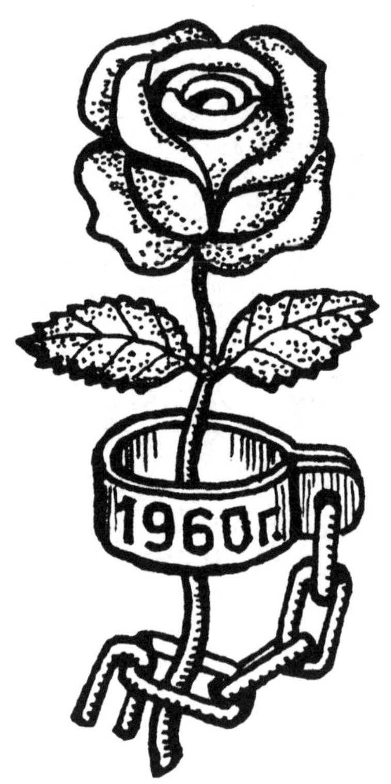

Obukhov Hospital Morgue, Leningrad. 1967.

The convict who wore this tattoo was killed in a brothel.

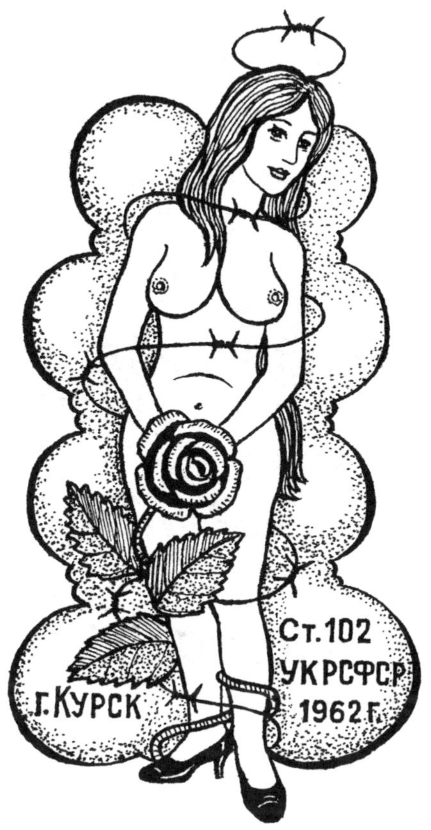

Isolation Cell Block. 1981. Hip.

The tattoo of a woman who, when she was seventeen years old, was given a ten year sentence for murdering the man she loved. She turned eighteen in prison.

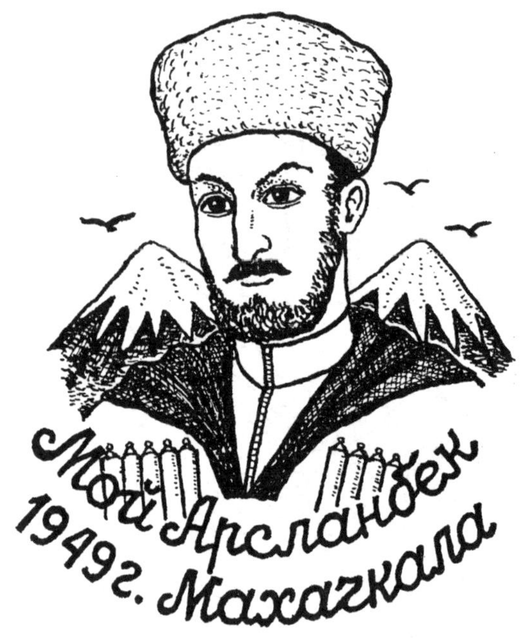

Isolation Cell Block No.2. 1949.

The woman who wore this tattoo, Galina, was convicted under article 136 of the Criminal Code of the RSFSR, for the murder of an Azeri man. He had attempted to rape her in the shop where he was the manager and she worked as a cashier. Her parents were arrested in 1937 and she was raised in a children's home. The tattoo depicts the man she loved. She claimed he was of princely descent, since he had the right to wear a white Circassian coat and fur hat. The tattoo was made in the Derbent Corrective Labour Colony by a Russian female convict who was imprisoned for forging bread rationing cards. Both convicts were later sent to a corrective labour colony in the Komi Autonomous Soviet Socialist Republic.

The acronym in this tattoo stands for **'You are really fine and wonderful'**.

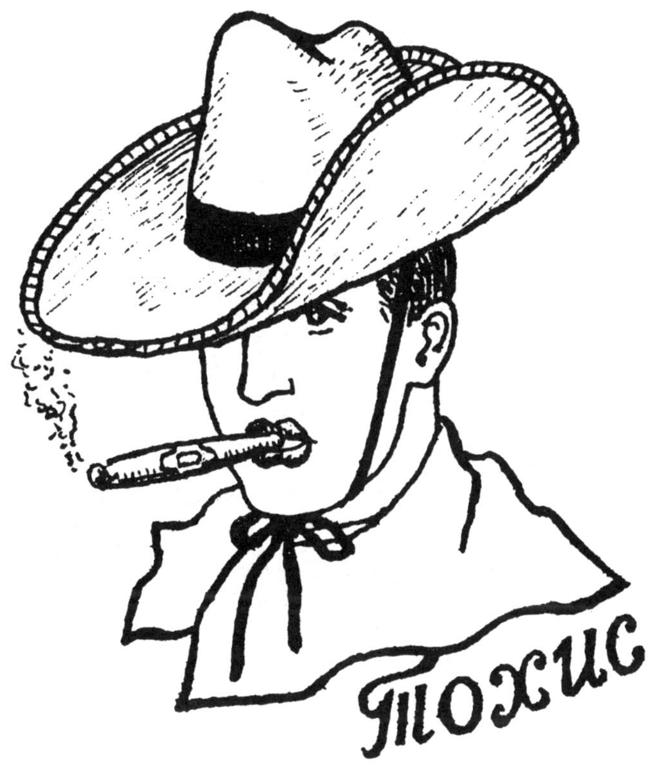

Corrective Labour Colony No.2. Shoulder.

The cowboy depicted was copied from a magazine.

'I shall take pride and delight in only one'

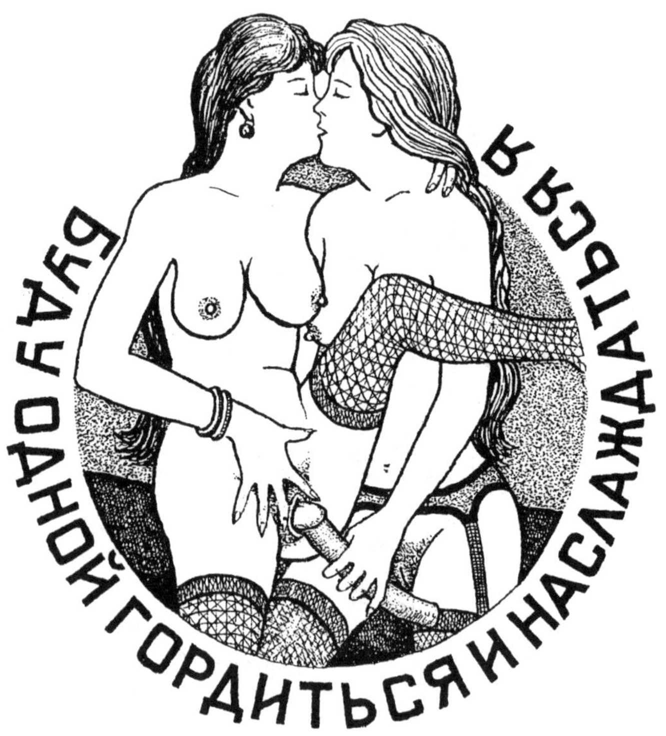

1992. Stomach.

Made by a vagrant artist in the Vagrants' Reception Centre at 1 Svechny Lane in Leningrad. The tattoo shows a variation on the theme of lesbian love, worn by a lesbian who was convicted of stealing narcotics under article 224 of the Criminal Code of the RSFSR.

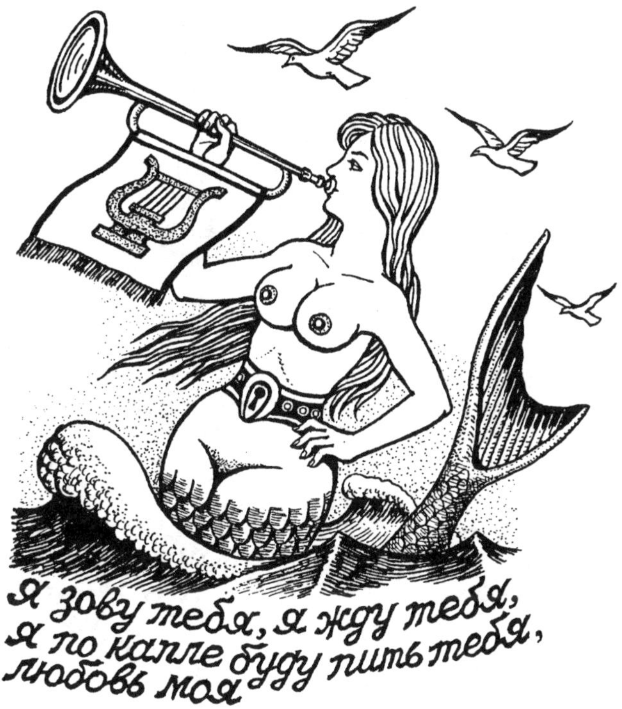

'I call to you, I wait for you, I will drink you drop by drop, my love'

Hip, stomach and occasionally other parts of the body.

A tattoo worn by an active lesbian, it was widespread in the 1970s and 1980s.

'Prison and the zone of the red-arsed **CPSU** cure women convicts of brains, so they won't get piles or get infested by nits and lice, or crabs on their cunts...'

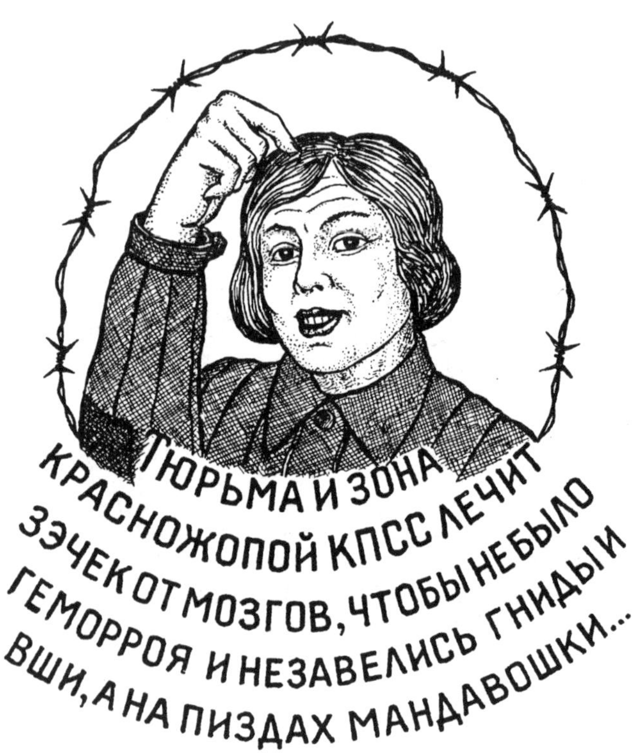

Special Reception and Distribution Unit, North Western Transport Department of Internal Affairs.

A hooligan tattoo worn by a woman with two convictions under articles 74 and 142 of the 1926 Criminal Code of the RSFSR and article 206 of the 1960 Criminal Code of the RSFSR.

The Georgian text reads '**Kolhida is a good country, but Russia is best of all!!!**'.

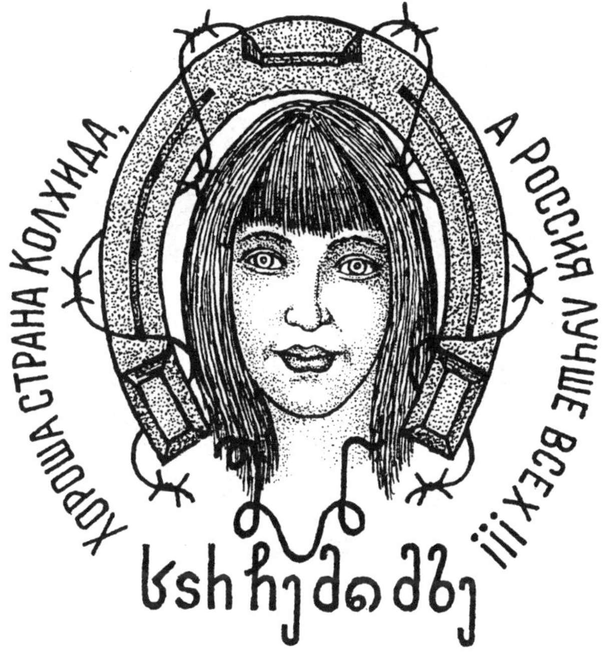

Hospital No.4, Kosinov Street, St. Petersburg. 1993. Stomach.

A tattoo from a woman twice convicted in the Georgian Soviet Socialist Republic for speculation. The horseshoe is a symbol of good luck – in this case hope for an early conditional release.

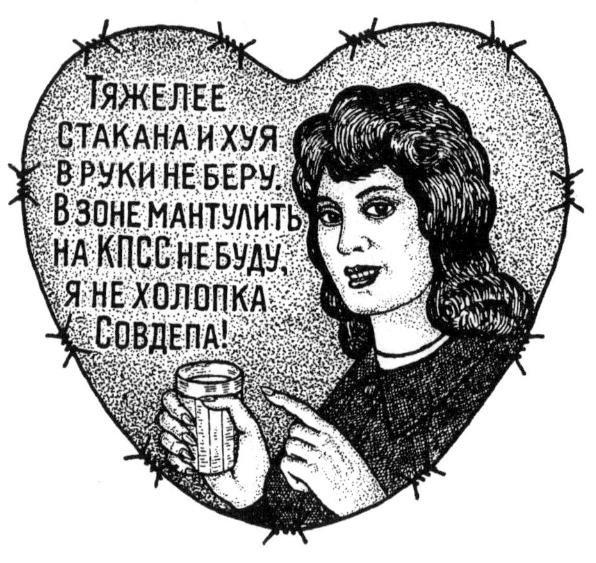

Vassilievsky Island Hospital Morgue, 85 Bolshoi Prospect, Leningrad. 1971. Stomach.

A cynical anti-Soviet tattoo belonging to Susanna Avilova, who was convicted of the theft of state property under article 92 of the Criminal Code of the RSFSR. She lived at flat 150, 4 Veselnaya Street in Leningrad and was stabbed to death by her lover, K. Gerasimov, a chauffeur, in a jealous fit of rage.

The German text reads **'Wherever the Russians go, the people and nature perish in poverty'**.

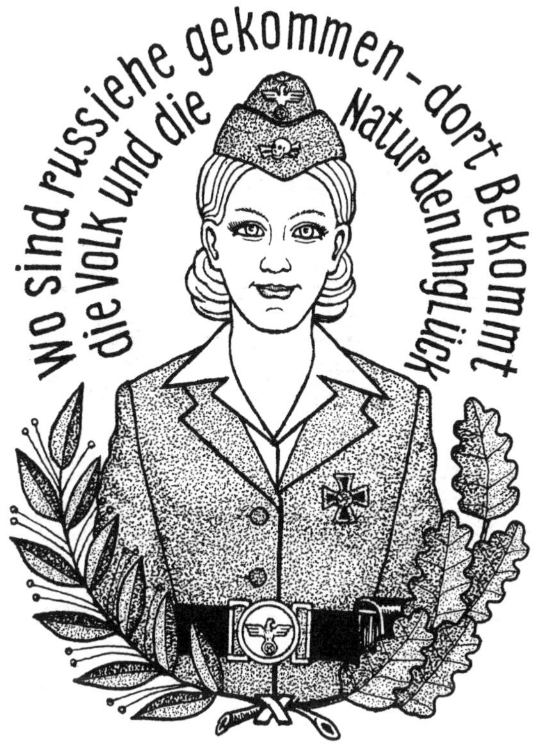

Obukhov Hospital Morgue. 1965.

The wearer of this tattoo was killed together with the driver of the Estonian registered car she was travelling in, when it was involved in a crash near the Leningrad Technological Institute. The man to blame for the accident, who was driving a ZIS-150 truck, was drunk and attempted to flee the scene, but he was detained by two members of a voluntary public order patrol.

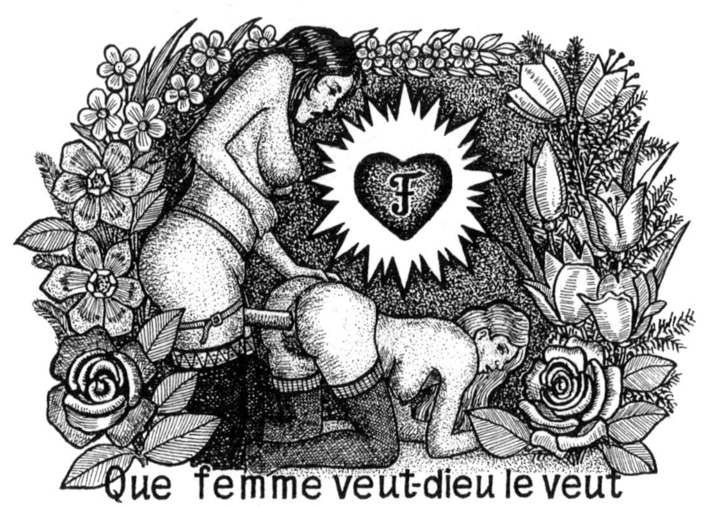

1993

A pornographic youth tattoo made by a vagrant professional artist, and worn by a twenty-three year old lesbian. The letter 'F' in the heart stands for 'free love'. The wearer of the tattoo also practises prostitution in order to support herself and her three year old illegitimate child, who lives with her. She mostly performs fellatio on her clients in order to avoid another pregnancy. As an active lesbian she has authoritative status as a sexual partner among passive lesbians.

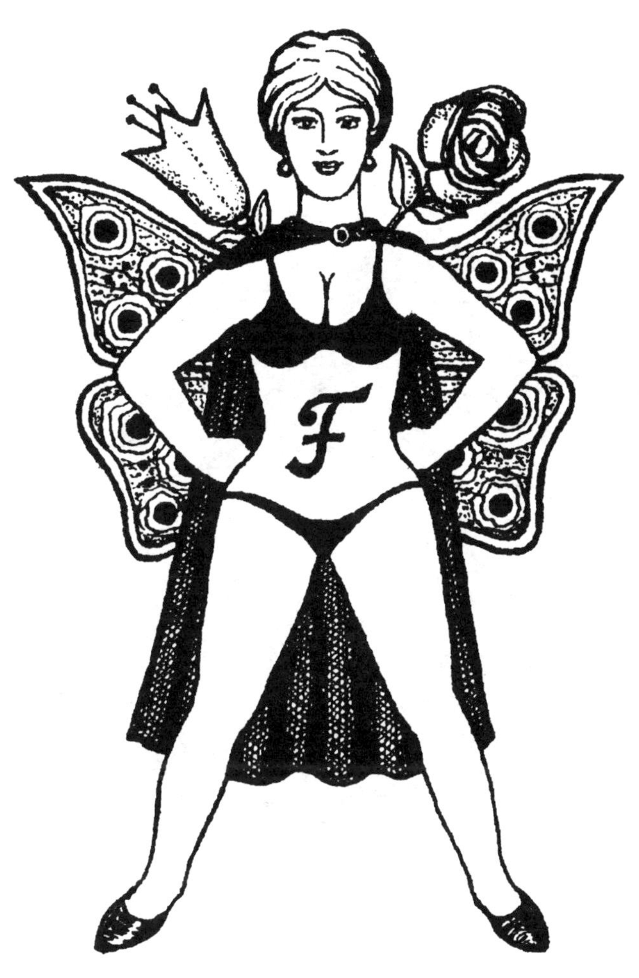

A tattoo from a young prostitute, a former ward of a children's home, who was convicted of vagrancy under article 209 of the Criminal Code of the RSFSR. Made by a vagrant artist in 1989.

The text on the left reads **'Girls, beware of AIDs and venereal disease!'**. The text on the right reads **'I am an Amazon!'**

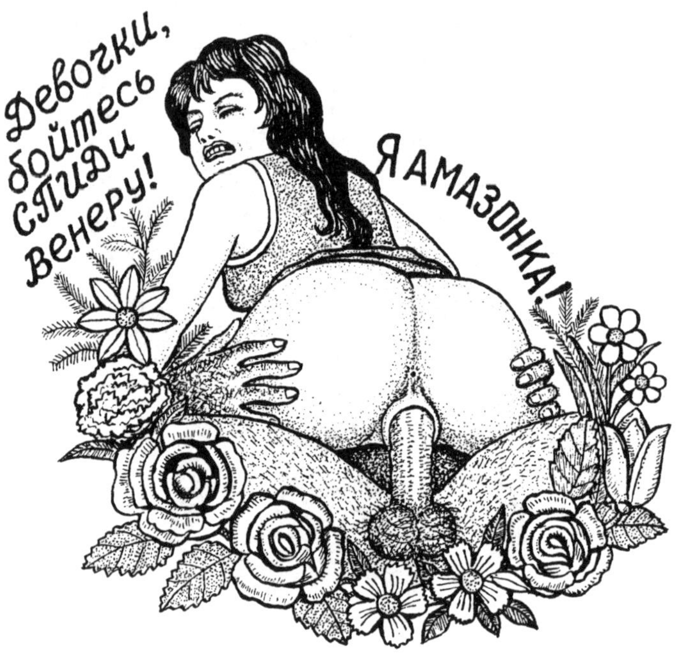

Leningrad. 1992.

This young prostitute's tattoo, by a vagrant artist, is called 'I am an Amazon!'.

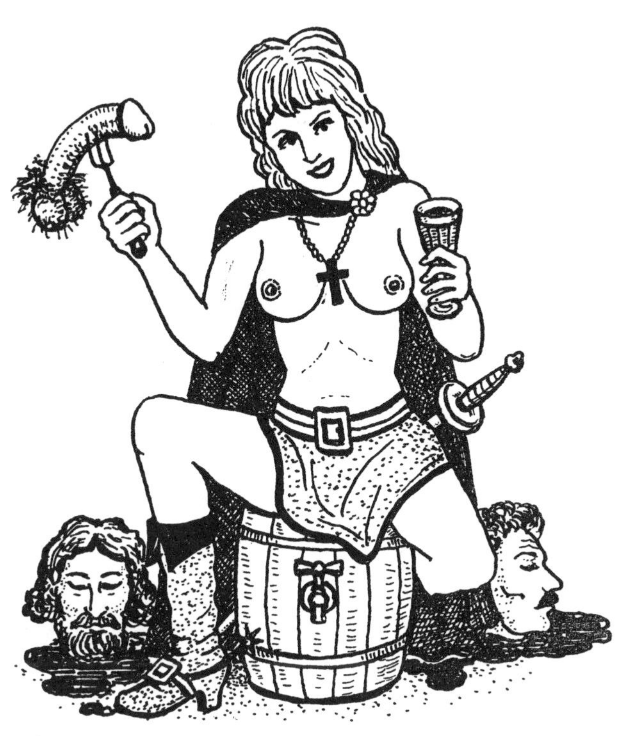

Leningrad Special Reception Centre. 1972. Stomach.

A female hooligan convict tattoo known as the 'The prick-eater'.

Photographs. Section Two

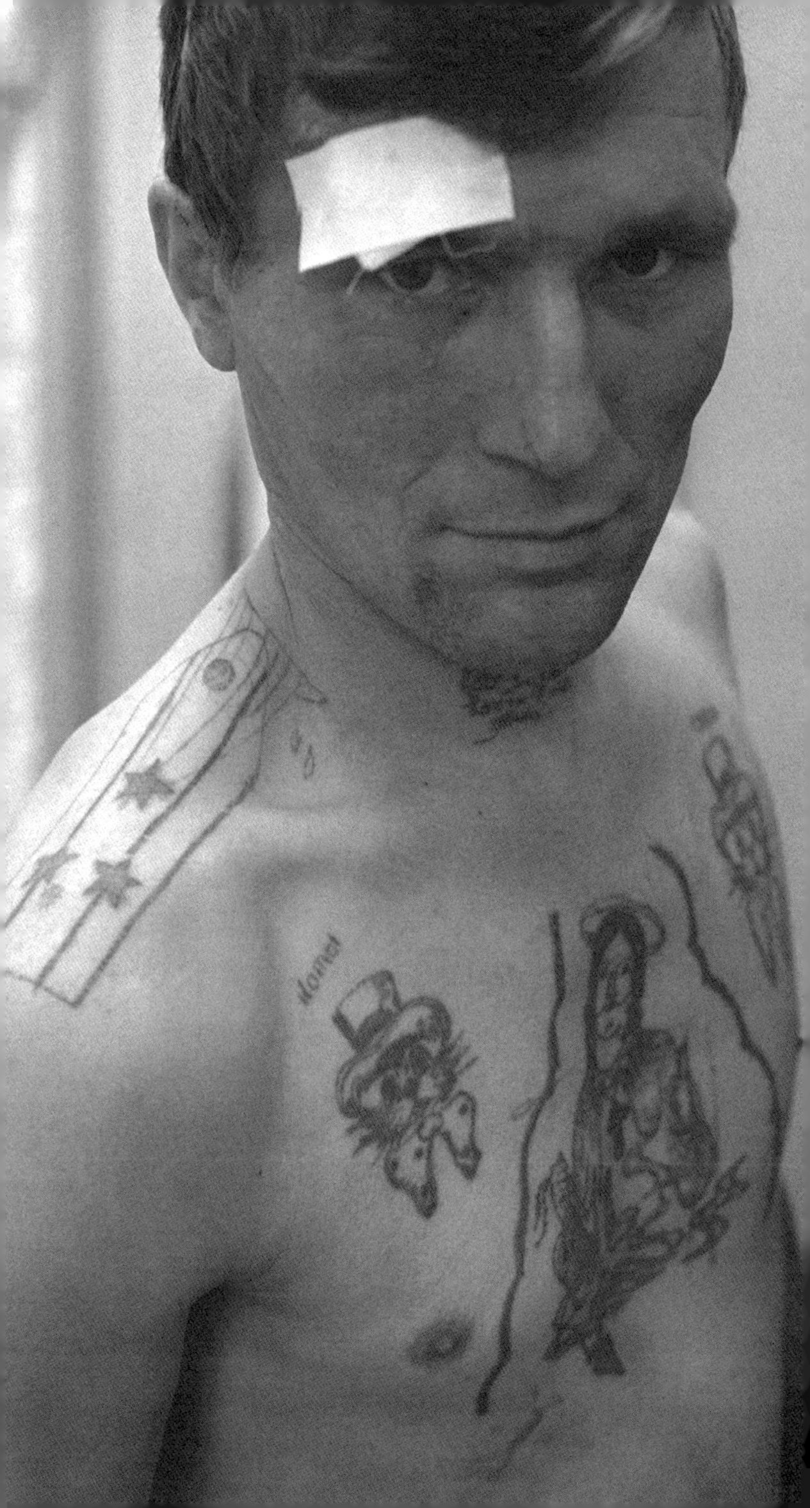

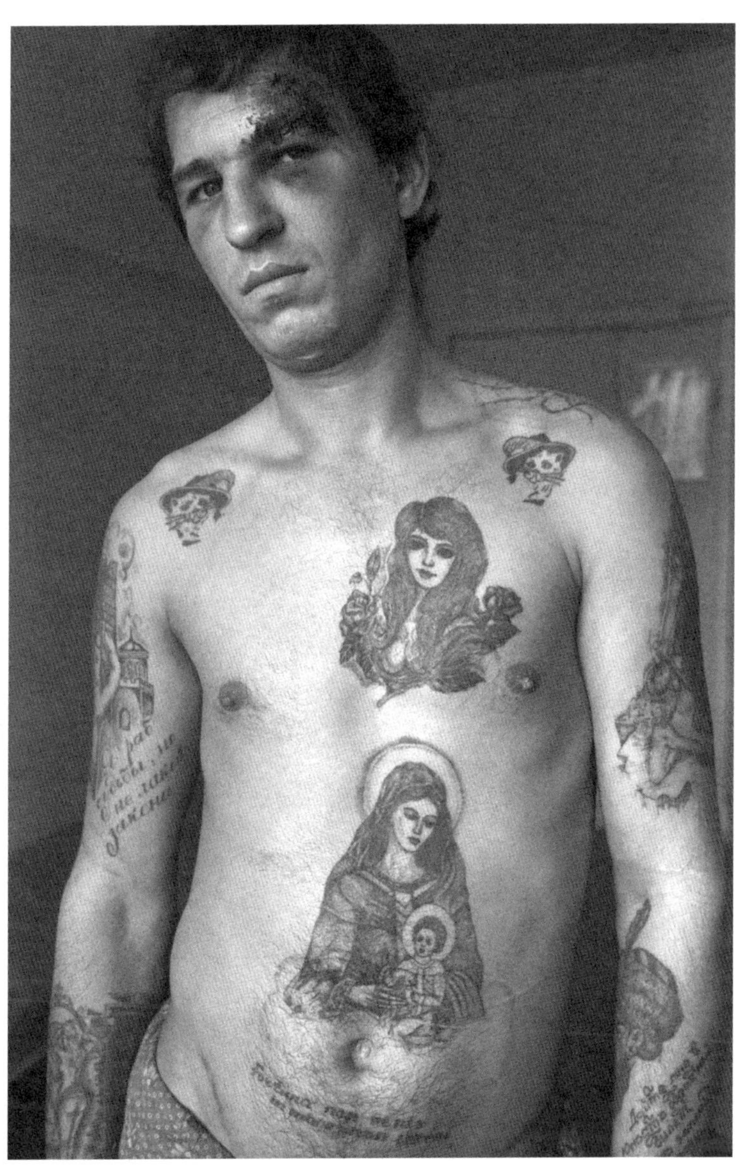

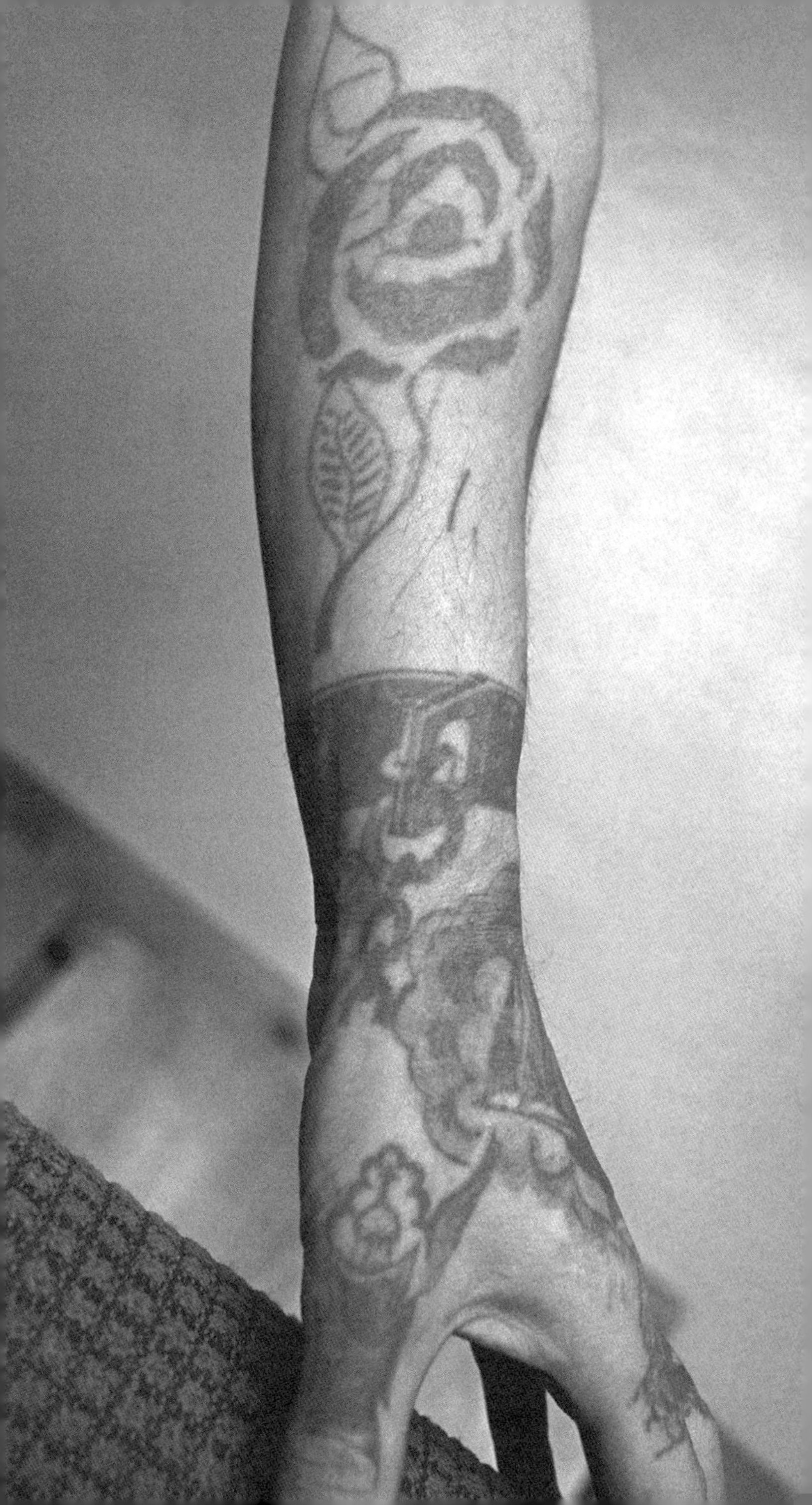

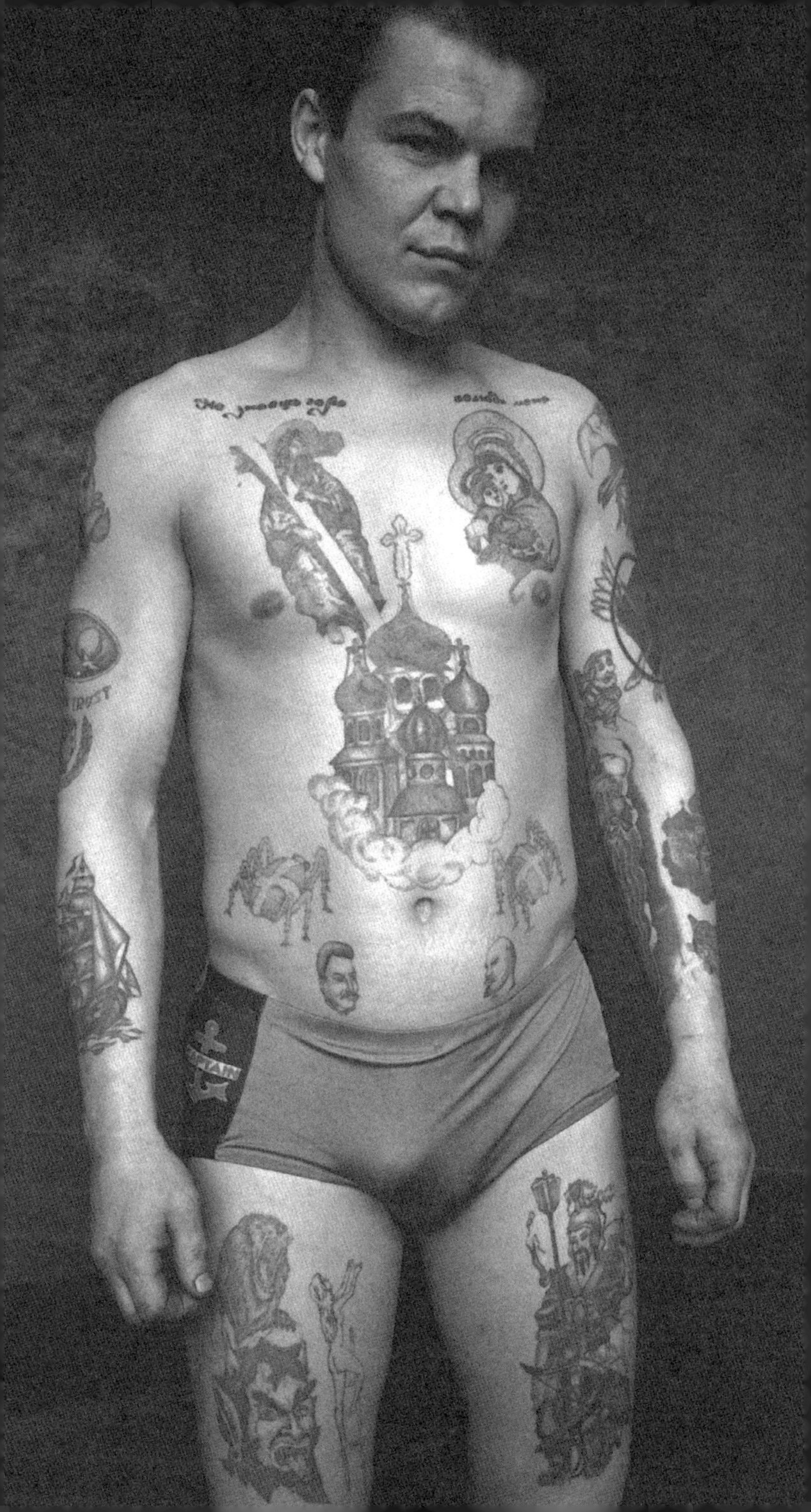

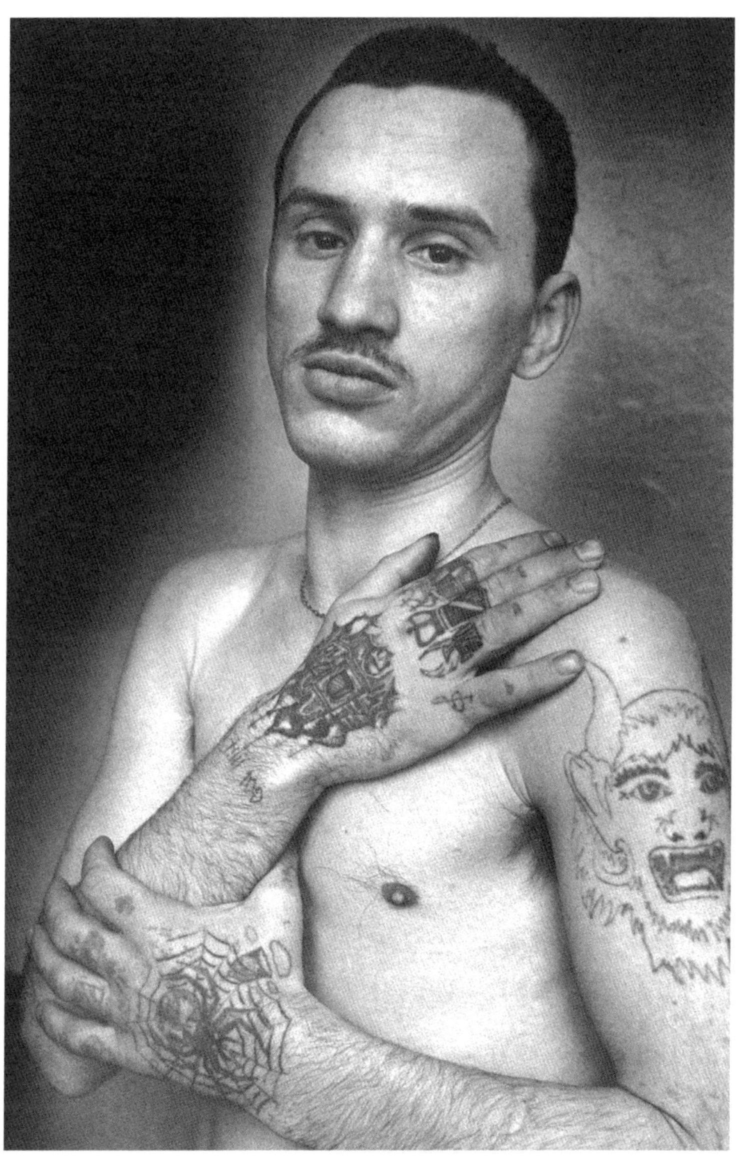

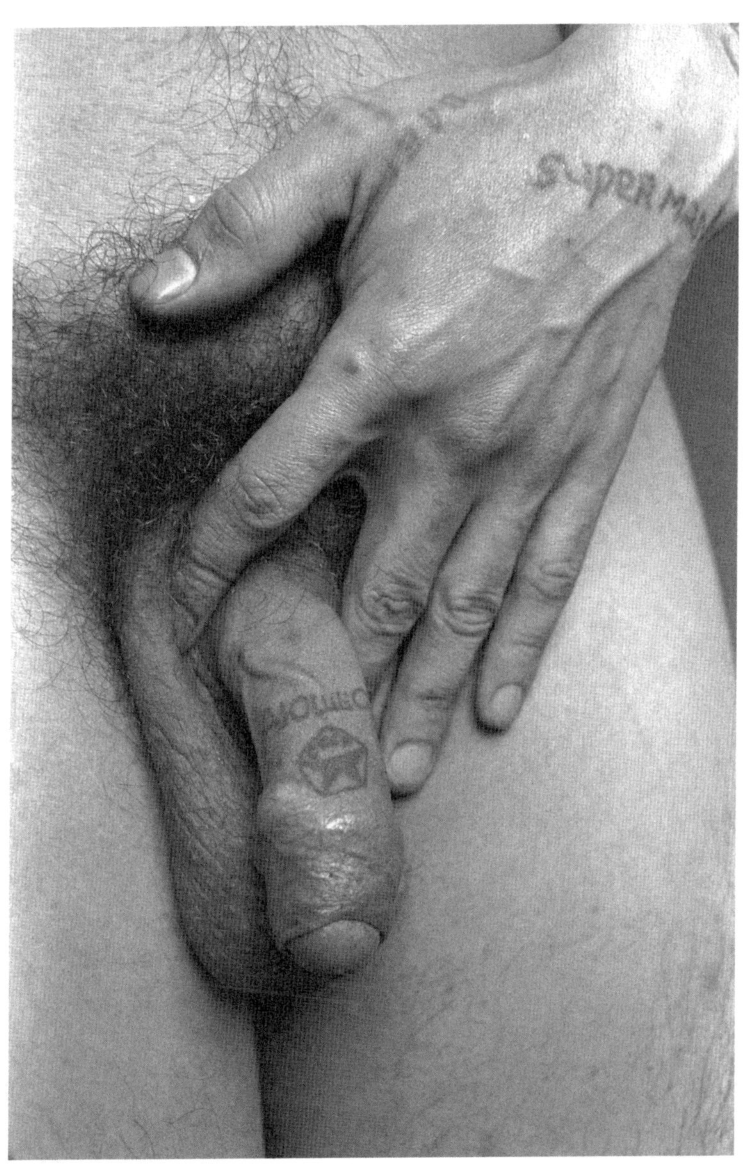

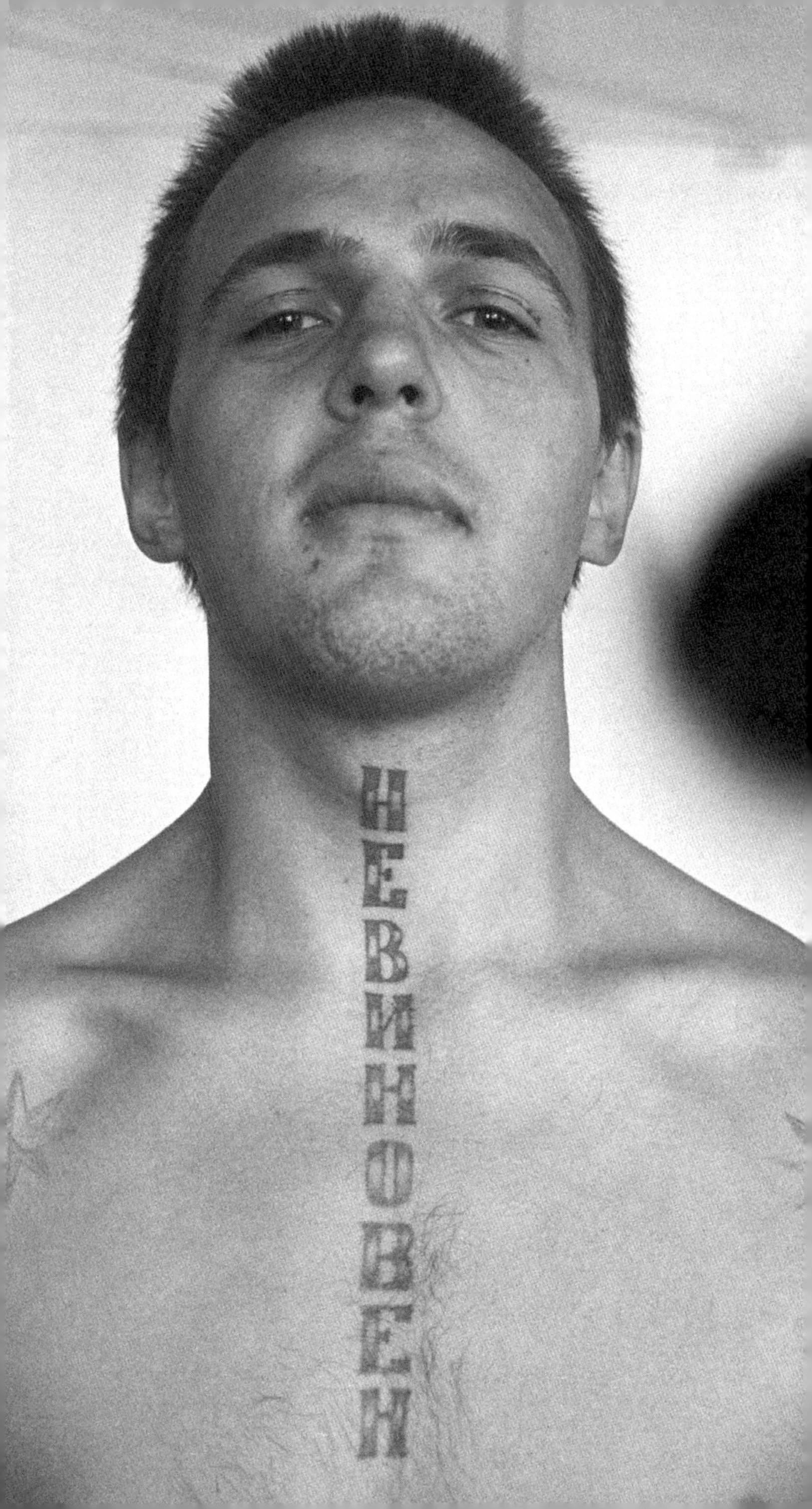
НЕВИНОВЕН

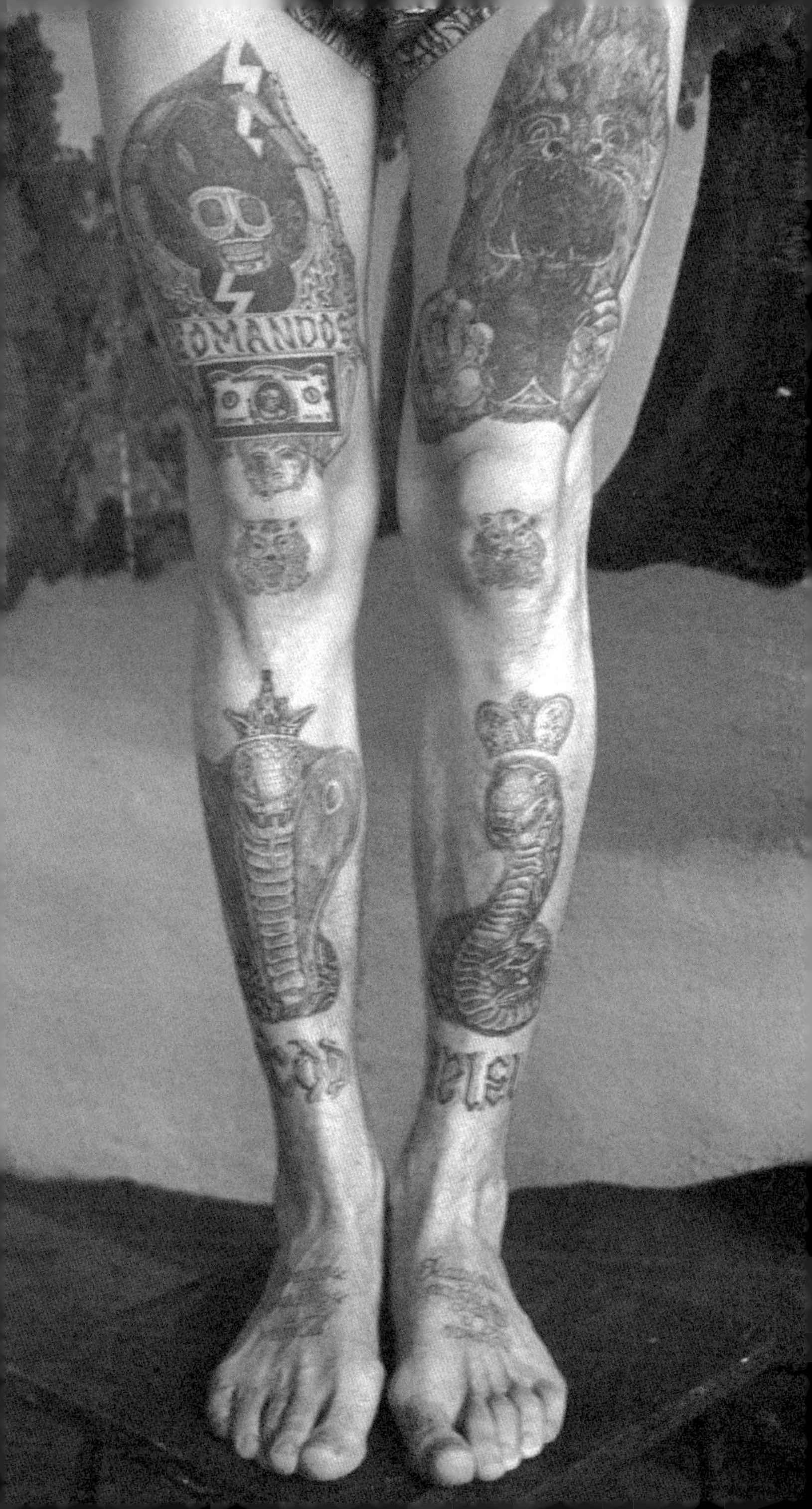
OMANDO

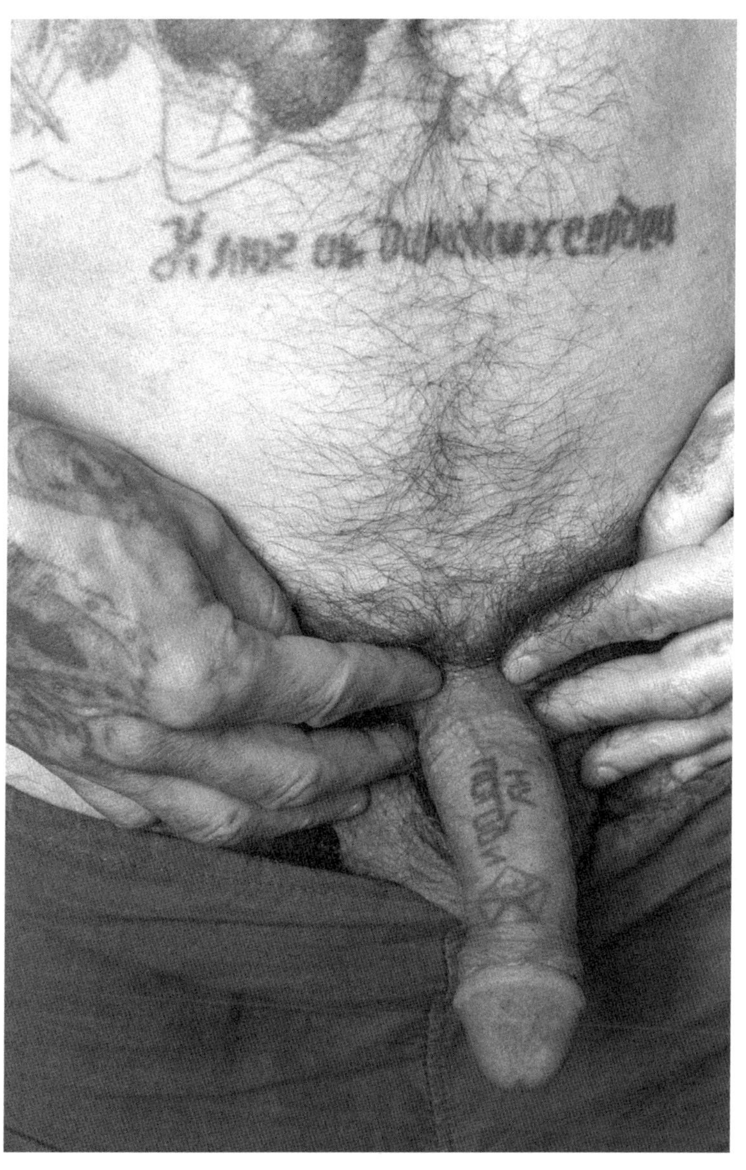

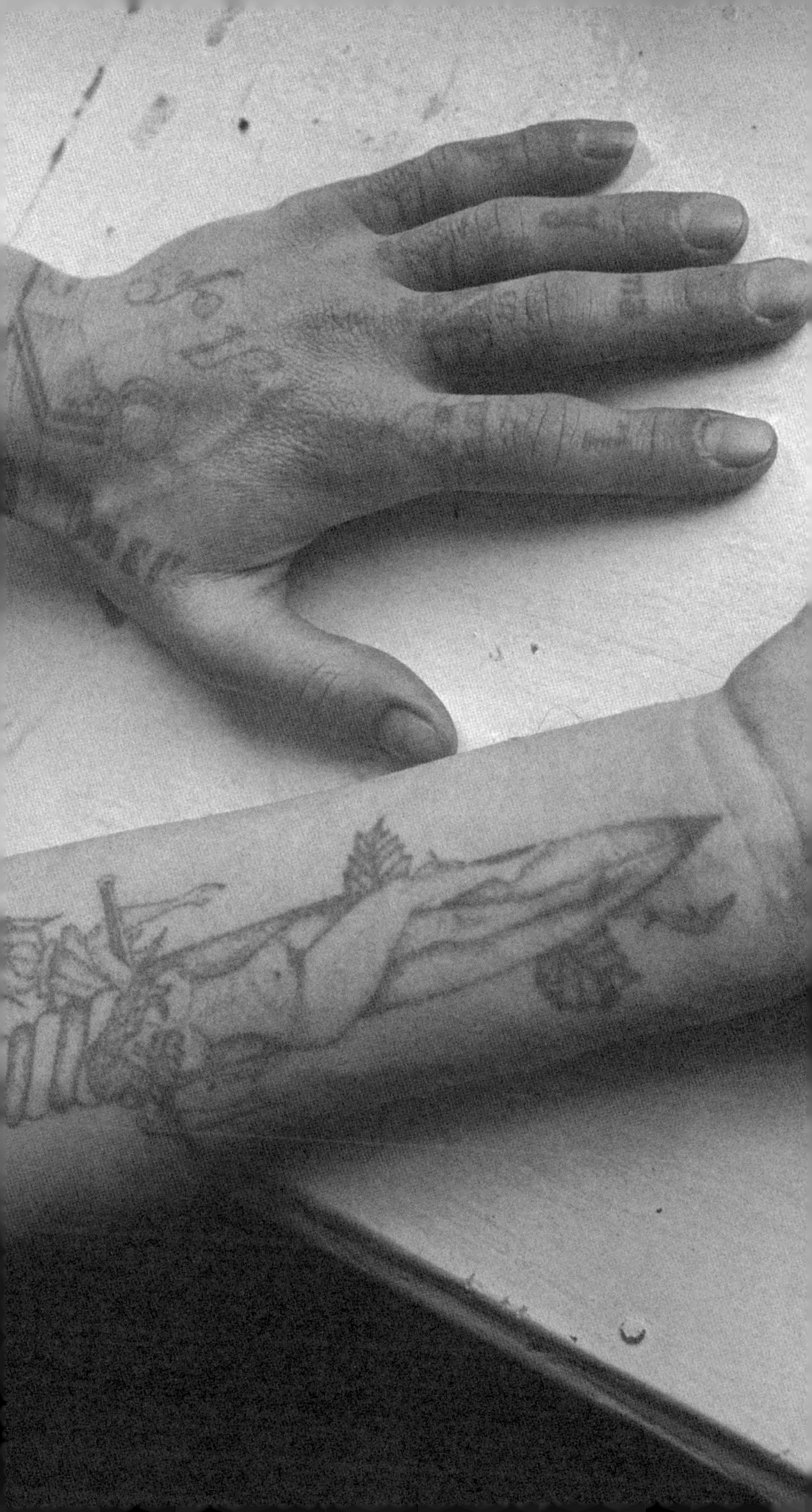

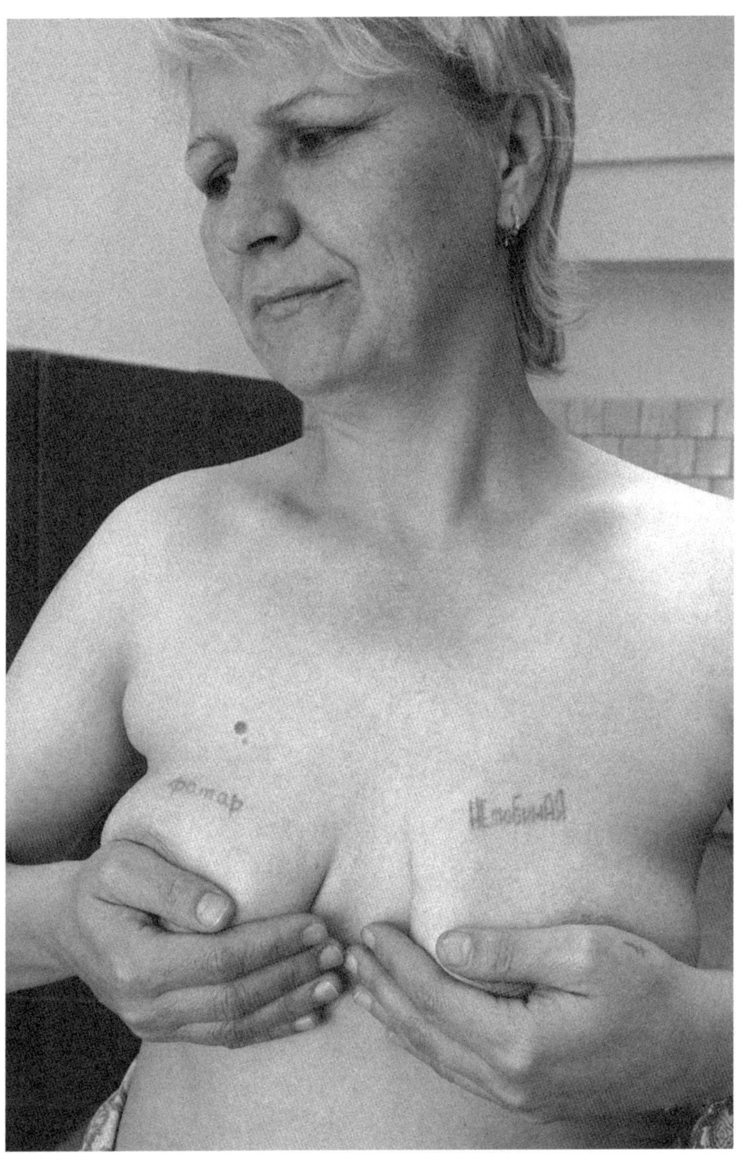

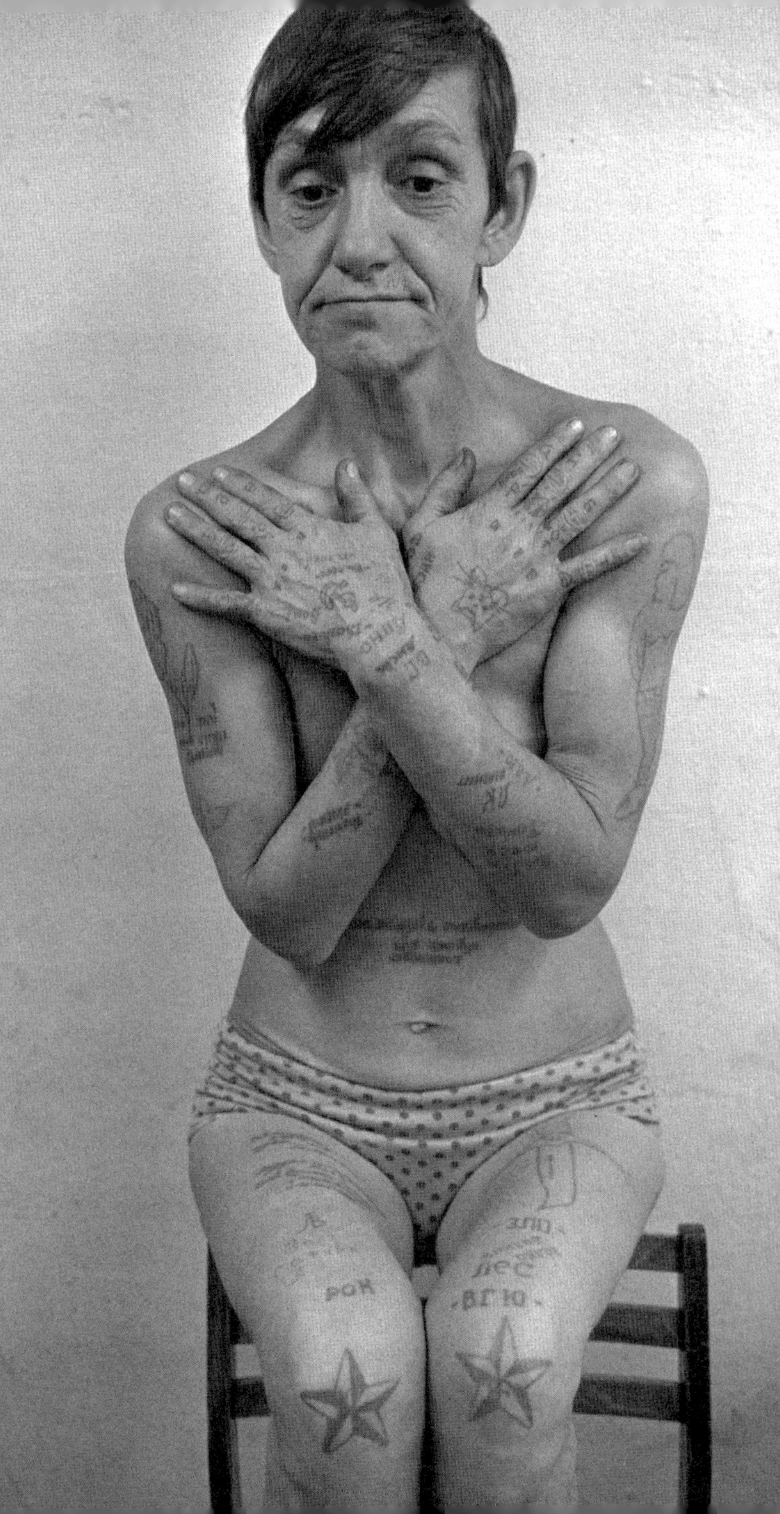

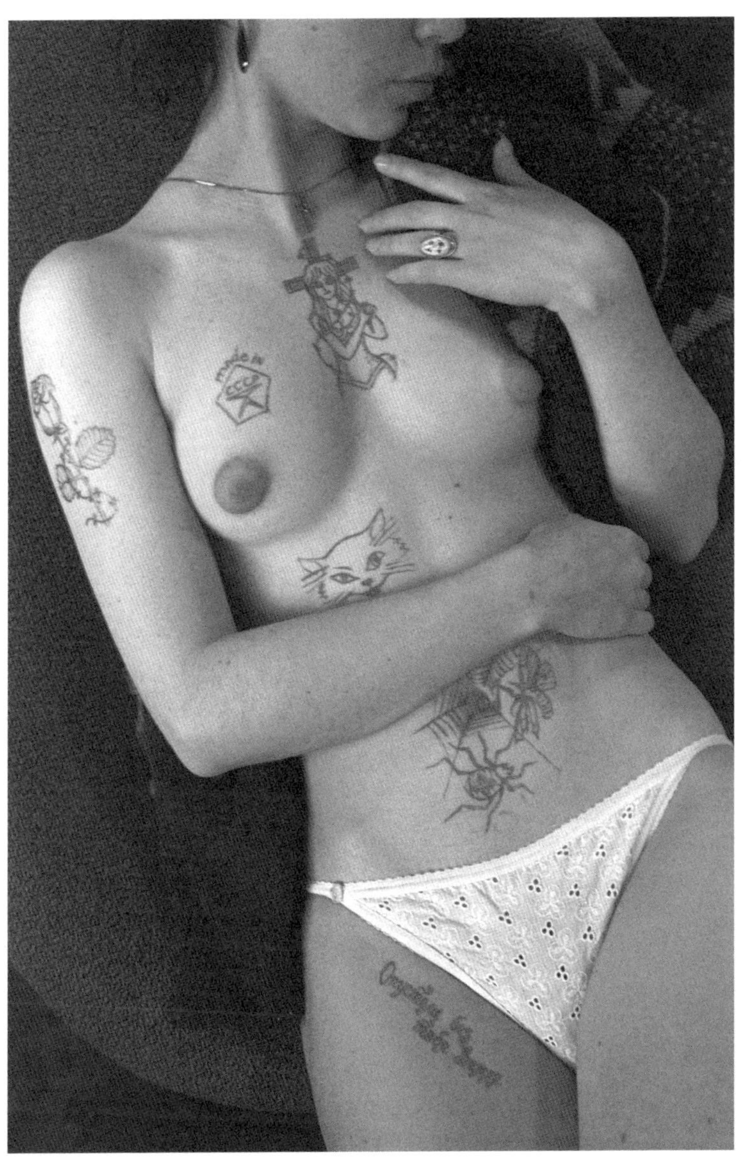

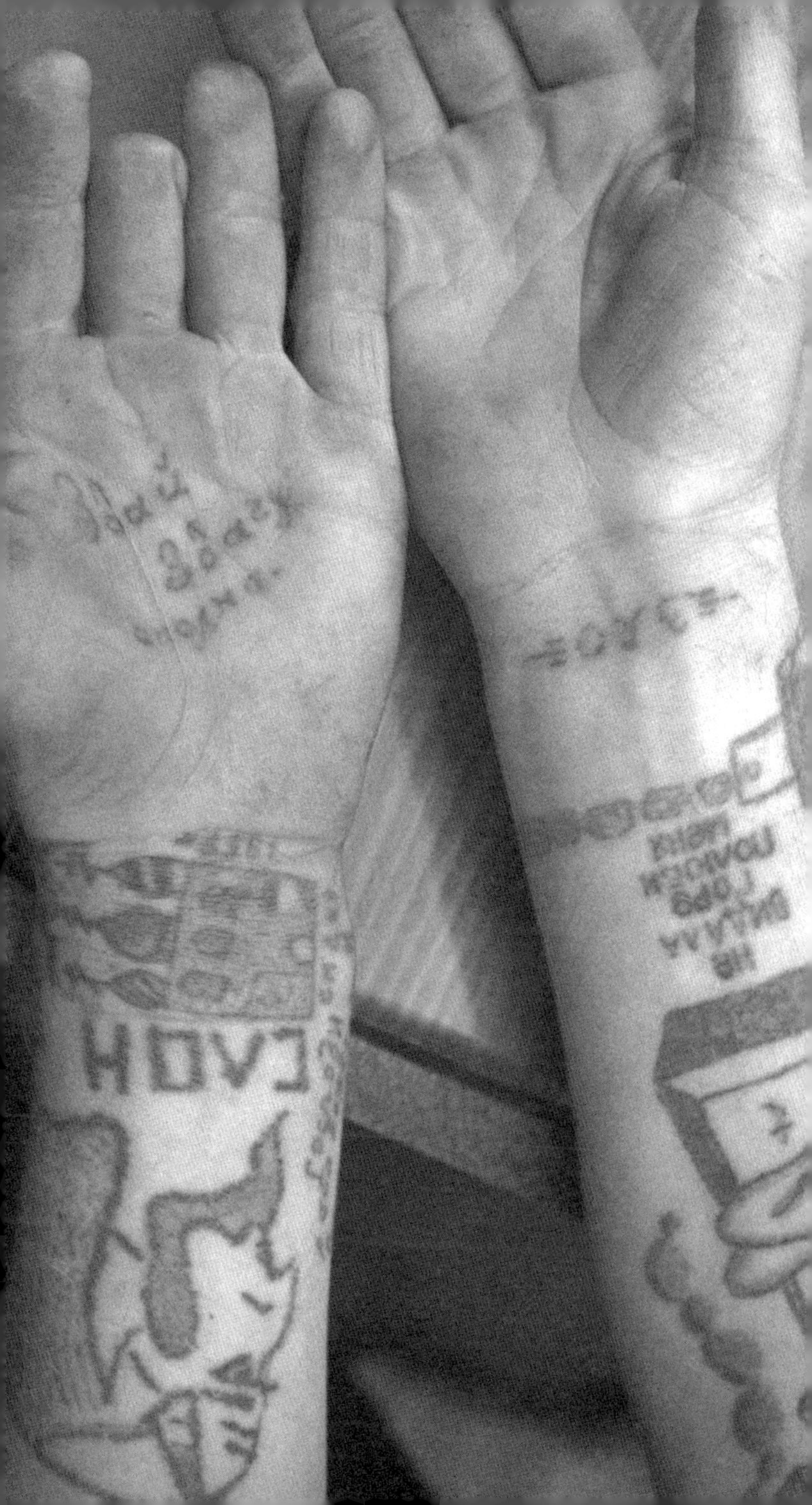

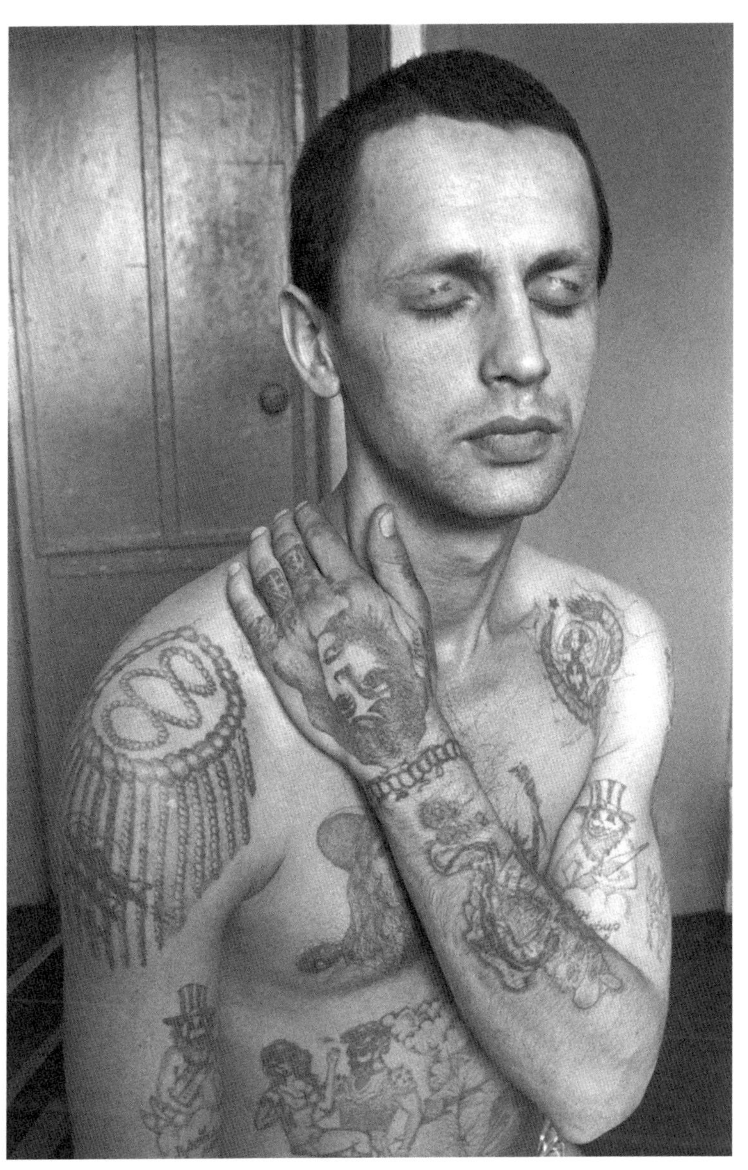

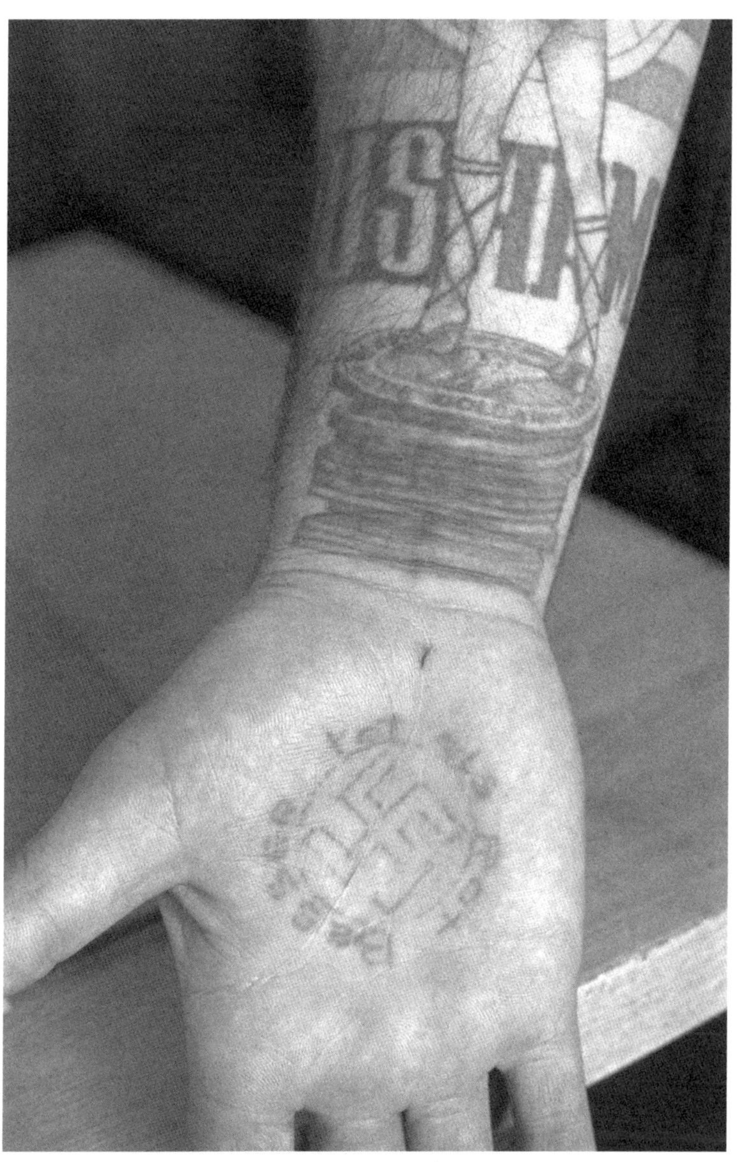

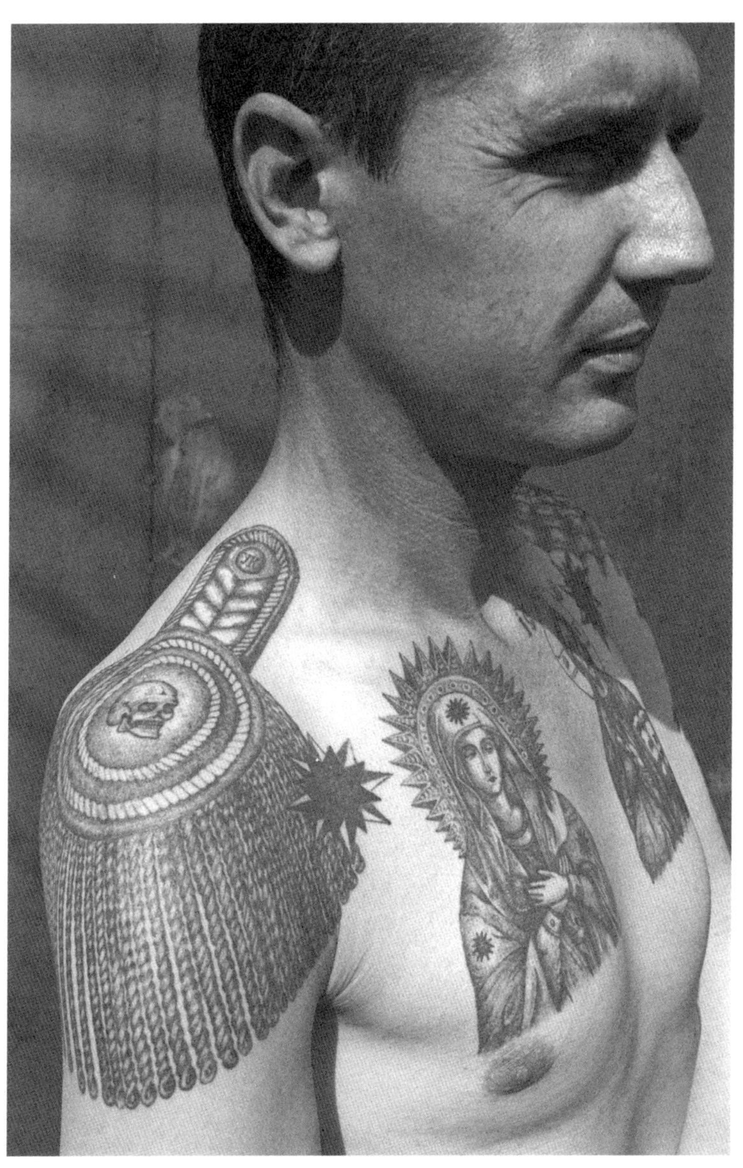

365

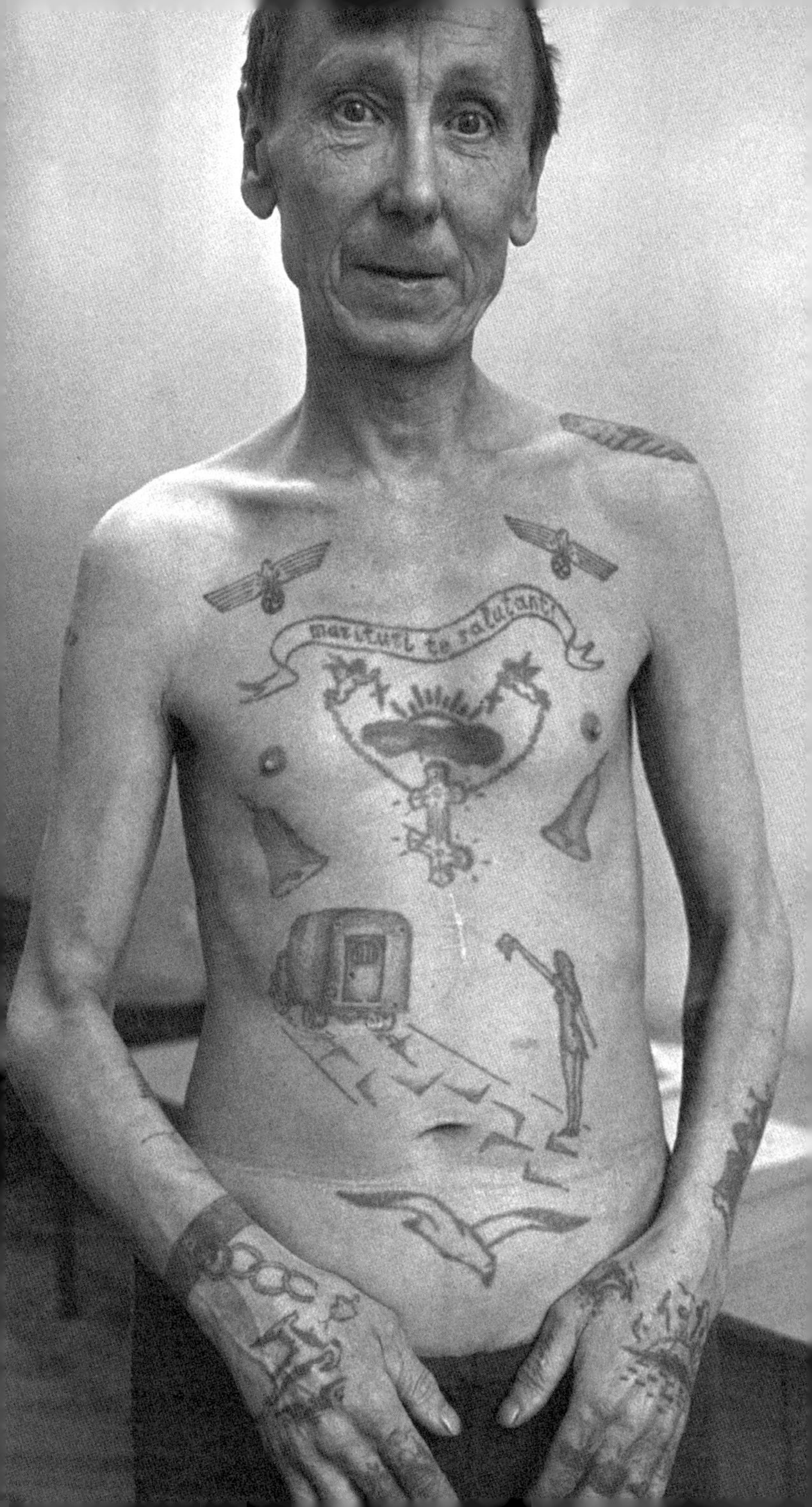

morituri te salutant

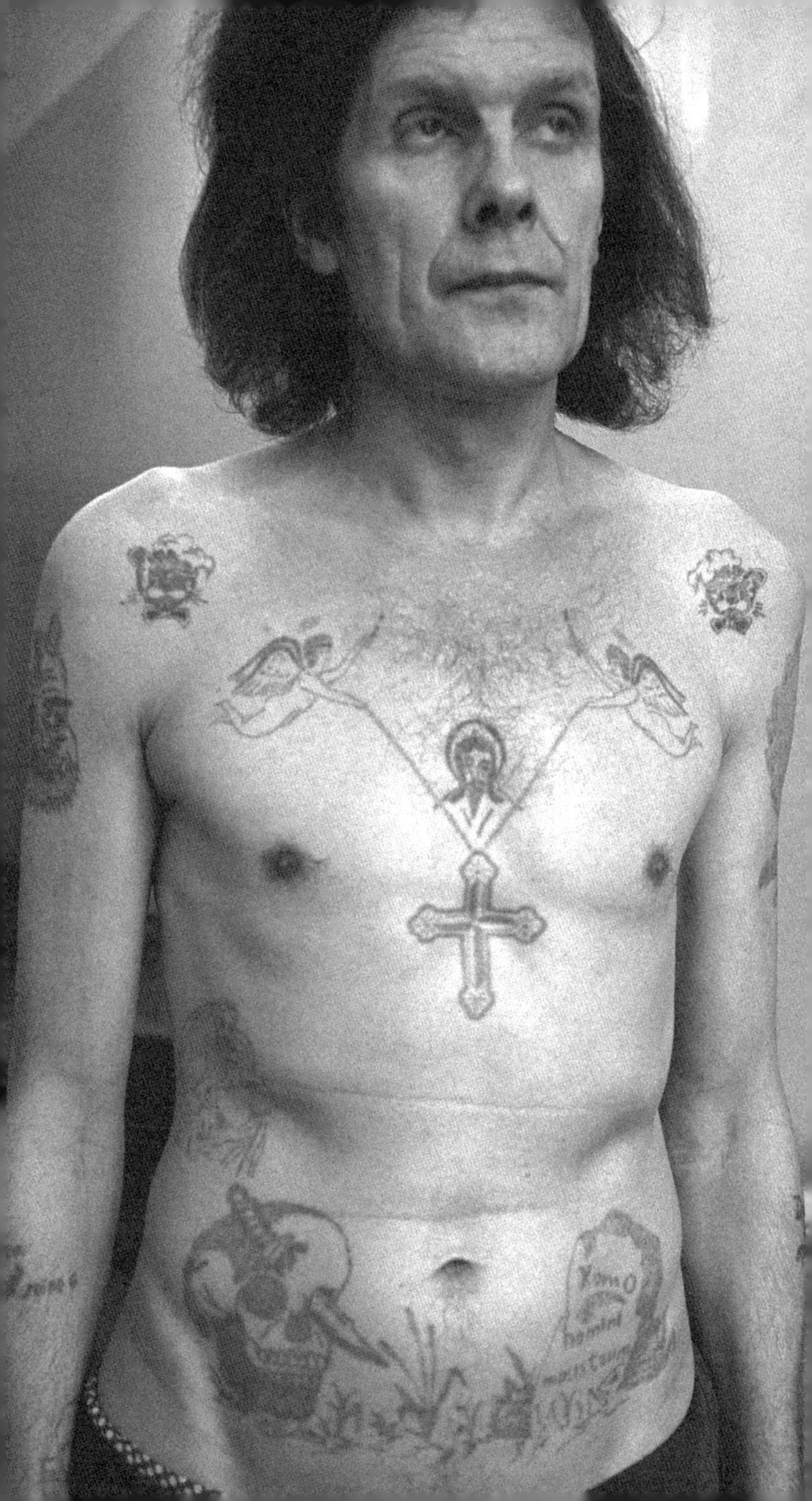

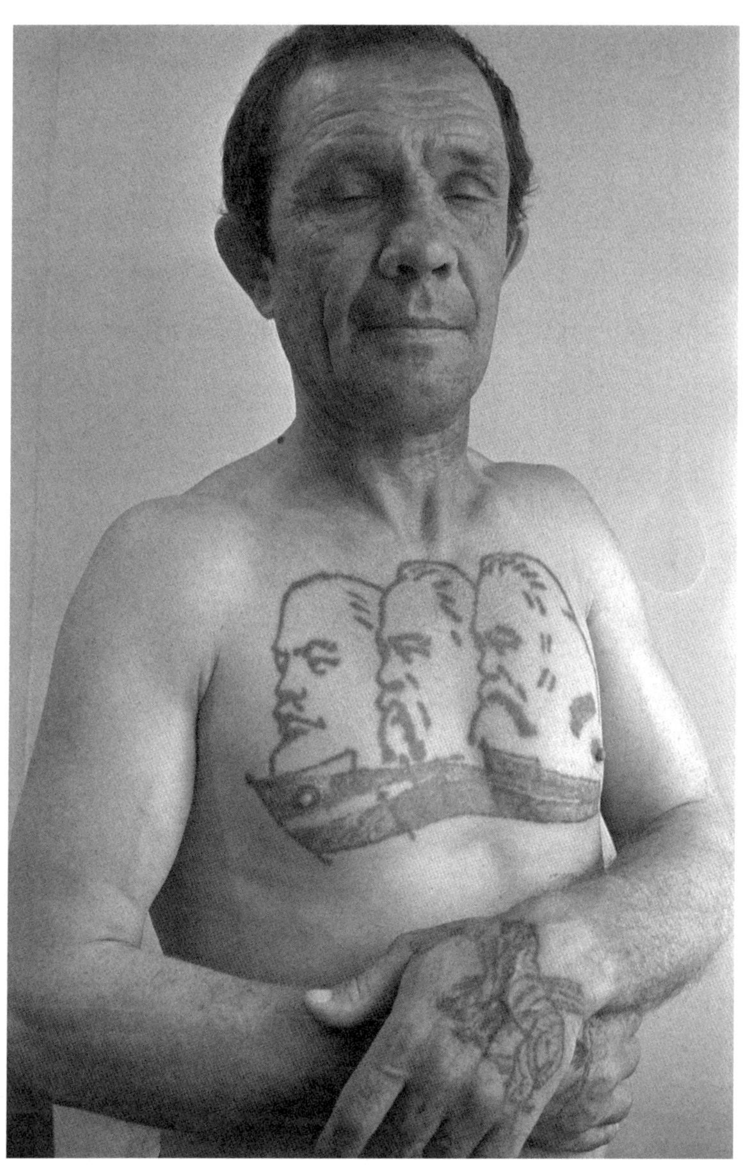

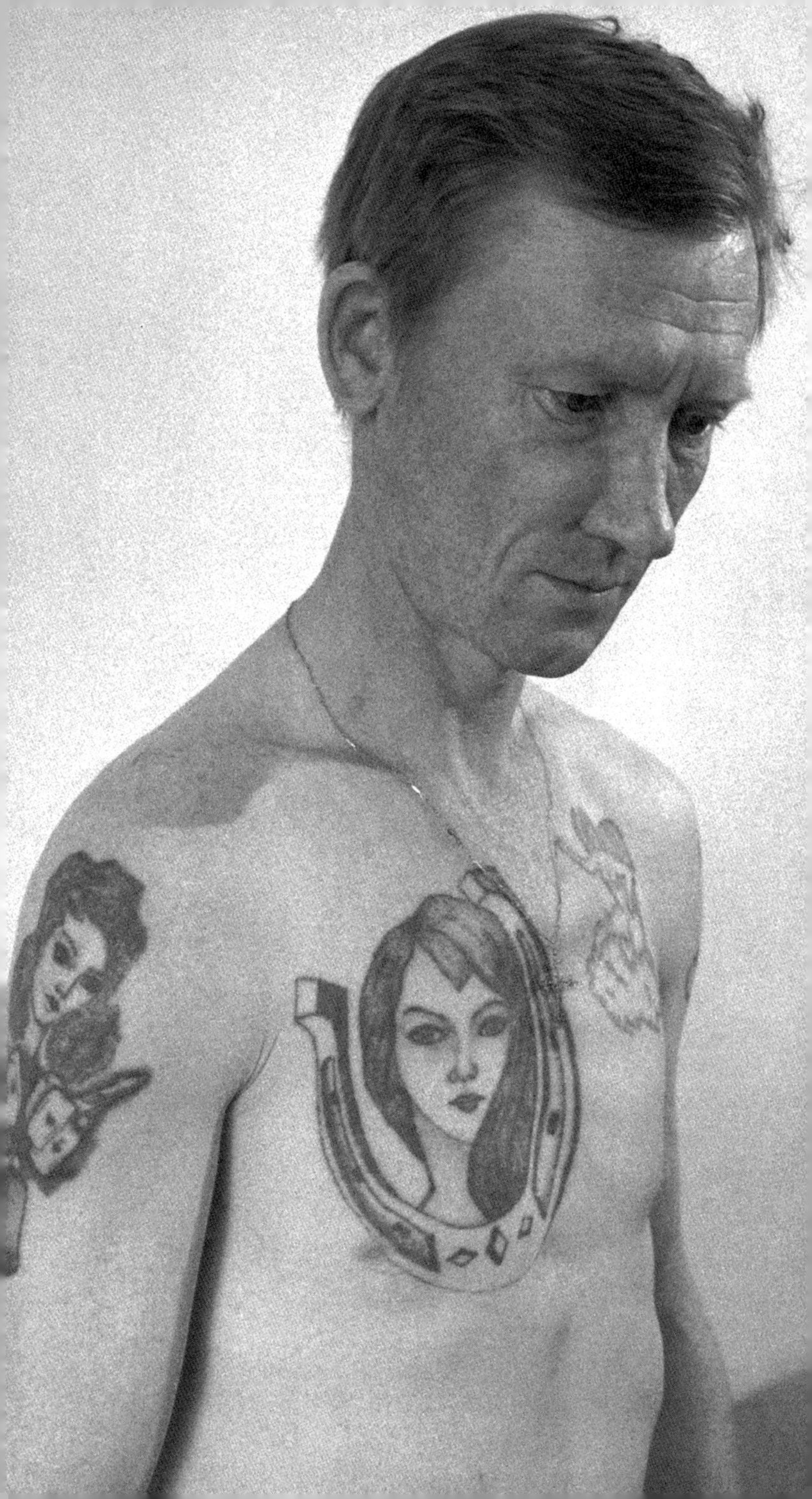

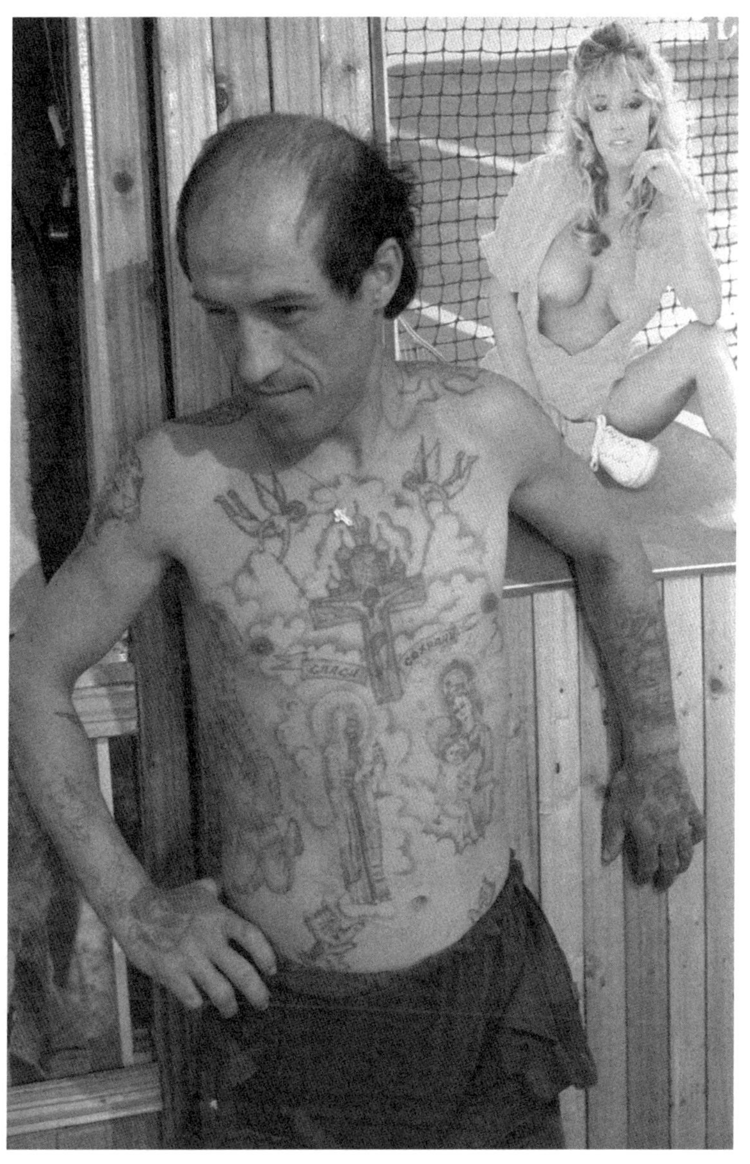

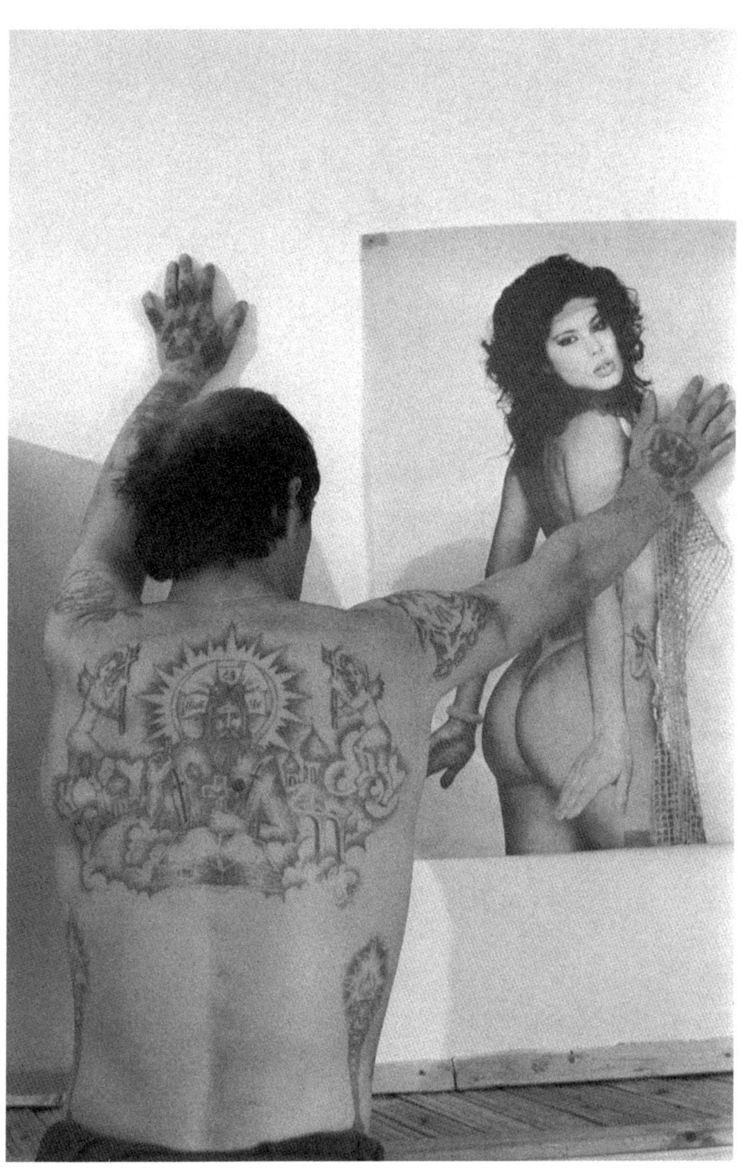

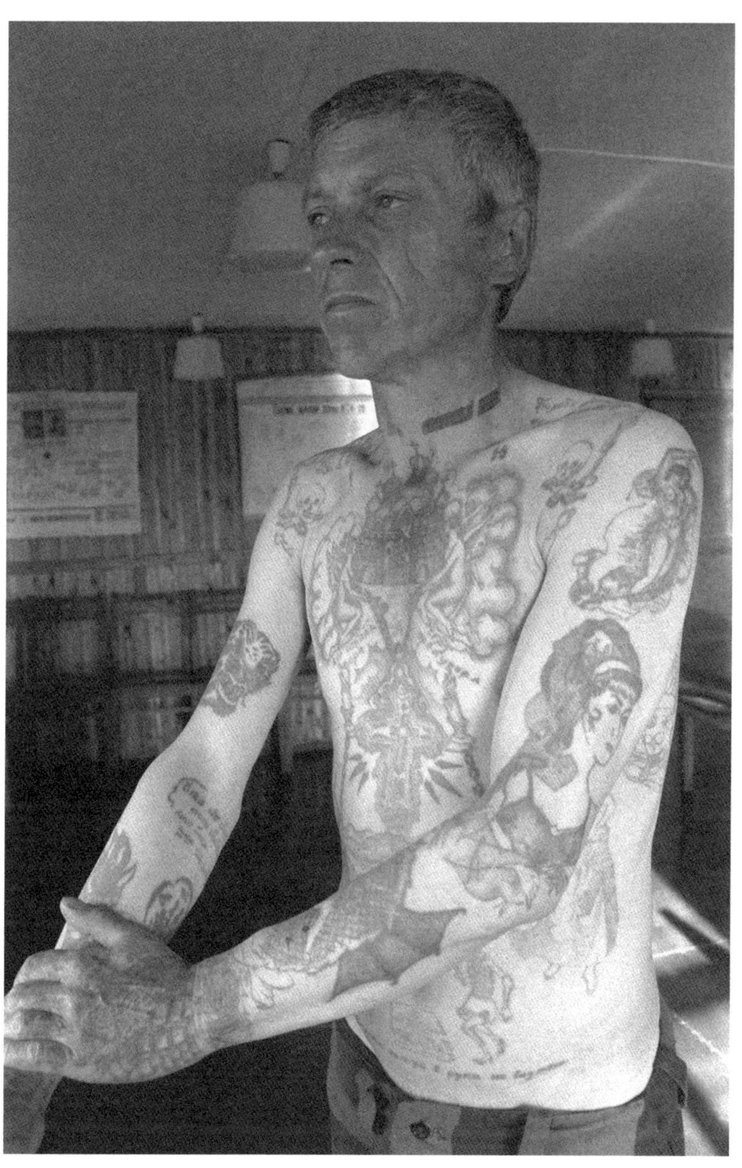

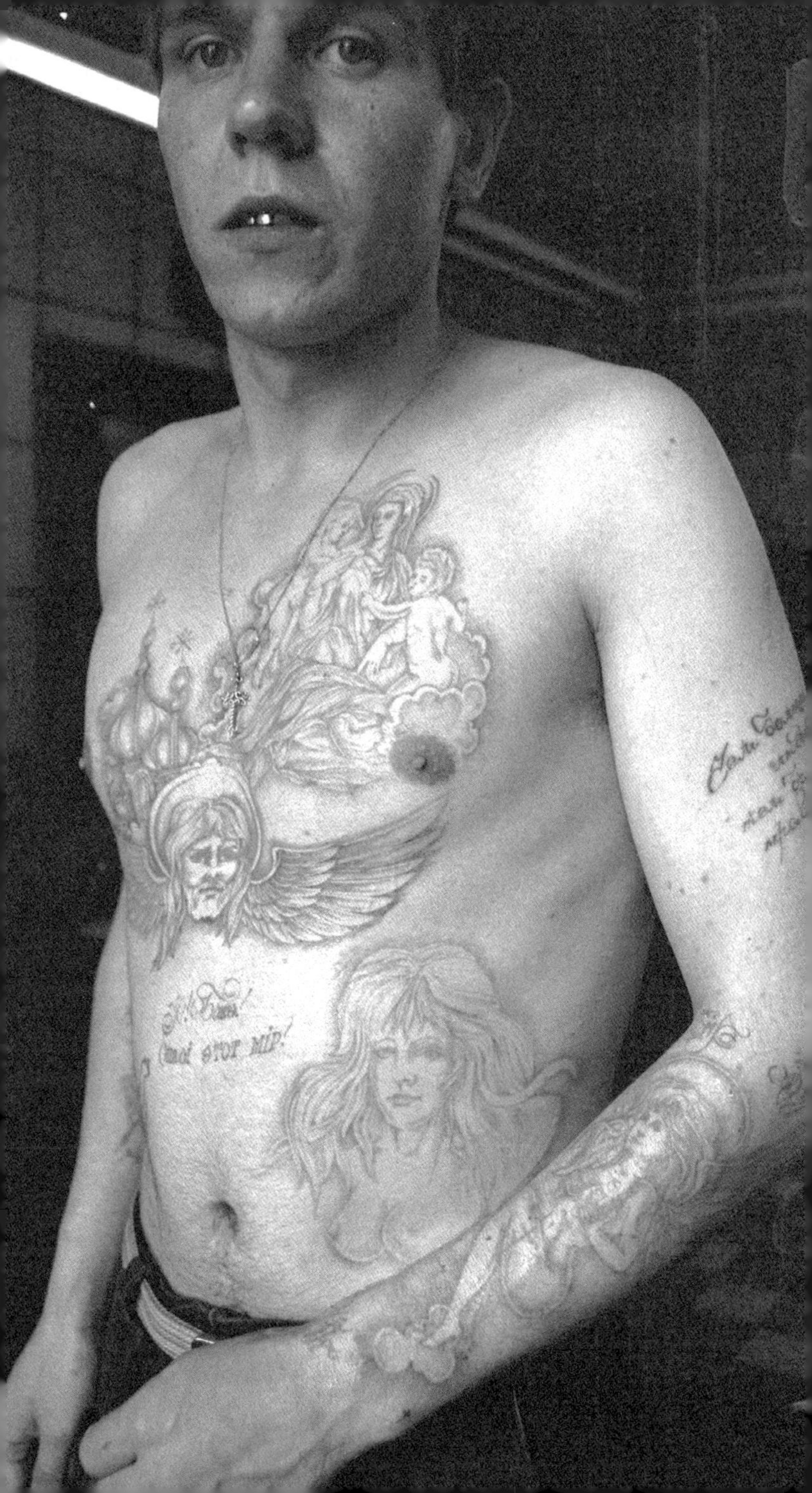

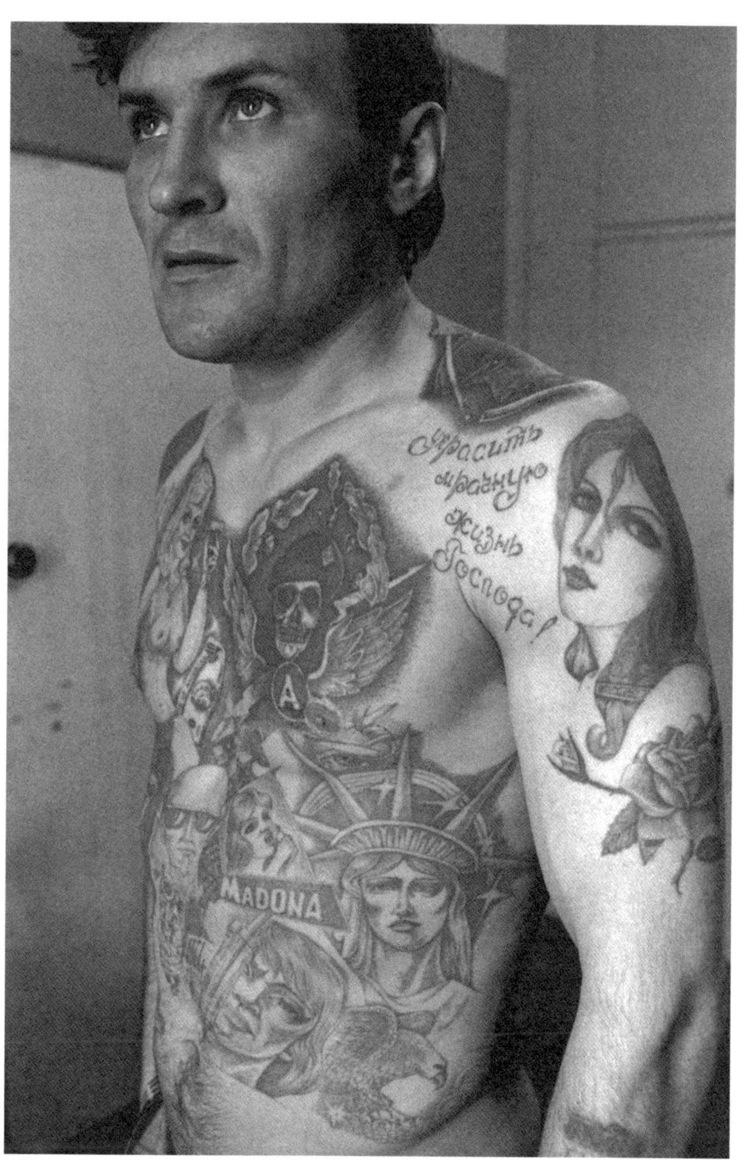
Красить
страшную
жизнь
Господа!
MADONA

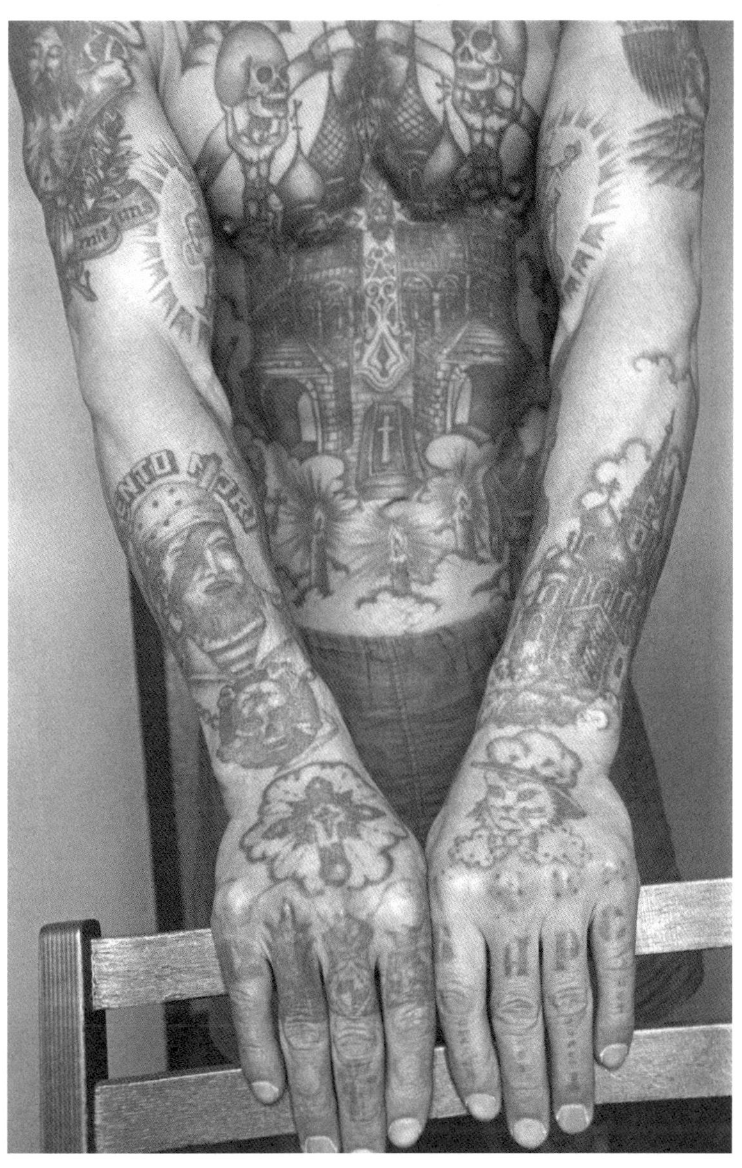

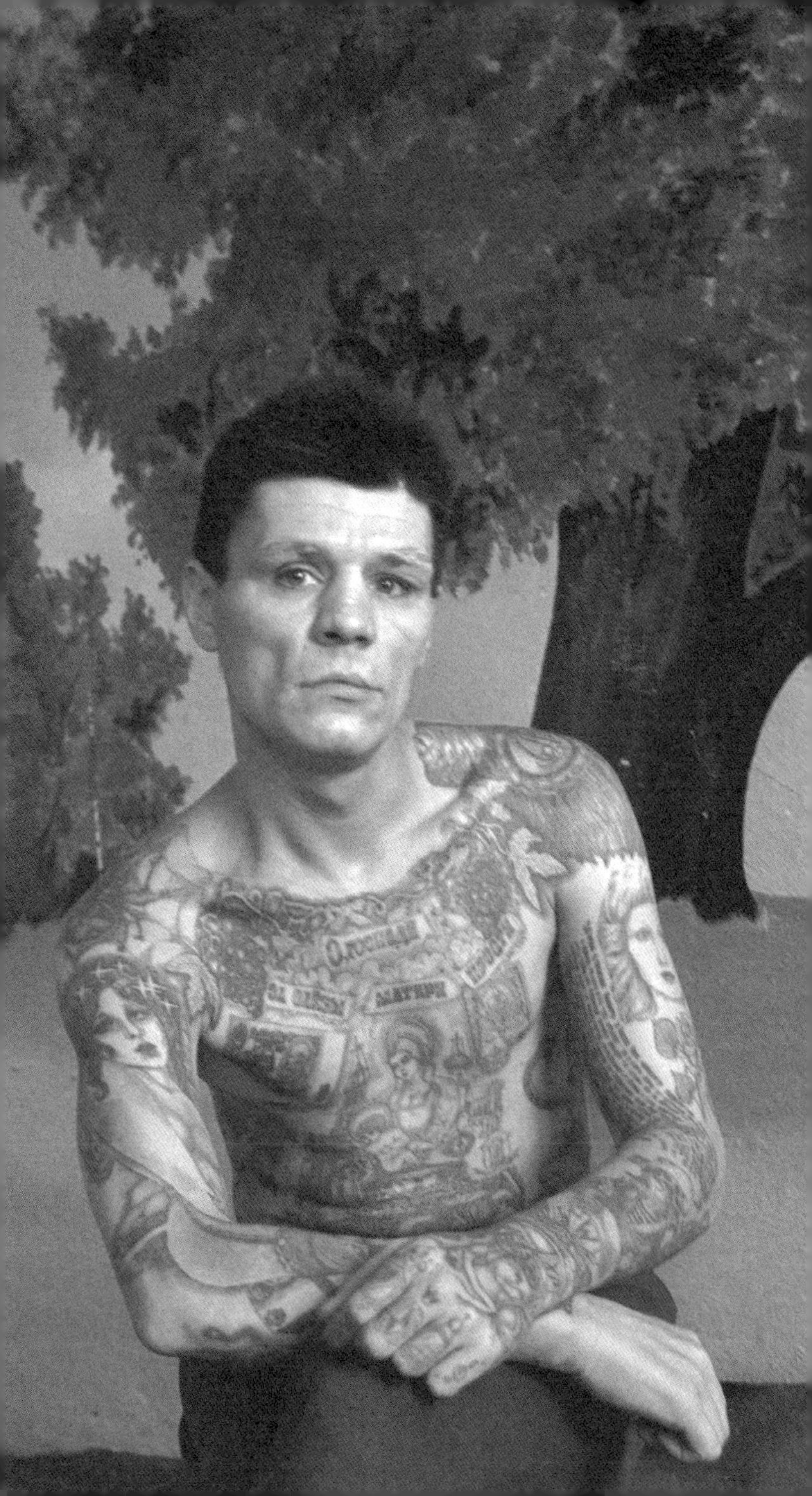

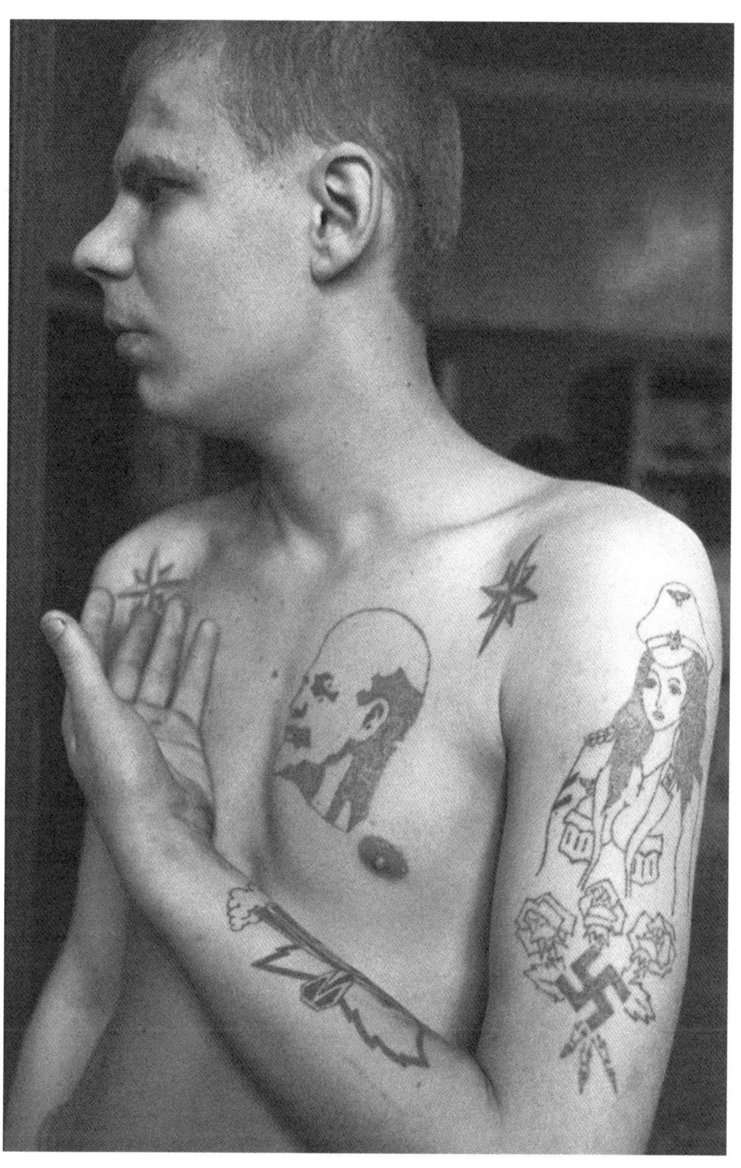

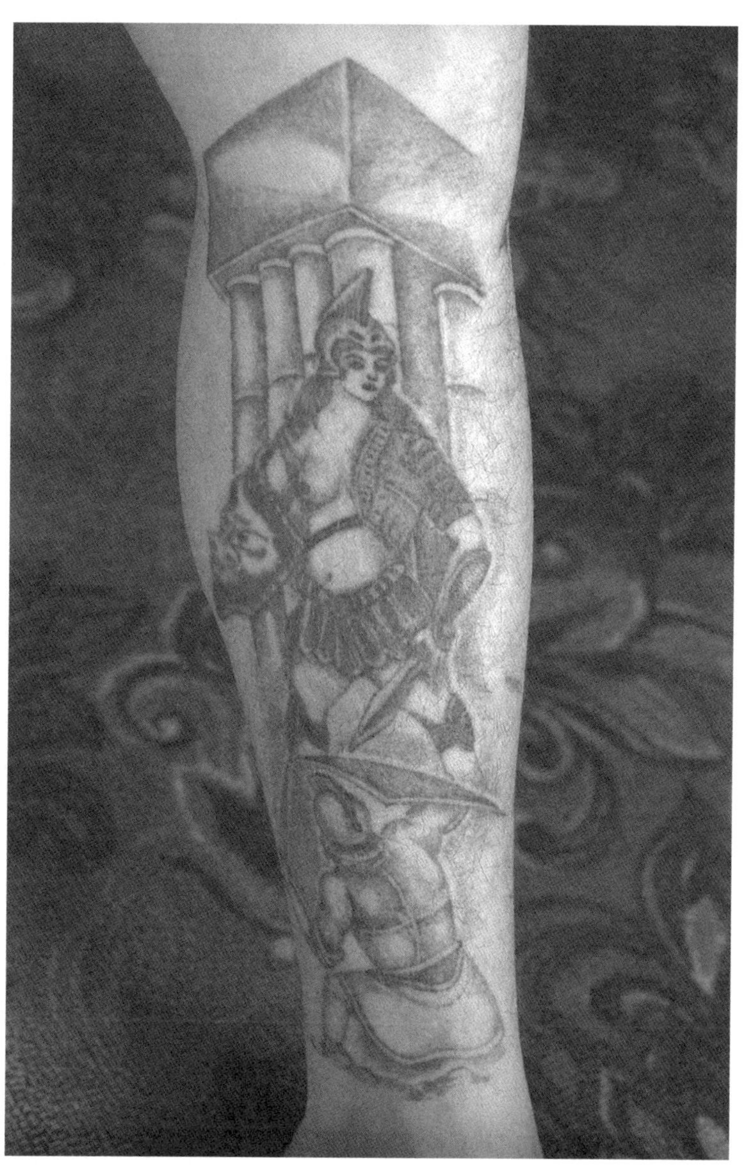

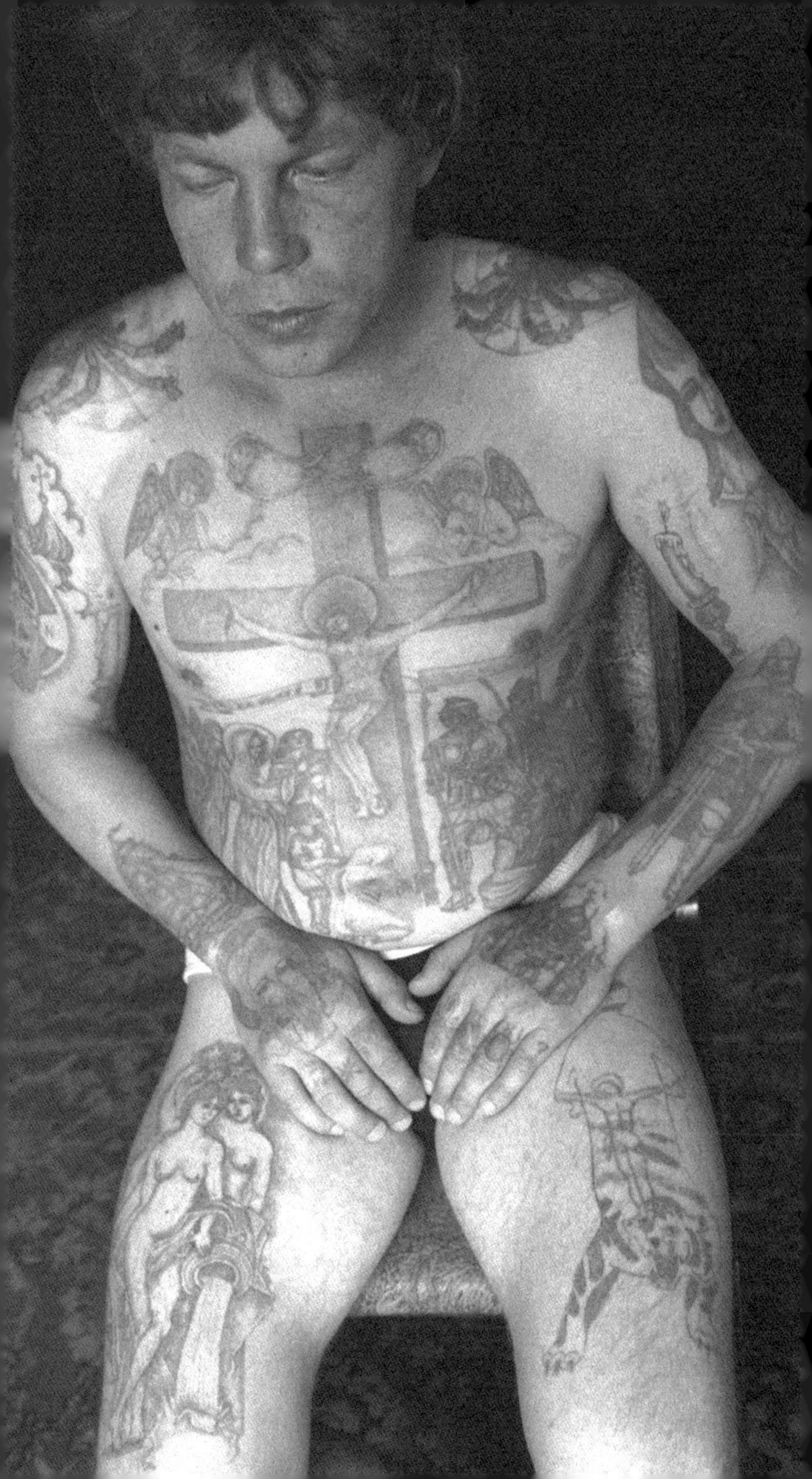

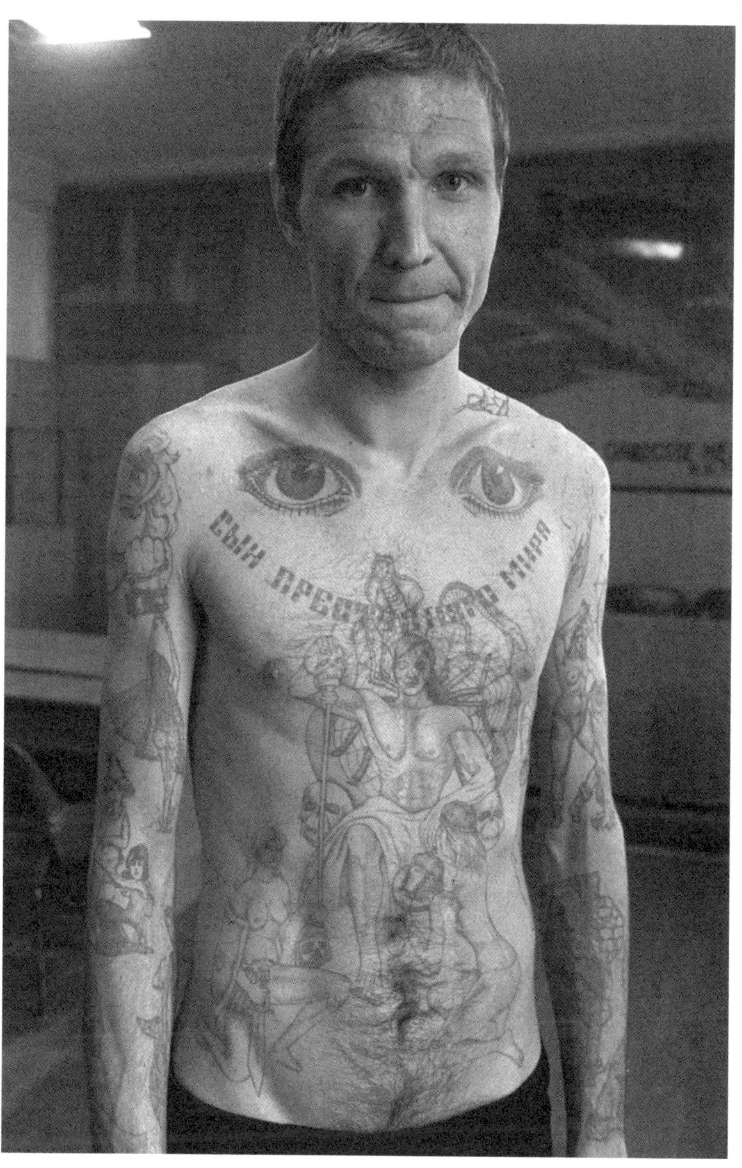
СЫН ПРЕСТУПНОГО МИРА

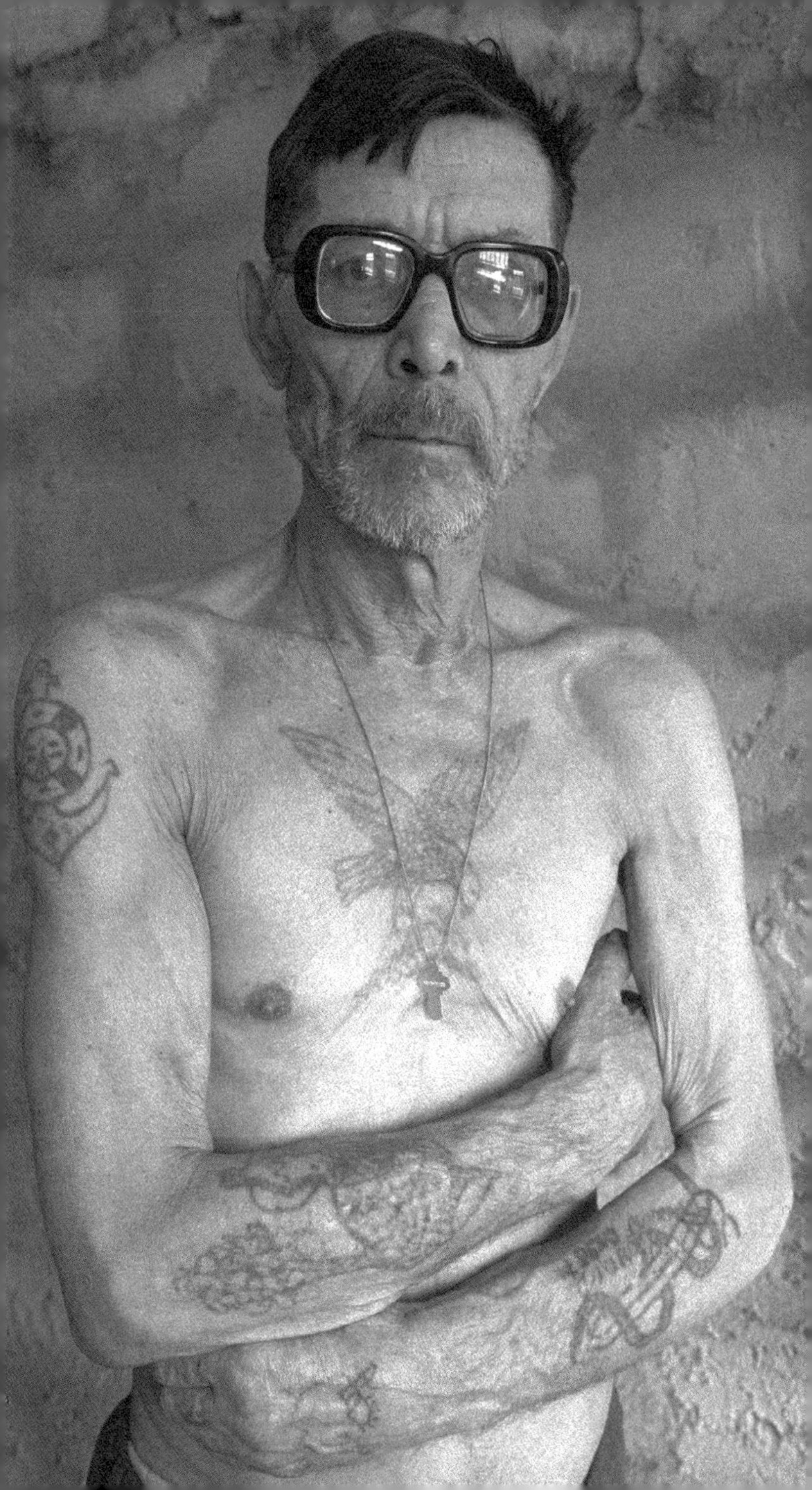

The photographs in this book were taken between 1989 and 1992 at the following locations:

Central Corrective Labour Colony, Sos'va Settlement, Sverdlovsk Region
Chelyabinsk Municipal Hospital
Corrective Labour Colony No.2 and No.8, Chelyabinsk
Corrective Labour Colony No.5 (Drug Addicts), Nizhny Tagil
Corrective Labour Colony No.40, Kungur, Perm Region
Female Corrective Labour Colony No.12, Kungur, Perm Region
Female Corrective Labour Colony No.40, Kungur, Perm Region
Female General Regime Corrective Labour Colony No.32, Perm Region
General Regime Corrective Labour Colony No.2, Sablino Settlement, Leningrad Region
General Regime Corrective Labour Colony No.5, Chelyabinsk
Interregional Prison Hospital, St. Petersburg
Juvenile and Female Prison No.2, Isolation Cell Block No.2, St. Petersburg
Special Regime Corrective Labour Colony No.14, Puksinka Settlement, Sverdlovsk Region
Special Vagrants' Reception and Distribution Centre, Chelyabinsk
Strict Regime Corrective Labour Colony, Lopatkovo Settlement, Sverdlovsk Region
Strict Regime Corrective Labour Colony No.4, Fornosovo Settlement, Leningrad Region
Strict Regime Corrective Labour Colony No.4, Obukhovo Settlement, St. Petersburg
Strict Regime Corrective Labour Colony No.6, Kopeisk, Chelyabinsk Region
Strict Regime Corrective Labour Colony No.9, Gorelovo Settlement, Leningrad Region
Strict Regime Corrective Labour Colony No.12, San-Donanto Junction, Sverdlovsk Region
Strict Regime Corrective Labour Colony No.40, Kungur, Perm Region
'The Crosses', Isolation Cell Block No.1, St. Petersburg

Russian Criminal Tattoo Encyclopaedia Volume II
Danzig Baldaev, Sergei Vasiliev
FUEL, 2006
ISBN: 978-0-9550061-2-8

Russian Criminal Tattoo Encyclopaedia Volume III
Danzig Baldaev, Sergei Vasiliev
FUEL, 2008
ISBN: 978-0-9550061-9-7

Drawings from the Gulag
Danzig Baldaev
FUEL, 2010
ISBN: 978-0-9563562-4-6

Soviets
Danzig Baldaev, Sergei Vasiliev
FUEL, 2014
ISBN 978-0-9568962-7-8

Russian Criminal Tattoo Archive
Danzig Baldaev, Sergei Vasiliev, Arkady Bronnikov
FUEL, 2023
ISBN: 978-1-7398878-0-3

First published in 2003
This edition published in 2009. Reprinted 2012, 2014, 2018, 2020, 2023

Murray & Sorrell FUEL Ltd
FUEL Design & Publishing
33 Fournier Street
London E1 6QE

fuel-design.com

Thanks to: Valentina Baldaeva

Printed in Belgium

Distribution by Thames & Hudson / D. A. P.
ISBN 978-0-9558620-7-6